The Invis...

Hungarian-born Gitta Sereny has twice before interrupted her career as an investigative journalist to write a book. The first was *The Case of Mary Bell*, of which Marganita Laski said in *The Times* that it "should be read not only for the moral problems it raises for every reader, but also for the moments of reality beyond imagination". The second was a "masterpiece" (*Daily Telegraph*), *Into that Darkness*, which was built on long talks with a man who had been Kommandant of the Nazi extermination camp at Treblinka, and which the late Philip Toynbee described in *The Observer* as "an admirable piece of research, conducted with great thoroughness and ingenuity, and presented with a most impressive and haunting dignity."

While still in her teens, Gitta Sereny was caught in Paris and cut off from her family by the Second World War. This led eventually to her working for a time with displaced children: an early experience highly relevant to the present book. Later she married the American photographer Don Honeyman and settled in London, where she has brought up a son and a daughter. The English newspapers for which she has worked most often are *The Telegraph Magazine* and *The Sunday Times*.

Gitta Sereny

The Invisible Children

Children 'on the game' in
America, West Germany and
Great Britain

Pan Books London and Sydney

First published 1984 by André Deutsch Ltd
This Pan edition published 1986 by Pan Books Ltd,
Cavaye Place, London SW10 9PG
9 8 7 6 5 4 3 2 1
© Gitta Sereny 1984
ISBN 0 330 29118 1
Printed in Great Britain by
Collins, Glasgow

Contents

THE INVISIBLE CHILDREN

Prologue

This is a book that should not need to be written. It is about something that should not exist and that, indeed, many people claim doesn't. It is, furthermore, about something for which blame cannot be laid—so simply—on God, or—so comfortingly —on a political party or on economic or national inequities.

The blame lies squarely on me and you: I who am writing and you, old or young, who are reading. It is we who in this last quarter of our rich twentieth century, in our enlightened Western world, have unthinkingly, recklessly and greedily created and supported an atmosphere of life which, it would appear, is intolerable to many of our children.

When life becomes intolerable to children, they fade. They do not necessarily fall ill, or die, but fade in other ways: they create chaos, throw tantrums, provoke disharmony, divide their families, become loners, fail in school, truant, steal, lie, dabble in alcohol and drugs, and finally run away.

A child who runs away is giving, loud and clear, a signal of alarm. Most runaway children, basically secure in their parents' love and ability to read this warning, return of their own volition after a brief taste of freedom and danger; but many don't. A child who *stays* away, believes that his or her scream for love has not been heard and may never be. It is a sick child and in order to find comfort—and, indeed, to live—it will seek the company of its peers, other sick children and even sicker adults: those who prey on children, either for financial or for sexual satisfaction. This is how the vicious circle of child prostitution is created and helped to flourish.

When people say that child prostitution is as old as the hills, they are thinking about something different from the huge industry it has now become. What is in their minds are the cases, rare now in Western countries but still commonplace in much of Asia and South America, where desperately poor and often mentally limited parents sell some of their children into service to enable the rest of the family to survive.

I don't think that I will ever forget the frozen-faced nine-year-old Indian girl I met a few years ago in a desolate hamlet up in the Peruvian Andes. She had been sold to the innkeeper for the equivalent of £10 (about $14). Her work, from five in the morning until late at night, included carrying heavy trays, scrubbing floors, and feeding the stove at least twice during the night; she slept on the stone floor curled around it. She also rendered regular sexual services to the innkeeper, aged fifty-one; his son, thirty-two; his grandson, fifteen; and to any customer who required them. The fee, paid to the owner (not, of course to the child, for whom it would have represented a fortune) was the equivalent of 5 cents.

These acts took place in a filthy, freezing stable behind the house. I came upon the scene by chance, hearing a child cry as I passed, and found myself spluttering with rage. The innkeeper got up, discreetly turning away from me to button his trousers. The little girl wiped her tears and pulled down her cotton dress—she wore nothing underneath. And both of them appeared nonplussed at my fury.

"You don't understand, Señora," the man said, patient and polite as all the people of the Andes are. "She is mine. I bought her." My interpreter, more knowledgeable than I about the realities of life in those parts, conscientiously translated my remonstrations but (while the child flitted out of the door) explained to me that "At least she is eating. If she had stayed with her parents, she'd most likely be dead."

The same explanations are proffered for the latest cause to be taken up by well-meaning conferences and our sensation-hungry media: sex tours to Asian countries where Western tourists are apparently provided with children of both sexes and all ages, ready to do their bidding. I have no personal knowledge of this traffic, its organizers, its clients, or its silent small victims. But I have seen a book—a world Baedeker of paedophilia—which provides names, addresses, phone numbers, and the most intimate personal descriptions of available "subjects" or "material" (both terms are used) in countries all over the world. It contained whole sections describing boys and girls from the age of three up, available for "posing for photographs or movies", "cuddle sessions", "friendly encounters with adults" and so on. The addresses range from London and Amsterdam, south through Germany and Austria, north to Scandinavia and across the different seas to the United States and Asia.

Small children advertized in such a book—including those in western Europe—are obviously made available through their parents: People like the fifty-seven-year-old grandmother in North London who hired out her granddaughters aged thirteen and eleven for sex-sessions in her flat. Three little school friends were also recruited and it went on for many months. Two men, one aged sixty-nine, one seventy-one, were finally convicted at a trial at the Old Bailey in London, and so was the grandmother who had supplied clients with condoms and passed the time in the next room watching TV. "We needed money for food," was her defence. But the judge must have believed her and sympathized with the two men, who both apologized in well-chosen words and public school accents, for all of them received minimum sentences. As indeed—at just about the same time—did the Chicago mother who, from the driver's seat of a car with one of her little girls aged eight next to her, had directed the other, aged eleven, "how to do it" with the client in the back. It was pure chance that a patrol car came upon that family. The man's defence: "But the mother offered me the girl."

It is not Third World poverty, nor the perversion of some parents in our own part of the world, that has brought about the problems we shall confront in this book: full-time child prostitution on a limited but still amazingly large and ever growing scale; part-time child prostitution on an immense scale in Western Europe and the United States; and child pornography against which laws now in force in almost every country in the Western world seem powerless. This commerce has not appeared out of a void, it is not forced upon an unwilling society. It is created by demand, catered to by people who make enormous sums from it, and can exist only because of the voluntary and often eager participation of hundreds of thousands of children of both sexes between the ages of eleven and fifteen.

I have spent a year and a half investigating the problem of child prostitution in Britain, America, and West Germany. Obviously, far more time and money than I was able to command ought to be devoted to the subject. The same kind of research should be done by experts in every country of the Western world so that a detailed picture can be obtained separately, for each country. For certainly the conditions I describe in this book—the same kind of children with the same problems, the same reasons, the same reactions, and the same clients (the most shadowy figures in this whole phenomenon)—can be found with slight variations in all countries in the West.

With the help of social workers, teachers and police who became interested and involved in the project, I met 161 boys and girls who are or had been, or were then active in full or part-time prostitution, and talked with 69 of them at length. Among the 161, and among the first short-list of 69, there were a number of schoolchildren who, more or less regularly, used weekend prostitution as a means of augmenting their pocket-money. These children continued to live at home, or in children's homes or foster-homes.

In this book I present detailed studies of twelve children who were engaged in full-time prostitution; a number of brief accounts of children in part-time prostitution or other sexual commerce; and one profile of an American pimp. For without understanding something about the pimp—the children's most important friend and enemy—we cannot even begin to visualize their lives.

The twelve children were chosen for a number of reasons, the most important being that they were people with whom I felt I would be able to establish the right kind of rapport; The project was not feasible unless we could talk together at length, and honestly. Also—and this was a decisive point—they agreed to my meeting their families and their families agreed to see me. Quite a number of other children also agreed to have me meet their parents, but the parents refused. In other cases social workers were certain that parents would eventually be willing, even eager to help and that, when they knew me better, I would be able to persuade the children to effect the introduction. But that was not the sequence I thought proper.

Even among these children, there were some who, as our conversations progessed, changed their minds on realizing what they had told me and what would *have* to be discussed with parents, however carefully I handled it. One or two requested that I speak to their parents "only on the telephone." I did as the children asked: their confidence and trust in me were the main prerequisites for this undertaking.

In the case of the children I write about who were in part-time prostitution, I did not seek out the parents, but social workers were always involved.

It is a mistake to assume that if children run away from home, the reasons are always dramatic ones: that they are invariably abused, beaten or neglected, or—the most common misapprehension of all—that if they turn to prostitution or criminality, they are merely reflecting parental examples or following a pattern. The truth is that although the decision to run away (and stay away) almost invariably grows out of long-term conflict with parents or parent-substitutes, these conflicts are by no means necessarily caused by cruelty or neglect. In fact, only a small percentage of the parents involved appear to be in any way asocial.

Indeed, many of the parents might be considered *too* respectable, even too caring. And the children, far from being limited in either intelligence or sensitivity, are apt to be over-imaginative, of above average intelligence, hypersensitive, shy and insecure. The child who runs away and stays away is invariably crying out for love.

I do not know how many such children there are, working full or part-time for the sex industry and on the fringe of criminality. No one knows. The only basis there is for a careful guess—and this *only* for those engaged in full-time prostitution—is an analysis of police figures for children who have run away and stayed away from home or institutions. This is certainly the most obvious approach, for ironically enough, the protective child-labour laws of our progressive societies have made it virtually impossible for children to survive by legal means away from their home base, and there are therefore no other records.

In America, an annual figure of between 750,000 and one million runaways is generally accepted (the media has often inflated it). The West Germans report around 20,000 runaways under sixteen (the age of legal majority varies from country to country, and in America from state to state). In England and Wales (Scotland is another story) the figure of juveniles reported missing fluctuates from year to year between 13,000 and 15,000.

These figures, which usually represent twice as many girls as boys, do not include the hundreds of thousands of male and female part-time schoolchildren prostitutes who—I am reliably informed by teachers and social workers—exist in all three countries. Nor do they include—and this raises serious questions about our attitudes towards children in care—children who run away from children's homes, community homes and the various kinds of correctional institutions. In all three countries, such children are listed not as "missing" but as "absconders." In England and Wales, recent figures for "absconders" added 6,514 youngsters under sixteen—almost half as many again—to the number of missing children, and we can safely assume that more or less the same proportion would be found in the other countries, and in other years.

The authorities in all three countries agree that the vast majority of runaways from home return after a few days: forty-eight hours on the loose is the average maximum. In West Germany and the United States, about 10 percent are believed to remain on the run—that is to say, 2,000 in West Germany and 100,000 in the United States excluding children in care. "But even that figure is not reliable," said one of the officers in the New York Runaway Squad, a small police detachment in charge of finding runaway children. "A lot of these kids are repeaters. They run away ten, twenty, even a hundred times, and finally parents give up and no longer report them missing. These are the truly lost. And many 'absconders' never go back."

In Britain the figures are even vaguer: about one-half percent of the total—no more than between seventy-two and eighty-five children— are listed by the Home Office as long-term missing in England and Wales. But this figure is meaningless: in addition to not including "absconders," it leaves out Scottish children, and workers in the field agree that the majority of runaways turning up in London are Scottish, most of them girls.

In each case I investigated, communication between children and parents had broken down or had hardly existed. Out of the sixty-nine children with whom I spoke at greater length, two-thirds came from respectable, often puritanical, backgrounds where any discussion of sex was taboo. Two-thirds, too, were disciplined from an early age— such as three or four years old—by means of physical punishment, often severe beatings with straps, whips or canes. Twelve of the sixty-nine children had been sexually abused in childhood, though some of them only marginally (i.e., not necessarily penetrated), by parents or relatives. Nine of them were from poor backgrounds, more than half were middle-class children, and three belonged to what is called "social class 1," the upper classes.

Out of the 161 pre-teenage children I met, 113 received only the most minimal weekly pocket-money: between 50p and £1 in the United Kingdom, 50 cents and $3 in the United States and 5.10 DM (Deutschmarks) in West Germany.

Many parents, including some of the excessively strict ones, showed themselves when I talked to them as loving and humorous people, desperate about their children and totally at sea about the whys and wherefores. "They teach us so many things at school which mean nothing for our later lives," said one father (to be echoed later by a child). "Why in God's name don't they teach us how to be parents?"

Here, in the final analysis, lie the seeds of the problem. For although it is true that money—too little or too much of it—plays a part particularly with the "part-timers," it would be absurd to ascribe what is so widely and so disastrously happening to so many of our children to this one aspect. It would be absurd thus to minimize the problem.

Almost every child I spoke to had at some time been asked to pose for pornographic pictures or to take part in porno-movies. Until two years ago in Britain and West Germany, and three in the United States, pornographic material based on children—about two hundred magazines and eighty films—was freely available in speciality bookshops and sex-shops in all the larger cities. Much of it, could be bought at railway station book-stalls.

Most of this material was and is openly produced in Denmark and Holland, but not all. "We found through our research that at least three of the magazines and several of the films were actually produced in America," says Dr Judianne Densen-Gerber, a New York psychiatrist who seven years ago almost single-handedly took on the battle against the child pornography industry. "The market for this filth is enormous," she told me. "They are all sick people, but what is worse is that the children who participate—we see them in our consulting-rooms—are invariably severely damaged by these experiences. It *had* to be stopped."

Dr Densen-Gerber's two-year campaign all over the United States, and in Britain a Private Bill presented in 1978 by Cyril Townsend MP, resulted in new legislation in both countries. This strengthened the Child Protection laws and fixed the penalties for offences against children (including the distribution of pornographic material brought in from abroad) at from seven to fifteen years in prison. But police in both countries feel that these measures are insufficient.

"All it has done," said one officer from Scotland Yard's Obscene Publications Squad, "is drive the traffic underground and raise the prices to astronomical levels. It [the material] now comes in sealed container lorries. Hundreds of them arrive every week, most of them from Holland, Scandinavia and Germany, and it's literally impossible to search them all."

In America, such material is smuggled in amongst sealed cargo and along the old drug route from Mexico. Magazines which previously sold for £2 or $3 in the States now cost £20 ($28), and the films have risen from £25 to £100, and in the US from $300 to $500 a reel. And back-street video companies, both in Britain and America, are said to be hard at work producing new material. Certainly, children I have talked to over the last year have taken part in such productions.

In West Germany, there are laws prohibiting the open sale of such material. Nonetheless, in a sex-shop in Hamburg's St Pauli I found openly displayed twenty-one child-porn magazines at 8 DM each, and a full selection of the eighty films I already knew from New York, at 25 DM each. "At those prices," said my Scotland Yard informant, disgusted, "it's worth it to the buyers to pay for a round trip by air to buy them in bulk."

Child porn, however, represents only a fraction of the child sex industry: a commerce with a billion-dollar turnover, which the police believe is part of organized crime.

I cannot say that I am convinced by this police interpretation as far as child prostitution goes. Pornography, no doubt, *is* part of organized crime. The production and distribution of magazines and films requires the kind of capital and organisation individuals cannot command. But child prostitution, with or without pimps, still seems to me largely the result of individual initiative—a situation which will, however, change very soon unless it is taken in hand.

In West Germany, many though by no means all of the worst pimps—and incidentally the drug-pushers too, though the two are not necessarily connected—are foreigners, former foreign workers. Ever since the beginning of the "economic miracle" in West Germany (now more than thirty years ago), and despite many efforts by the churches, civic organizations and hard-working enlightened individuals, these immigrants have been treated by much of the community, especially the older generations, with contempt and condescension. A sad perpetuation of this attitude is that many of the girls who, by necessity, sleep with these men, use them, serve them, and often claim that they are "kinder than West German pimps," admit to feeling physically repelled by them.

There are marked parallels in the American problem. Here, and on a much vaster scale, it is the blacks who feel themselves to be second-class citizens. It is almost exclusively blacks who are the pimps of white teen-aged girls. "The highest ambition for our young blacks, where it used to be to become a Panther, now is to be a pimp," said a teacher from a remedial school in Detroit, now almost entirely a black ghetto. "If they make it, they are admired and envied."

"Nobody had ever talked to me like he did," admitted one thirteen-year-old, trying to explain her feelings for her first pimp. "He was so gentle, he had so many words, he knew so much, so much about me too and what I felt. He opened the world for me."

"They are the scum of the earth," said one police officer.

It is difficult for those who are confronted with the consequences of these liaisons to control a violent reaction against pimps. While I was researching this book in New York, the body of a young girl, Helen Sykes, was found in a ditch near La Guardia Airport, mutilated. "My God, I've known her since she was fourteen," said Youth Counsellor Trudie Peterson, who for two years worked at "Under 21", a "crash-pad" for runaways in the Times Square area run by a Catholic priest, Father Bruce Ritter (it is now known as Covenant House). "The way the papers make her sound now," said Trudie, "is as if she was just dirt." She cried. "She wasn't like that at all. She was a beautiful delicate girl with red hair and fine skin, who went through a hell of foster-homes in California from when she was two and ended up a runaway at fourteen. All she was, was too fragile—a born victim."

It was never discovered whether Helen's murderer was a pimp or a trick. But no doubt, like most, she was brought into "the life" ("the scene" in West Germany, "the game" in Britain) by a pimp who persuaded her that he could give her what they all crave—love, a relationship and some sort of stability and structure in her life. The illusory nature of this love and stability, and the awful dangers, only emerge later, when the sweet-talk ends and the beatings begin.

The legal impediments to indicting pimps in America and West Germany are incredible. In Britain, the problem is financial rather than legal. All that is needed is evidence of living on immoral earnings, and courts accept police testimony to this effect. But in order to make an arrest, British vice squad officers have to spend weeks on observation and can only arrest a man when they are satisfied they have a case. "And how except in isolated cases can we afford the number of officers it would take to really do the job?" demanded one Scotland Yard official.

In America and West Germany, the courts require corroborating evidence: the act of pimping has to be witnessed and corroborated by the victim, i.e., the girl, for whom it is of course extremely dangerous to testify. The extraordinary New York Pimp Squad, started experimentally in 1976 (described more fully in the American section of this book) has been relatively successful. In the course of their first three years, twenty-nine pimps were sent to prison on the complaints of girls under sixteen, and eight on those of girls aged sixteen and seventeen to mention only those directly connected with this subject. Nonetheless, it appears that success such as this comes too dear; According to latest information, the pimp squad is being faded out—a great relief, no doubt, to New York's "gentlemen of leisure," as the pimps like to call themselves.

"Here it is almost impossible to convict a pimp," said a police official in Berlin, "because it is almost impossible to get any girl to testify. That's why we use our limited resources to get the others, the drug-pushers. There we get evidence in plenty."

In Britain, the problems are still far more individual, and so is their resolution. The coloured pimp is still the exception, not the rule. Indeed, unlike adult prostitutes, few of the young girls will admit to having a pimp at all; they call them boyfriends, and fantasize that the lives they live together are normal. But in England, too, the incidence of child prostitution has increased dramatically over the past years of depression, with increasing financial need on the part of the children, and with demand. Much of the "demand," at least in London, is now from foreigners, many of them Arabs. This is not because they are particularly perverse but because, as one of them said to me, "Firstly, we do not know how old an English girl is, and secondly, you see, it would not be wrong at home to be with very young girls."

Girls in London voiced few complaints about their foreign clients (called punters in England, tricks in America, *Freier* in West Germany). They seem to dislike the native ones more. "Well, they are creeps, aren't they?" said one fifteen-year-old who has been on the streets for just under two years. "If they want to do it with kids, they are creeps."

The fact that child prostitution in West Germany appears—quite erroneously—to be almost entirely associated with drug addiction is the result of a vicious circle. Police tend to concentrate their limited resources on pushers. It is these cases which get into the newspapers. The press, anyway—quite understandably—finds the drama of drug addicted youngsters easier to demonstrate than that of young girls and boys who voluntarily choose to be prostitutes.

Perhaps the most extraordinary thing about the whole phenomenon of child prostitution is that with just a few remarkable exceptions, such as the New York Pimp Squad, virtually all police forces and many official social service agencies in all three countries tend to pretend that child prostitution does not exist.

If it is difficult to get the authorities to admit to the existence of young girl prostitutes, it is, again with a few exceptions in New York and Berlin, virtually impossible to obtain any official information about boys. It is not that anybody denies that there are boys around who offer their sexual services, but—a curious version of sexism—they don't refer to them as prostitutes. Even in West Germany, where they have an identical term for girl and boy prostitutes, *Strichmädchen* and *Strichjungen* (*Strich* strip which in this instance has the double meaning of edge of the pavement and the verb *streichen*—to prowl), people usually add that the boys are not "doing it seriously." They are "rascals" or "just fooling around."

While it is true that a considerable number of boys appear to be "fooling around"—if that term can be applied to part-time prostitution in the case of boys any more than that of girls—there are many others for whom it represents their only source of livelihood. And oddly enough, I found that it is the young boys who become more, and more quickly, corrupted than the girls. On weekend nights they can be found by the dozen in front of the railway stations and in the bars and discos in Hamburg and Berlin; in New York on Third Avenue from 52nd to 59th Street; and, in spite of very efficient sweeps by the West End police in London, on the "Meat Rack" in Piccadilly Circus, in the Piccadilly Underground station and in a number of well-known pubs in the residential districts of Kensington, Mayfair, Chelsea, Bayswater and Queensway.

The main concern of the authorities—at least in Europe—appears to be to scare the boys away, move them out of sight, discourage open soliciting. No questions are asked as to why they do it, who they are, why there are so many of them and how they can be helped. Perhaps it requires more major shocks such as the discovery of young boys' buried bodies in Houston, in Berlin, in Chicago and in London, although one does wonder how many children actually have to die before the words "resources" and "priorities" begin to be applied in a new way.

For the present, in all countries, the commerce continues to flourish. In America, aside from well-known pick-up points in all major cities, a toll-free "Outcall" telephone service, openly advertized in a number of publications and functioning on a computerized basis across the country, offers males of all ages and types, with all specialities on demand, within twenty-five minutes. Their services can be charged to a number of major credit cards. And most of the "males" offered are young boys. Somehow the authorities and the public seem able to keep their eyes shut to the latent violence of some homosexual relations and the danger which these children—many of them basically not homosexual at all, just lonely, poor, foolish or greedy—run.

And all of us seem equally adept at somehow not seeing the newspaper advertisements in all our countries by which girls offer, or are offered for, sexual services under the labels of massage, modelling or escorting. In Britain, a number of respectable magazines and papers still accept such ads. In America, where there has been more publicity, some now refuse to accept them, but others still do. In West Germany and in Austria some of the biggest-circulation press publish whole pages of explicit ads offering young models, "with leather gear," "strict," "special attire," "youngest," "just from France," "young Thai," "boyish and young" and so on. (Austria's largest circulation paper *Die Krone* caused sensation when they decided in the summer of 1983 to accept no further "sexual" ads.) All the young girls I talked with in West Germany—children, every one of them—used these pages "very successfully," they said, to advertize their services.

The children who speak in this book did so voluntarily and in full knowledge that it was for the purpose of a book on child prostitution. I approached none of them directly. Each was known either by a teacher, a social worker, or a police officer who agreed to act as intermediary for me. I wanted no child to be confronted with the necessity to think about my proposal unwarned, in my presence, and as a result feel either pressured to accept or embarrassed when refusing.

My first conversation with each of the children I met was held in the presence of the person who introduced them to me, or else that person was within call. The children were told from the start that they would receive no material reward if they agreed to talk with me. Of the 161 children I met, this affected the willingness to continue of only two, one boy and one girl, both fifteen years old.

Among the first short-list of sixty-nine children, the median age was fourteen and a half, but there were several considerably younger, a number who were already fifteen, and several just sixteen. One—a very special person—was a young adult when I met her. She volunteered to be part of the project and had such a special story to tell that I felt she had to be included. Nine of them were on the point of giving up "the life" or had already done so. Among the children I finally chose to write about at length, two had recently given it up. But both were under pressure to go back.

My talks with the parents or parent-substitutes were mostly about their children's early years: we talked about their running away, but in a few cases they couldn't bring themselves to mention prostitution and I never brought it up unless asked.

In the cases where girls were working for pimps, I offered to pay their daily "quota": the minimum of between $150 and $300 they had to bring to the pimp every night. Three of the children in the book, who very obviously could not be subjected to the risk of punishment for non-delivery, received this "quota" from me—two for several days, one for several weeks. The three who took money on several occasions returned some of it, saying it was "too much," or "I'll manage," or "I don't want you to give me any more. He can go to hell."

Each of the "interviews"—for lack of a better word—took place under conditions as quiet and comfortable as I could manage, most of them in my hotel room in different cities. All these children relish, and relax in, luxury, so I deliberately stayed in very good hotels. In London, where I live, my meetings with the two children I write about at greatest length were at my house. They met my husband and our young daughter and were considerate and careful of their feelings. Others again I saw in hotel rooms, the homes of social workers, or talked to over long meals in quiet restaurants.

Basically what I was doing was using the experience I had gained in two professions: that of social work with children, which I did during and after World War II, and that of investigative journalism which has been my work over the past twenty years. I don't think this kind of research into the lives of children in distress should be or can be conducted by anyone who has not had experience of actually working in the field of child care.

Even so, the work was difficult and presented me with ethical conflicts I never quite resolved. I knew my own motivation for doing this book. I was appalled by the problem, the extent of it and the point to which it was not only being ignored but deliberately suppressed by the authorities. I was and am convinced that opening it up to public examination is the only way that authorities can be forced to act, parents can be helped to exercise greater control on themselves and watch for danger signs in their children, and children—who I hope will read this at an age when it has some meaning for them—can be warned of what is in store for them, should they be tempted to choose this tragic path.

Nonetheless, I never ceased to doubt my right to delve so deeply into these fragile and vulnerable personalities, particularly because they are so open to adult sympathy and help and therefore, also, so open to misuse or abuse. Yet without the questions, there could be no answers, no understanding; and without direction, dialogues such as these would merely reflect and indeed intensify the chaos of their minds and emotions.

In each case, my intention, and that of the intermediary who had brought the youngster to me, was to use these conversations to begin—or in some instances to continue—the process of turning the child around, back towards normal life. The arrangement between me and the intermediaries was that once my own work with the child was done, he or she or someone found between us would continue to work with the child. I hoped that no child would be left high and dry when—as all the children knew—I had to leave.

At the time of writing the last pages, six of the twelve children, all of them now several years older, have stopped prostitution altogether and are back in more or less normal life. Four have been lost touch with, both by me and the social workers who cared for them. We are continuing to search for them and hope that, if we don't find them sooner, perhaps this book will bring them back to us. One girl—you will meet her—is in prison. One, still a child, is in care.

I am proud of my profession and the newspapers I have been associated with over the years. But I am appalled at how many people in the media, in the unceasing search for sensation, take it upon themselves to risk the reputations and even the lives of children in distress by unnecessary identification and photographs in newspapers, and even fully recognizable pictures on TV and in films.

Two German documentaries on the subject of child prostitution, both excellent and instructive in their way, resulted in girls staying away in droves from VD clinics they had been attending because some clinic social workers, with the best intentions and assured that the anonymity of the children would be respected, had collaborated with the film-makers. The girls had then—in spite of this undertaking—been identified in the film. One fifteen-year-old for whom there had been some hope injected herself with an overdose after she had been shown in yet another film on drug addiction and child prostitution. "It isn't worth it any more," she said to a doctor who was called to attend to her, lying on the ground in a Berlin subway station. "Everybody has seen me now; everybody knows me. What could I do, where could I go?" She died.

In Britain, photographs of a young boy were shown on a famous BBC program as part of an excellent documentary on child pornography. The boy's mother had a near heart attack. And the boy, as well as some others from the same town who had been part of a porno-ring described in the documentary, were ostracized by the community. In the end the families had to move. The harm it has done to the children, their parents and their siblings, is incalculable.

Finally—I describe this in some detail in the forthcoming pages—an American TV documentary actually used a thirteen-year-old girl, interviewing her full-face and paying her to take part in an arranged encounter with the pimp from whom she had fled. A microphone hidden under her shirt enabled the nation to listen to the conversation. Afterwards, the pimp was arrested. "We had to get her out of town," said a furious New York police officer. "We've got her hidden away. If she as much as shows her face in New York, she is dead."

Everything the children in this book have said to me is on tape, as they knew it would be. But locations have been changed where necessary and so have names and physical descriptions. Their introducers and their families, they themselves and I (who also hold the releases they have signed) are and always will be the only people who know their identities.

What needs to be read, and known, and understood, is what they say—what has happened to them and why. Who they and their parents are is immaterial. It could be any of us and any of our children.

Part One

AMERICA
The Life

1

"It's just business"

One o'clock in the morning, on Madison Avenue in the Fifties: the unmarked pimp squad patrol car comes to a screeching halt behind a lilac Cadillac with California licence plates, stopped in front of an all-night delicatessen. Two of the three officers are out, one at each door of the Cadillac, before their own car has fully stopped. The man in the driving seat, a tall black about thirty-five years old, is dressed in cashmere: white polo-neck sweater, beige car coat and gloves. His passengers—shopping in the deli—are two blond girls in trousers and fur jackets, one grey mink, the other red fox.

"Getting your supper, are they?" asks the plain-clothes officer. The driver calmly hands over his licence and smiles. "They are always hungry," he jests, his tone self-assured, humorous, even friendly. "They've been hungry all across the country!"

From across the pavement, through the plate-glass windows of the store, the girls had looked very young. "Could be fourteen, fifteen," said the sergeant who had stayed in the car: the pimp squad is considered to be so vulnerable to pressure and accusations from the public that they always patrol in threes, rather than the usual two, and always with an officer. The sergeant shook his head. "Look at him," he said, "a professional, a real pro. Whatever their ages are, their papers will be perfect."

When the girls emerge from the shop and their faces can be seen more clearly, he changes his mind; they are young, but they look used. "Sixteen at least," he says, "and not new at it. Anyway at sixteen, God help us, they are of age in California; we wouldn't be able to touch them. All we can hope is that they get a good look at us and that when he takes off those cashmere gloves after a few weeks and let's them have it square in the kisser—which he will—they'll come to us."

The girls produce their identity cards before they are asked. "Got nothing better to do than hassle peaceful citizens, have you?" asks red fox with a withering look of contempt—Barbara, aged eighteen, according to her perfect card. But grey mink—Jane, nineteen, from San Francisco, her card says—smiles. "Is that a nice way to welcome us to the Big Apple?" she drawls sweetly.

"Everything strictly kosher," says the detective on his return. "Can't book the guy because he's joy-riding with two beautiful girls, even if their IDs are probably phony, and he's got *pimp* stamped all over him."

The pimp squad came into existence in 1976, the brain-child of Sergeant George Trapp. The reason for its existence cannot be simply to "get" the pimps: not because they wouldn't like to, but because it is too often impossible. Pimps, like everyone else, have their rights under the law, and proving them to be in default of the law can take hundreds of man-hours. In America, a pimp can only be arrested upon sworn evidence from one of his "ladies," and it is extremely dangerous for prostitutes to provide such evidence. A vengeful threat by a pimp, I was told by a police officer, "is the equivalent of a Mafia 'contract' and there is no limit in time."

He described what happened when an American television company and a famous crisis centre in New York collaborated in a shocking case of irresponsibility, concerning thirteen-year-old Bianca while she was in the centre's care. They persuaded her to allow herself to be filmed talking to her former pimp. The child, carefully primed in advance, wore a miniature microphone under her shirt and steered the conversation in the desired direction, so that the pimp would incriminate himself.

"I told you I ain't going to force you to do anything that you don't want to do, you know," the pimp said to Bianca, in sight and hearing of the programme's several million viewers. "I ain't beating up on you, because you don't . . . you don't need all that shit. I believe all I have to do is just talk to you cool, you know . . ." Not unexpectedly, he was arrested shortly after the programme went out. But he had time to send a message to the child, as a result of which the police—who had not been told in advance of the programme's content—spirited her away. "She was lucky we could be so quick," said the police officer. "The message was that she was dead."

Bianca was kept hidden in Catholic institutions away from New York for two years, and "every time she ran away, which of course she did, the whole state was alerted and we had to have every police officer in this city on the alert for her. If that girl comes to harm," the officer said, "the people who conceived this outrageous idea and the charity who permitted her to be used for it while she was in their care will be as much to blame as whoever does the actual deed."

Certainly the pimp squad's avowed aim is to prosecute bad pimps (which leaves aside, for the present, the question whether all pimps are evil men, and invariably bad for the girls). But—and herein lies the ambivalence of their job—the only way to do this effectively is to create an atmosphere of trust between themselves and the prostitutes.

It is the job of *other* policemen to pursue and eventually to prosecute the prostitutes for soliciting, for being a public nuisance, or on some other pretext. Such action is fairly pointless, of course, because there is ample proof that no prison sentence has ever deterred a prostitute from going back on the street.

In its most practical, realistic and also idealistic aspect, the pimp squad's mission is exactly the opposite. By its very existence, it can act as a kind of control of the pimp–prostitute relationship, a brake on the violence it is prone to. At the same time, the squad's ultimate goal is to eliminate, by due process, at least the most villainous among the pimps.

To achieve this double purpose, they must play a triple role: they must retain their role of authority figures, dangerous if needs be (like all American police officers, they are armed even when off duty). In spite of this, they must also be seen, to some extent, as the prostitutes' potential friends and allies—and this cannot be faked. They must be capable of feeling this way, and of making the feeling known to the girls. Finally, they need to be exceptionally perceptive about individual pimps. They may—as some do—loathe them as a group, and dislike them as men for what they are. But in order to do their job, they must be able to distinguish amongst them: between better and the worst, or at least the bad and the not so bad.

All this demands from Sergeant Trapp's famous squad an exceptional degree of intelligence, insight, balance and integrity. It also requires a liberal and unconventional attitude from above. Few American cities have been able to duplicate New York's endeavour—and indeed, as this book is finished, the New York Pimp Squad itself seems to be doomed.

When I was researching in New York City, Sergeant Greenlay was one of the police officers who worked for the Runaway Squad, which is in charge of identifying under-age children on the loose and returning them to their place of origin. "What the pimps all share," he told me, "is a basic contempt for the women they use. They are just meat to them, to be sold over the counter."

And this "sale over the counter" actually happens. Not so long ago two girls of fifteen, accompanied by a police officer, flew back to the Middle West from New York. Three months before, a pimp using the name of Earl had driven them, with two others aged fourteen, to New York in his Cadillac. The day after his arrival he sold the fourteen-year-olds—they were American Indian children—to a pimp from Boston for $200 each, while the fifteen-year-olds went to work for him on 32nd and Madison.

Alvin, a pimp with whom I discussed the incident, expressed amused surprise at my surprise. "It's business," he said, "just business." We were sitting at the bar of the Pork Pie, a pimp hangout on 50th Street between Broadway and Eighth Avenue. The darkness of the place—there was virtually no light except for two spots over the bar and the flashing colours of a pin-ball machine and juke-box—was emphasized by the fact that all the customers, except for two girls—one very young and blonde—were black. There had been a moment of silence when I entered the place. But the conversation, —to all appearances mostly fruity jokes and expansive gestures,— was quickly resumed as I sat down at the bar and ordered a glass of wine.

'What are you *doing* here?" the barmaid, also white, hissed out of a corner of her mouth, as she assiduously wiped the impeccably clean surface in front of me. I said I was hoping for the glass of wine I had ordered. She looked stunned. "Can't you *see* this isn't a place for you?" she whispered. None of the customers seemed to watch or listen. ("You bet your life they heard every syllable and watched your every move," said George Trapp, horrified when he heard the story later.)

There were eleven men, sitting or standing in groups, and two girls: the little blonde, probably an under-age youngster, and a red-head, slightly older. Three of the men were quite old—white hair, canes and crumpled clothes. These were former pimps, men with a past but no future, silently waiting to be offered drinks and equally silent if offers were not forthcoming. The two white girls—manifestly belonging to a tall, lissome youth with smooth brown skin, a light tan coat, an open lacy shirt and a gold and silver medallion on a silver chain—said nothing. They stood back, listening. They didn't interrupt or speak to each other, even when the man began a tour around the tables, his street vocabulary almost a foreign language to me.

The only other person sitting at the bar—I had deliberately sat down near him—was a rather small man with an intelligent face, who gave the impression of enjoying some standing in his world. He exuded assurance, calm and a disconcerting cold humour. He introduced himself as Alvin. ("That means nothing," said my police friend. "Hardly any of them use their real names. They pick one out of movies or magazines.")

It did not bother him at all to talk to me when I explained what I was doing. He made it clear, though, that anything beyond chit-chat would have to be for "a share in the royalties." If I wanted to know what the life was all about, he knew more about it than anyone else. (Slim was to use almost identical words when I met him a few days later. And Rachel said, "They are all incredible show-offs—they all know *every-thing*. They not only know all about their business, they know all about everything in the whole world . . .")

I said that I already knew quite a bit. "Then why are you here?" he enquired. "And what do you know, outside the usual newspaper nonsense about pimp brutality and so on?"

"I know, for example, that many of the girls I've talked to claim to love their pimps." He was silent. "But it seems difficult," I went on, "to associate that concept with the auctions I understand you hold here, and elsewhere."

If I wanted to talk about love, he said after a moment, it would be on the basis he proposed or not at all. As for what I called "auctions"— "That's business, just business." There was nothing brutal about it, nobody hurt the girls and they were there of their own free will. He pointed to the two free-willed, silent creatures near the door. "You don't see any chains on *them*, do you?" He asked it loudly, and laughed at the girls' pimp who had just passed us. He joined in Alvin's mirth with a deep belly-laugh. "Chains?" he repeated, and danced a little jig. "You in chains, girls?" he called across the room, and they too laughed, with a shrill note.

"A player passes on a girl," said Alvin, in an instructing tone of voice, "because he's too busy elsewhere; he can't give her the attention she needs."

The "passing on" is actually unlikely to happen in as visible and obvious a place as the Pork Pie, I was later told by a black under-cover police officer. "It really is like an auction—they usually do it in small tucked-away bars. The girl is put up on the bar." Dressed? "Oh yes, unless it's slow going, then they might pull her skirts up and tell her to show her tits. But more often than not," he said, "it goes very quickly and in an atmosphere of fun."

"*Fun*?" I asked.

"Fun," he replied, drily.

I don't know what happened to the fourteen-year-old Indian girls in Boston. But the fifteen-year-old girls' quota, for nine hours on the street, was set at $250 dollars. This was collected by Earl each night, except for the customary $5 for coffee, sandwiches, and the taxi home. During the autumn weeks, they would testify later, their average was "ten tricks a day, at thirty dollars each." In later November, as the weather turned raw, their earnings fell off. The third time one of the girls—she was 5 feet 2 inches tall and weighed 103 pounds—came back with less than $250 she was stripped, strapped across a bed and —in front of the assembled stable of four girls—beaten with a wire coat-hanger until she fainted.

"That's one of their ways of "kicking ass," said Sergeant Greenlay. Usually, he added, in addition to the methodical beatings, the girls being disciplined are subjected to humiliating public sexual acts—perversions they are made to perform in front of the stable and often other pimps.

By the time these particular fifteen-year-olds were picked up, just before Christmas, they had received two more savage beatings. I saw the police photographs of their injured backs, deep weals running from the waist to the knees. "The wounds will heal," Sergeant Greenlay said, as we went through their collection of hundreds of such photographs. "But the scars will remain forever. They are marked for life."

For child prostitutes, however much they may deny it, fear plays a large part in their life with pimps. Maria, whom her foster-mother had described to me as the "most beautiful baby she'd ever seen," was still beautiful when the pimp squad pointed her out to me, twelve years old and standing at the corner of Madison and 33rd Street at one o'clock in the morning. She was small, slim, with a short smooth haircut, and exquisitely dressed, all in beige—trousers, boots, sweater and an expensive short fur jacket, her skin as golden as her clothes.

She looked angry, not frightened at all, when Karen, the police-woman with us, jumped out of the car and pulled her in. "You took me in three days ago," she snarled, "and you took me in last week. What is this, a conspiracy?"

("In her case, and with other very young ones too," said George Trapp, "we deliberately take them in quite often to let their pimps know that we've got our eyes on them. It's the only protection they've got.")

It was explained to Maria that this time all that was required of her was to mind her manners for a little while, and try to give civil answers to my questions, after which she'd be let out where she was picked up.

She was very wary, very guarded in her replies to my careful questions. To be picked up as a runaway and sent back to wherever she had absconded from—foster-home or an institution— was routine for her. She could handle that. "She's been sent back four times," they'd told me, "but no walls, no locks can hold her. In twenty-four hours, sometimes less, she's back."

She could also handle being questioned about her pimp. "He's fine," she said, her body pressed into a corner of the back seat, her face dead, her voice without expression. "I'm happier than I've ever been."

What she could not handle easily were questions about her mother. Was she seeing her mother? She shrugged. Did she phone her some-times? She shrugged. Did her mother know what she was doing? That provoked a convulsive arching of her body and a hiss, like an angry cat. It gave me goose-pimples. Karen raised her hand—was it to warn me, or Maria? I didn't know and nor did she, she later said. I changed the subject, swiftly.

How did she feel about her foster-mother? "I love her," she mumbled, "I love her best in the world. I'm going to spend Christmas with her"—it was the first information she had volunteered. Also for the first time she looked me fully in the face. "I've bought her a present," she said. "A watch."

(I spoke to Cherry, her foster-mother, after Christmas, to ask about Maria's visit. "She phoned," she said, "Christmas Day, it was. She said she wanted to come but he wouldn't let her. She was crying so hard . . ." she too was crying, ". . . she sounded just like she did when she was five.")

Sure her pimp gave her money, Maria said, her eyes once more turned inward. Sure he bought her clothes. "Look at me: anything I want. I only have to ask." Sure, he was good to her, took her out, fed her good. She shrugged. "I love him, sure."

Yes, he had other ladies. They all lived together in a big apartment on the West Side. She, as the youngest, was pampered by everybody. It sounded cosy.

Could I come and see the apartment, meet her pimp and the other girls? She looked up, wide-eyed. "Are you crazy?" she asked. She turned to Karen (although there were three police officers in the car, she never addressed or looked at the two men) and repeated, "Is she crazy?", then just ignored the suggestion.

Did she have a quota? No, of course she didn't have a quota, why should she? He trusted her. Did she work every night? Yes of course she worked every night. "Just from ten to four," she said.

How many men? She shrugged—stupid questions. It wasn't the hours or the men that mattered, but what they paid and I should have known. She didn't say that—she didn't have to, her shrugs said it all. She made about $400 on a bad night, $700 to $800 on good nights. Alan, her pimp, brought her to work in his Caddy and picked her up when she was through. For the first time she showed feeling when talking about her life: he looked after her, she said, with pride.

Two years later, now in an institution for her own protection, she told me: "Alan was a shit, a double-triple shit, and I was scared to death of him. . ."

2

"Life was a pit"

Eleventh Avenue and 42nd Street in New York on a wet winter night: locked warehouses and garages, heavily fenced against intruders. A few primitive diners and empty sidewalks as far as the eye can see, the only sign of life the changing traffic lights. It is about as desolate a place as one can imagine.

"They call it the sink," said Cassie. She was fifteen, with a rounded face, her only make-up the thick, shiny light-blue shadow on her eyelids. Slim and of medium height, she had long, fair, very clean hair, and although it was November was wearing only the tightest of tight white jeans, a thin white polo-neck, a little unlined white leather jacket and shiny white boots. A remarkable-looking girl.

It was Ray who had "turned her out" on Eleventh Avenue. Ray, her sixth pimp.

"Big Daddy was my first pimp," said Cassie. "I met him in the bus depot, up home."

The bus depot in downtown B—— is dingy. When I saw it, a toothless old man was listlessly sweeping the floor while four kids, their transistors turned to raucous rock music, threw chewing-gum wrappers in the wake of his broom. He noticed, but didn't even turn around. "Why don't you kids behave yourselves?" said a fat black lady a few seats away. "He hasn't done nothing to you."

"Go fuck yourself," one boy replied conversationally, and all four laughed, their laughter high, provocative and unamused. And after a brief parley they carefully laid their beer-cans on the floor next to their chairs and watched the dregs seep out. "Hey you," shouted one of them to the old man, "Wipe up the shit."

"They don't mean nothing," said Cassie, hearing the story, "they're just bored." Boredom was something she was an authority on: her capacity for it was instant and unlimited, her concentration span on anything outside herself close to zero, except when she spoke about "the life," which she had been engaged in for three years when I met her. "When you were down at the depot," she asked, her voice suddenly alive, "did you see any macks?" (a term used for pimps) "Because that's where they hang out, in the bus terminals."

In fact, I thought I had. There were five black men lounging about, all probably nearer forty than thirty, none of them with luggage or giving the impression of waiting for a specific person. Also, although they didn't sit together, it was evident that they knew each other; there were nods, winks and occasional words from one to another. The most conspicuous of them was a really sharp looker, elegantly attired in white trousers, a white turtle-neck sweater and fawn-coloured jacket (both cashmere, I was sure) and camel-coloured bootees which looked hand-made. ("Oh he was a *player*," said a pimp in New York to whom I described what I had seen. Players are the highest category of pimps.) He really was a very impressive-looking man, clean, prosperous and self-assured. What's more, he had an interesting face, the kind of face one might trust.

Cassie was twelve years old when, truanting from school, she met Big Daddy one October morning. "Life was a pit," she said.

She had been waiting for a girlfriend who was coming to stay with her. "Her father was a doctor, and they had lived near us a few years before and then moved west," she told me. "I guess his being a doctor made them acceptable to my mother, because she was one of the few girls I was ever allowed to have in the house. She was a real exception."

Big Daddy had sat down a little way from her. "He was sitting across from me," she said, and laughed, remembering—it seemed with delight—that moment two and a half years before. "He's beautiful. He's tall, he's got long hair but it's styled nice, you know."

Frizzy hair? "He has it rolled—really nice. He's got a beard. And he's very slim. So he's sitting there and, you know, like when you know somebody's looking at you, you start getting self-conscious about yourself? Well, the way he's looking at me gets me sort of nervous and I get to doing all sorts of stuff. So he gets up and goes some place and then he comes back and sits down beside me and just starts talking. I can't relate to what he is talking about because, you know, when people have that accent, like a city accent, and talk low because they don't want anybody to hear, you can't really understand what they are saying . . ." What Cassie, the child of sternly racist parents, means to say is that the tall, slim, bearded man was black and spoke black language.

What did she look like that day?

"I was really tanned from the sun all summer. And my hair—it wasn't artificially bleached like now, it was real dark blonde, like I am naturally."

Oddly enough, despite her exaggerated make-up and sophisticated clothes, it was the word "natural" that had sprung to my mind as soon as I saw her.

She had been brought to me by a New York Port Authority police officer whom I shall call Dan. I had been told that he, like a number of others I was to meet, was an officer of the law who did not just enforce it but who cared, especially, about the hundreds of youngsters arriving off the buses in the Terminal concourse (where many of them try to spend their first night), or drifting in the nearby streets. So obviously young, they are readymade victims for the predators lying in wait, and it was part of Dan's job to prevent this. He is black, a university graduate with degrees in sociology, psychology and literature. On his desk in the small room shared by the Youth Officers on the second floor of the Port Authority Building on West 40th Street, there were books by Freud, Tolstoy, Schumacher and Faulkner. He had put Cassie back on the bus she arrived on, paid her fare and watched the bus leave. "Of course, as I knew she would," said Dan, "she got out at the first stop, hitched a ride to the nearest subway and took an express to Forty-second Street. It's hopeless—if that's what they want to do, they'll do it. We can't *force* them not to. The only way is to get them never to *want* to do it, or to stop wanting to do it."

I was then at the very beginning of my research. I had not yet fully realized that these children present a problem which virtually no police force anywhere in the Western world had been able to solve. They are children who cannot bear to live with their families and who will not stay in institutions. There *is* no place for them to go.

*

Half an hour after Dan had left me in his office, the door opened. "This is Cleo," he said, and gave her a little push in my direction. "That's Gitta." Cleo was the name by which she was known in the "life".

The preliminary fencing—"Yeah, and why are you going to do a book like that? Yeah, and how much money are you going to make off it? Yeah, and who's going to read it?"—didn't go on for very long. She *wanted* to talk. Indeed, given a neutral but caring adult, she was desperate to do so, and this was to prove true later of almost all the children.

On that first day she wasn't prepared to speak about her background, her parents or her battles with them, and much of what she told me about her beginnings in prostitution was part-fantasy. The fantasy did not relate to people or events, only to places. Her home, she said, was out west, and her meeting with Big Daddy had happened in Los Angeles. All of her story, that day, was given the golden glow of Californian life, which represented her dream of glamour, freedom and warmth. As we became friends, starting the very next day, she corrected the story and later, wherever she could, took me to the places she described, and wrote down descriptions of other places I hadn't been able to see for myself. And she told me that her real name was Cassandra, though her family called her Cassie. But to everyone on the street, she was Cleo.

"I looked like a regular beggar that day I met Big Daddy," she said then. "Pair of old faded jeans, rips and patches all over. I had on a pair of mountain boots, I think, chain belt and, you know, these hats that Billy Jack would wear. I always wore a braid on one side and beads all the way up it. No—" she said, "I didn't wear make-up." And she didn't know about pimps. "Not really, except once my uncle said something. My mother's Italian—he's in the Mafia."

(Her mother, desperately wedded to respectability, would later haltingly reject that. "Well, he's an American," she said. "Mafia, I don't know . . ." she added, sounding unconvincing. "He is . . . he's . . .", and then she stopped.)

"We aren't allowed to bring up his name in our house," continued Cassie. "But I was staying with him once, and he was reading in the paper about some guy in Florida who was killed by a pimp, and I asked what was a pimp and what was prostitution." The uncle avoided answering. "I had the wrong idea," she said. "I knew that girls sell their bodies, but I didn't know exactly how they'd go about it, and I wasn't sure whether it was legal or illegal."

Anyway, she asked the "beautiful tall bearded man" in the bus station what his name was. "He said, 'Well, you can call me Big Daddy' "—she laughed. "He was very sweet. You can get a first impression of somebody and after you get to know them that impression changes. But that first impression I got of him stayed through the whole relationship." (This, it turned out later, was not true.)

"He started to talk about marriage and about how much there is to learn, and he talked about life in general, and nobody had ever talked to me like that. So I started really listening and we started to really have a conversation. He was really nice to me, and I liked him a lot.

"He gave me his phone number, and when my girlfriend arrived soon after, I had so much in me—this guy put so much in me—I was thrilled and I felt good, real good about myself. She was a good friend, you know, I'd known her since I was nine, so I was very happy to see her just then and I told her right away about this big guy. He was . . ." she hesitated for a moment, "he was the first black guy I'd ever met. She's going 'Yeah, yeah,' and I'm saying that he was a black man, but really nice. I told her he said to call him Big Daddy and she says, 'He sounds like some kind of pimp to me,' and I felt she was insulting him.

"A couple of days later I decided to give him a call. I wanted my friend to meet him. He told me to meet him at such-and-such a place, and when she saw him—just the way he was dressed, you know—she says to me as we walked up to him, 'He's a pimp!' I don't know how she knew. I was scared, but we had a coffee with him and we talked. And then after my friend had gone back home, I saw him maybe once a week. He'd give me things to think about, like he'd say, 'I want you to think about this—' like, being married, or being this person or that person. 'You need to learn to think,' he'd say, 'how people live, and what they are.' "

He had told her quite soon that he was a pimp. "I still couldn't believe it. I said I knew about prostitution, but I didn't really, and I guess he knew, because he told me the real side of it, his side and what it was all about.

"And then one day he said 'Do you want me?' I didn't know what he was really getting at, so I said one way yes, but in another way no. I was in an awful spot. I was mad over him. And he said, 'You could be my lady and I'll put you down here and everything will be cool. You don't have to worry about no police.' He explained it all to me thoroughly, like 'Don't ever get in a car with more than one guy, and check the licence plate before you get in.' And he said the money didn't matter.

" 'I don't care,' he said, 'if you bring in five dollars a night, as long as you're out there trying. Because some nights the police will be out there, and some nights you won't feel like working. The money doesn't matter to me, it's you that I'm concerned about. If you feel strongly about me, the money will come in naturally.'

"I said I didn't believe him, and we both laughed. And afterwards I said, 'Okay, I'll check it out for a week.' So I went home and got into a big argument with my parents, so I'd have a reason to leave . . ."

By "leave" she meant run away. Cassie had already established a pattern of running away which was to continue for over two years and involve countless police searches, and eventually a year's stay in a Catholic maximum security institution. "Maximum security—ha!" she said. "I ran away from there too, eight or nine times."

Her troubled relationship with her parents exploded, she thinks, just before she was twelve and found out that she was adopted, as were her brother Bob, seven years older, and her sister Sally, six years younger. Her mother had had a car accident when she was young, and was unable to have children.

"I don't know how old Bob was when they adopted him," Cassie said, "But I was four months old and Sally was two weeks."

Cassie's mother later insisted that all three children had always known that they were adopted: "We always talked about it openly." But Cassie said that wasn't true. "I found out when I was just twelve. And when she told me, something happened. I just couldn't accept it."

Had her mother told her anything about her natural parents? "She said the place I was born at was a hospital for unwedded mothers, for victims of rape. You'd be there either if you were a rape victim, or a fifteen- or sixteen-year-old who couldn't keep the kid, for financial or other reasons. I was unwanted, anyway. That made me feel real good! I remember, when I got mad at my parents, I used to say something like 'Well, if you didn't love me, why did you adopt me?' Something like that, something to do with being adopted. That used to make them shut up from yelling at me. You know, just something to hurt them, to get them off my back."

Would they answer her?

"No, they'd just shut right up. There were many fights with my parents—my father was always whipping us with his belt—he was really whip-happy."

*

"When my father was away," Cassie said, "it was my mother who beat me: she used to pull down my pants and smack me with a wooden paddle. But usually, if we did something, she would say, 'You wait until your father comes home,' and we'd know that meant a whipping, at least once a week, if not more."

("Well, they have to mind, don't they?" said her mother, sounding despairing—her voice always sounded despairing. "They have to learn it.")

"I can remember getting whipped when I was four or five," Cassie said, and went on to make a disconcerting distinction. "Before I was four they just spanked me, you know." Spanking, she explained, was being slapped on the bottom with the hand; whipping was being beaten with an instrument. "One thing, I didn't mind me being beaten so much. But later it hurt so much to see my little sister be beaten, hear her screaming."

More than half the children I talked to, in America and elsewhere, were beaten—or "whipped"—regularly from a very young age, usually by their father at their mother's direction, and hours after their offence.

Cassie didn't know how babies were made until she learned at school, also when she was twelve. She was six when her sister was adopted. "All that week when I came home from school my parents had been asking me, 'Do you want a little sister? Do you want a little baby sister?' And I said Yeah. Yeah, you know, it'd be fun instead of my dolls. And then they said, 'You're going to have one.' So that confused me and so I started thinking, How can they do this?" She had been sent to stay with relatives when they actually went to get the new baby. "And then one day the door opened and there they were, carrying Sally."

("We were so careful about it, you know," said her mother. "We told her for a long time before, and we tried to make her part of it, like one is supposed to do.")

"I liked her a lot, but then I got really jealous of her. It was all *her*—it was always Sally—it still is, you know. It's not me or my brother, it's Sally. They changed, they definitely changed. Like when I was real small, they kissed me goodnight and good morning, but that stopped after Sally came."

Did she think her parents loved her?

"I hope so. I don't know. I think they do. They have to. I mean, they don't have to, but after fifteen years of me being their daughter, I think they have something for me. I love them very much and I respect them, but I just can't get along with them. We can't live in the same house. They don't want me to grow up, they don't want to let go. . . . About this adoption thing—I think perhaps that was just the last straw. I know that after they used to whip me, they'd always say, 'We did it because we love you,' That confused me about what love was, you know.''

Cassie's parents live in a pleasant residential neighbourhood on the edge of the sprawling city. The houses are ranch style, roomy, each one set in its own pretty garden and equipped with a basement "playroom" or "family room." ("My dad after supper takes his six-pack of beer and goes down to the cellar," says Cassie. "I think he gets high. What else can he do?")

Their house, into which they had moved six months before I visited them, is immaculate. Cassie's mother explained the move by saying: "The taxes are lower here than in our last house. That was much larger—a colonial." Cassie's explanation is different. "They've moved four times in four years," she said. "Every time Mom didn't like the people I went around with, we moved." The moves were not caused by money troubles—Cassie's father is a hard-working man who has always earned a good living as a crane-driver—but by fear. Fear for Cassie, fear for their own reputation which her conduct threatened, and finally fear of Cassie, who had gone beyond their control. She had become a mystery to them, a stranger—the stranger who, in fact, she was by birth—and they were afraid of her.

(This fear of children is, again, not uncommon. Ten out of twelve sets of parents I spoke with admitted to it. "Once you've tried everything," said one mother, "what else is there to do? You tell them nicely, you tell them angrily, you *ask* them to be good, you *tell* them to mind. You try to find out what's wrong—you talk to them, their teachers, the social worker, the priest, the doctor. In the end you feel defeated." It is a very special defeat, engendering a feeling of impotence like no other—and very obvious, impossible to hide. Children despise it, as they depise the fear which their contempt generates in the parents.)

The living-room in Cassie's parents' house is straight out of *Beautiful Homes* Magazine, with an artificial log fire, low tables, two comfortable settees, nice chairs. On one low table stood a handsome vase of artificial roses. On the dinette table were four orange placemats and another arrangement of artificial flowers which matched the mats. There was instant coffee in flowered Pyrex cups, chicken sandwiches with the crusts trimmed off, and a white-iced chocolate cake. "I bought it," said Cassie's mother.

She is Italian by origin, a slim little woman, small-breasted, small-waisted, small-faced. Her hair, beautifully cut in a short bob, is full and blonde. Her eyes are brown, darting and tired. She was wearing well-cut slacks and an expensive-looking white sweater, and was made-up so carefully it might have been done by a professional.

It was obvious at once that she was aching to talk to me on her own. "Go shopping or something," she said to her husband, "and don't come back for a couple of hours or so." He is a huge man, stomach bulging over his belt, large face, large hands, large everything but his voice; he seldom speaks and when he does he mumbles. When he came back three hours later, he was freezing and looked as though he had stayed out in the cold in front of the house all that time, just waiting to be allowed back in. "We haven't finished," she said sharply, and sent him out again.

A little black and white dog had run in with him, and jumped up on me. "Out!" she cried, her voice high, almost out of control. "Out—get him out, Harry!" I reassured her: it was all right, I liked dogs, he was sweet. "No," she said, "he's an outside dog, not an inside dog. And Harry knows it."

Later, on our way to the car when they were going to drive me back to the hotel, we walked past the dog, who was in an enclosure in the garage. I stopped to admire him: he was particularly attractive. Standing up on his back legs and cocking his head to look straight at me with warm eyes, he looked astonishingly human. When I said so, she stopped, put a finger through the mesh way above him, too high to touch him or be touched by him. "The kids love him," volunteered Harry, in a rare burst of information.

Cassie's mother wanted to talk about herself but had no technique for doing so; she had never been asked real questions, only stock ones requiring or allowing only stock answers. These she had at the ready: the kids had it good—they loved them, they gave them everything kids should have or could need.

What, I asked, do kids need?

"Talk, good food, education, a home and of course, love. They have to have plenty of love," she explained. "Hugs, too, kids need that."

Had she or Harry talked to the children about sex, I asked. "Sex . . . yes, of course. Well I told them . . . I gave them books to read."

Not true, said Cassie. It was in her school's health class that she learned the facts of sex. "My mother never talked about it." But, I asked, was she aware, as she grew up, that such a thing as sex existed—that her parents had a sexual relationship?

"I couldn't ever think about them having any kind of sex—it didn't fit them," she said. She had never seen them kiss. "Just a peck on the cheek when he comes home. But they must love each other, because they've been married so long—twenty-six years." She said that in exactly the same defensive way she had said earlier that "They have to love me."

"Do you enjoy sex?" I asked her mother.

"Well, you know," she answered, "I've got this pain. I don't know what it is; they've given me creams and all that, and I put it in, but it still hurts a lot, so no, I don't really enjoy it so much since then."

Since when had she had the pain?

"Oh, about a year. . ."

But before that?

"Well, I never . . . you know . . . well, of course, I liked it all right, you know, but not all that much."

Her husband sleeps now in what used to be Cassie's room. She married him when she was twenty-four and he was a year older. "Love? Well, no. Oh, I *liked* him, you know, but love—no, I guess I didn't love him." She paused. "I . . .I don't like his personality, to be truthful . . . intellectually," she added, the word sounding incongruous.

What about his personality?

"The way he—you know—I just don't like his way of talking . . . of thinking. I don't know, it . . . it so irritates me."

In fact, he can rarely bring himself to talk. "My mother doesn't *let* him talk," said Cassie's brother Bob, and Cassie added: "He is always made to feel so stupid, it has always got to be her, what she thinks, feels, says, orders."

"I've been thinking of leaving him," Cassie's mother said. "I've said perhaps we should separate, but then I change my mind. I said to my mother more than once—not that we talk, my mother and I—but I did say, 'I think I'll separate,' and she said, 'He's a wonderful man.' "

"He loves her," said her son. "He worships her. I tell you, if I have one wish, it's that I find a girl I can love as much as my father loves my mother. He carries her in his hands."

What things *look* like is incredibly important to Cassie's mother. She has constructed an "appearance" life, and everything that doesn't match that pretence existence she so despairingly clings to must be moulded to fit or be rejected. Or rather, as she can't really reject either—for that wouldn't be "right" according to her magazine conception of what is "right"—she battles and rages to force into existence the image she so desperately needs to be the centre of.

In the process of doing this, she has forgotten, ignored, suppressed the fact that all these figures which people her life are human beings, individuals with the potential of independence from her. She rages against their independence, requires them to be *hers*. If twenty or thirty years ago she had had access to someone with interest and insight, perhaps she could have learned to listen, to hear and to give: She is not incapable of loving, nor of gaiety. She is not intrinsically frigid or dry. But whatever was once in bloom within her has shrunk, if not withered.

Harry appears too inarticulate and massive to be a sensitive lover. "My father was strong, he's a big man. And he used to use all his strength," Cassie said. "I used to count when he beat me—the longest I got to was seventeen." Seventeen blows with his belt ("dunked in water," she added). Once she was five years old her mother considered it the father's duty, not hers, to punish the little girl. "I did have an educational paddle," she told me, "but I hardly ever . . . I can't *remember* using it, certainly not often. Anyway, I preferred for their father to punish them when necessary. Often? Oh no, hardly ever. Cassie? Oh, I don't know—once, maybe twice he spanked her."

"I did . . .", Harry paused. For a few moments the three of us were talking together. "Perhaps . . . I sometimes thought that perhaps I spanked her too hard." He has his own kind of honesty. Again, if there had been the time and opportunity long ago, he could perhaps have been reassured about his own value as a man. Thus enabled to speak, he would have spoken the truth. "But I didn't spank her often—I don't know, maybe six times."

"Six?" said his wife. "I don't think it was that often."

"No, probably not," he agreed quickly. "Less . . . four."

"Two, I thought," she said.

"Yes, perhaps two times," he accommodated his estimate to her requirements.

"Ha!" said Cassie. "Well," she conceded, "perhaps it wasn't every week—maybe it was every two weeks." I pointed out that over eight years that would add up to some two hundred beatings. She laughed, embarrassed at this monstrous figure. "No, it can't have been that many. But two, or six—that's ridiculous. It happened all the time."

However often it actually happened, the fear or perhaps the anticipation of it was in her bones throughout her childhood years. The memory—less of the pain than of the confused feelings it aroused in her—is part of the nightmare her life became.

I visited Cassie's parents three times. The first time her mother sent her father out, the second time he was out working, and the third time I asked him to drive me back to my hotel. "We'll both drive you," said his wife, and only desisted when I said bluntly that I wanted to talk to him alone, as I had talked to her.

When we were by ourselves, he did at least try to speak, but never to the point of fluency, and never to say a word against his wife. She is the driving force in this set-up, but because he loves and needs her, they are locked inevitably together in their deficiencies. "She's so pretty," he said about Cassie. "She was so cute. We wanted her so bad. I don't know—I just don't know what went wrong."

As I talked to more and more girls and their families, that was a sentence I was to hear time and again. When it "goes wrong," parents hardly ever know how and why it happened. In the Middle West, I talked to two girls—Julie and Anna—and their families. Julie's mother kept saying, "We never stopped loving her." And Anna's mother insisted, "I loved her," as if love explained everything, as if love justified and excused everything.

When I met Anna, she too was fifteen. After more than a year on the streets, first in her own midwestern city and then in Chicago and New York, she had left "the life" and come home of her own volition. "Those days" were when she was just thirteen, already a tall curvy girl with long, dark-blond hair, big soft brown eyes and a heart-shaped sensual mouth. With that strong face, sturdy body, and wide, intelligent forehead—her IQ was 170—she can never have looked like an obvious teenage pick up. Nonetheless, twenty-four-year-old Sonny saw her walk along a street, and "knew."

"I was standing near a bus-stop," Anna said, "and he was walking his dog. He walked up to me and said, 'Hey, what's your name?' And I said, 'Who me? Anna.' And he said, 'Here, will you hold my dog for

me while I go into the dry-cleaners?' So of course I did, and when he
came back, I expected that to be the end of it. But it was only the
beginning."

He took her to MacDonald's. "People are always taking me to
MacDonald's," she said wryly. He bought her an orange juice and
asked whether she walked the streets. When she said no, he told her
she could make a lot of money doing that, and asked whether she
wanted to go to New York with him.

"I said 'No, I'd never do that, never!' I was pretty shocked." It
wasn't the idea of leaving home or even her home town that had
shocked her. "But that he thought I might be walking the streets, or
wish to be a prostitute—that did shock me. I had read a lot about
it,"—she is a great reader and, unusual for a thirteen-year-old in those
parts, was acquainted with Emile Zola's novels. "I'd heard a good deal
about it, too," she said, and added drily: "It didn't seem like a very
desirable profession."

When Anna was small, she and her mother had been close. "I used
to take baths with her and crawl into bed with her on Sunday
mornings." Her usually over-adult voice went dreamy. "I remember
one time seeing a string between her legs and I told her." She laughed.
"And then she told me about menstruation. But later . . ." her voice
changed, "I could never talk to her about sex. Never. Sex was taboo."

And yet, in this intelligent professional household, it was finally
also sexual confusion and ambiguity that led to Anna's catastrophe.

"My parents' marriage didn't last," she said. "My mother just
couldn't live with my father after a while. She was only twenty-one
when she married him, very shy, very unsure of herself, and he was
fourteen years older. He was, I think, terribly unhappy about himself
after he came out of the Korean War. My mother was working her way
up, but he just couldn't get anywhere. And he couldn't express his
unhappiness or anger. If he got mad about something—anything, like
it didn't rain and his garden was drying up, or because it rained too
much, or whatever—he'd just clam up and not say anything to my
mother for days. Silence was his method of punishment for us, too,
later. He was good with his hands, he made things and he gardened
. . . He really did love me, though—" she said this abruptly and
somewhat defensively "because I was his first child. My sister was born
three years later, kind of to keep the marriage together, I think. After
she was three months old, my mother left him for the last of many
times. I was kind of afraid of him, I think. When I was eight, he got

married again, to a nurse, older than he was. We saw him every other week or so.''

The reasons for Anna's fear of her father had been buried deep in her mind for years. They lay in three particular experiences, the first when she was four, before he remarried. She thought it was the first holiday outing she had with him, alone.

"He was giving me a bath in a bucket and soaping me all over and then, you know, saying he was going to wash my pussy. I was standing up in the bucket and he washed me between my legs. I don't remember whether he tried to . . . to touch me. But,'' she added quickly, "he was a good man, basically. And he really loved me,'' and she repeated, "even more than my little sister.''

The second occasion was not long after his remarriage—she was still only eight. "One of my father's sisters had a farm and many kids,'' Anna said, "and we used to go up there and sleep over, sometimes, and have fun. They lived quite near my grandparents' farm.

"It was on one visit we went up there, we were looking at coats for my aunt in a catalogue or something. There was a picture of a sexy young lady modelling a very pretty coat. My aunt, she looked like a farm wife, kinda worn out and stocky, and I pointed to that photo and I said, 'Wouldn't that be a nice coat for you if you got back in shape?' And that really insulted my aunt, so that night my sister and I were driving with my step-mother and father, and my father pulled off to the side of the road and started asking us very accusing questions.

"My sister was only five and we started crying, and we didn't know what he was talking about because . . . '' she stopped for a moment, "because it seemed to be not only about the catalogue. He said that our aunt and her family had felt terribly insulted—terribly 'shocked,' he said—and that my grandmother never wanted to see us again. It was terribly crushing and I felt just totally trapped . . .''

As it turned out, it wasn't just Anna's thoughtless remark to the aunt that had upset the family. "The next day my father took me into his room and told me they had also been terribly insulted because I had fondled their dog's genitals. The cousins told him that I had said I wanted to be a veterinarian and had to know about this. I didn't know what to think because I didn't even remember doing it.''

Did she now remember fondling the dog?

"No, not at all. I wasn't the type to do things like that.'' Following this accusation, Anna said, she was kept away from her cousins—"in exile''—for quite a while. "And my grandparents wouldn't speak to me. I'd get taken up there to see them, but then nobody spoke to me. It's funny—" she returned to the business with the dog—"I don't remember doing it, but I don't remember denying it either. I remember feeling terribly confused about the whole thing, terribly guilty . . ." She sounded desperate, still.

Not long after the bad experience on the farm, her father started having long private talks with her, about her developing body and getting her periods. "It really just grossed me out to hear my father talking about it," she said, and throughout the time she talked about these memories her face was pale, she sweated, squirmed around in her chair and played with strands of hair. "He didn't do it just once, either. It happened several times, as if, you know—at least that's how I see it now—he was forcing the conversation that way."

The worst of these experiences—she only managed to get to it after dozens of talks, and even then only in passing—happened when she was ten.

"I was in his room and he started undressing or something," she said. "And he said, 'Annie, have you ever seen a man naked?' And I turned around to face the wall and said, 'No.' He said, 'Well then, turn around,' and I said, 'I won't—I won't turn around.' He put his shorts on and I said, '*Now* I'll turn around'—I could probably hear him or see him out of the corner of my eyes. And he said, 'You just don't want to see my penis,' or something like that. That gave me a very, very funny feeling. And it scared me, because I knew it was something out of the ordinary, that a normal man wouldn't do, that wasn't normal for a father . . ."

On the last day I spent in Anna's home town—after a week of talks we were good friends and she was much more at ease—I asked her whether she thought it possible that her father had in fact sexually interfered with her, or at least tried to.

"I think it might be entirely possible," she said, thoughtfully. "He might have done something—something more than I said. Something I put away in my subconscious."

And when later, with her knowledge and permission, I talked to her mother, I was taken aback when this quiet sensible woman asked suddenly, before I ever mentioned this story: "Was Anna relieved when her father died?"

Anna, in the final analysis, was lucky: she is a girl who attracts love. I think even Sonny, in his own hapless way, loved her. And as we shall see, at the most critical moment of her young life she was finally rescued by love from a totally unexpected source. Most important of all, however, her mother truly loved her and Anna always knew it.

Julie, on the other hand, like Cassie, was desperate for love all her life. Her mother claimed that "we never stopped loving her," but Julie was always frightened of and for her mother.

She is a small girl, only a little over 5 feet tall. She is slim, with a round, child-like face, a tiny waist and a warm voice. Everything about Julie is soft, tentative and shyly alive. Everything she says manifests curiosity and humour, and it seems impossible to think of her as a prostitute. Yet when I met her she was just sixteen, and had been in "the life" for three years, suffering experiences which would, one would have thought, have destroyed someone twice her age.

When she left home at thirteen, after a final traumatic occurrence, she was immediately recruited by Irving, also a small-time pimp. He installed her in a room in a run-down hotel in the city centre, and explained a few things to her. "You know," she said, "what a trick would do, how he'd come up to me and approach me." Did he tell her how much money to ask for? "He said not to take anything under twenty dollars." Did he say she had to do anything men asked for? There was a long pause before she answered, "Yeah."

The first day she made about $60. Wasn't that very little? "You see," she said, "I didn't dare go out on the street because I was sure my mom had called the police." So Irving arranged for the desk clerk to provide the tricks. Did the pimp pay the desk clerk? "No, I turned a trick with him." she said. And who were the men the desk clerk sent up? "Well," she said, "there were a lot of . . . kind of bummy old men staying there . . . " That must have been pretty terrible for her, wasn't it? "Yes, it was."

Although Julie's family background is rather more middle-class than Cassie's—her father is an accountant and her mother dabbles in the decorative arts—there is a good deal of resemblance in their home circumstances. Her mother, too, has a mania for moving, creating in each house an identical and obsessive order. "Everything had to be in its own little place, everything was always immaculately clean." Also, just like Cassie, Julie was beaten "from the time I was—I don't know—three, four?" she said, and added in her soft voice: "I guess I was pretty bad. My mother would say, 'You'll get your spanking when Daddy gets home.' And then he'd put me across his knee and give me three, four hard whacks on my bottom. It happened at least every other day or so until I was ten."

Why just ten, I asked. Did her mother say, "Now you are ten, you won't be spanked any more"?

"No, I think it was more I was getting better, perhaps." She reflected for a moment, then said, "It was funny, you know—it was my father doing it, but I always thought it was her, because it was her that gave the orders to do it."

As well as the spankings, Julie was punished by her mother's screaming rages and then by silences. "When she was *real* mad, she'd give me the silent treatment. She'd scream, 'I don't care about you, do what you like—' and then she just wouldn't say anything at all for hours, sometimes a whole day. Every day I did something that made her be silent—real small things, a spot on my dress, a moment's delay if she called me, a toy out of place in our room." Until Julie was eleven, she and her brother, two years younger, shared a room.

"When I was five we moved to a duplex. The top was like an attic and that was our bedroom. I thought my mom made us sleep up there because she didn't like us," she said. "I was always on my guard, always tiptoeing around trying not to make her angry. The thing was, she just wanted me to be this perfect little girl—I don't know, maybe it was the perfect little girl she thought *she* should have been and wasn't, but it was real hard for me to do it. I was hearing all the time how awful I was. I remember one day—I guess I was about six or seven—I'd dressed up and put on make-up, you know, make-believe, and I came down to show her and she slapped me and called me a whore. Later I had phases of breaking things—I didn't *want* to break them, I just did. Anyway, I broke a glass and she got real mad. I was trying to apologize. I followed her to the bathroom and there she was, cutting off her hair. Whenever she got really mad, she'd start cutting off her hair. I was trying to make peace with her but she wouldn't let me. She was screaming and I tried to take the scissors away but I couldn't, so I went to the neighbours and they called my dad."

The majority of girls who become child prostitutes appear to have suffered childhood traumas associated with early sexual experiences. This doesn't mean, of course, that any child who suffers such experiences necessarily becomes a runaway or a child prostitute. But it does demonstrate that the violation of fragile child sexuality, if it is combined with other family tensions or emotional deficiencies—whether in the child or in the family—makes the probability of catastrophe in puberty extremely high.

"When I was little we had this baby-sitter," said Julie. "She was sixteen and she'd baby-sit my brother and me on weekends when Mom and Dad would go out. Well, one day she decided my brother and me were going to play—as I remember, she called it 'doctor.' She told me to lay down and take off my clothes, and she told my brother to try and put his penis in me. That wasn't long after we'd stopped having baths together because my mother had said we mustn't touch each other."

Had they touched each other? Was that why her mother had said it? It would have been quite normal, I said, if they had. She didn't answer. In every child I spoke with who had had such experiences, the guilt engendered by parental reaction endured.

"My mother sat in our bedroom and said I wasn't supposed to touch his penis and he wasn't supposed to touch my vagina."

Were those the words her mother had used? "Yes. So you see," she went on, and it was almost like talking to someone who was sleep-walking, "it was real weird because I was so scared of my mom, but I was so scared too of the baby-sitter. When I said I wouldn't do it, she said she'd tell my mom when she came back in the morning that I'd been bad and then, when we woke up, we'd get a spanking. So my brother tried but he couldn't, you know, and she stood there and laughed and laughed—it was real weird."

Could Julie remember what she felt? "The thing I remember was just closing my eyes and trying not to think of what was going on."

But didn't she tell her mother when she came home? "No, because I was so scared of her, I thought she would blame *me*. But then it happened again and again—five times altogether."

Five times? "Yes. And a couple of times she took her clothes off and she was rubbing against my brother, you know? And I asked her, 'Can I go in my bed?' and she said 'Yeah, go ahead.' So I just . . . covered up my head."

And when the girl left the room, did she and her brother talk about it? "No."

Never? "No, You see, my mother had told us that we weren't supposed to touch each other and then that had happened, and we were feeling real guilty . . . I don't know . . . we . . . I just couldn't . . ." She stopped.

And what finally brought it to an end? "Well, you see they didn't go out every weekend, so she didn't come every weekend, maybe every

two or three weeks; so it went on for a very long time. The last time
something happened . . . in the living-room . . . on the floor . . ." She
couldn't bring herself to go into any further details. "I . . . that's when
I told my mom and she told me never to talk or think about it again.
So—you know—I didn't. I guess I blocked it out. I've always wanted to
talk to my brother about it but I just didn't how to approach him on it,
so I haven't."

Did her mother seem to blame her? "No," she said, sounding very
weary. "I don't think so. It was just never spoken of again. . . ."

3

"My mother was freaking out"

It was soon after Cassie's discovery that she was illegitimate and adopted that she met a group of Hell's Angels and fell in love with one of them. It was Bud who first named her Cleo, which later became her street name. "After some goddess or something," she said. "He had long, long hair, really hippyish, and he had a big bike." These groups of motor-bike-roaring hippies—some of them middle-class college drop-outs—terrified people at the time.

"Five, six, seven of them would come up the road, leaving a cloud of smoke behind. I'd look out the window and think, 'Oh my God, I've got to pretend I don't know them!' But then of course I couldn't do that. And they'd give my mother evil eyes and they'd say for me to come to a party with them. And my mother's freaking out, she doesn't know what to do. You know, she's going, 'Oh God . . .' And so I'd go and come home like four or five in the morning, and later when my father came back, he got to know, of course, and I kept getting beatings and beatings and beatings. But me and Bud, we got really tight, really tight. He was my first. . ."

Until then, Cassie had been pretty good at school. "My grades were in the eighties," she said. She never liked gym—she didn't think it was important, and skipped it whenever she could. "I got in lots of trouble over that. One class I always wanted to do was algebra, and then English. I wanted to do journalism later, and business courses." The courses she skipped and over which she got into trouble were art—"I wasn't interested"—and science. "I just never went." But she loved typing. "I used to sneak in there even when I wasn't supposed to." And she was very active on the school paper. "The journalism class wrote it up once a week—I loved doing that."

The trouble she got into for being "not interested" and for truancy resulted in several temporary suspensions, and later two different schools expelled her. Did she care? "Yes, I did," she said, sounding very young. "I liked school."

Obviously every child I saw was different. Although there were a number of things most of them had in common, no one case is more "classic" than another. Nor would I wish to claim that the children I chose to write about represent a norm in this abnormal group.

At the same time it is one of the phenomena of child prostitution that—contrary to what one might expect—most of these children are above average in every sense: they are intelligent, imaginative, warm, curious and loving. They are also very much individuals, with a very special need for freedom.

Thus Julie, too, enjoyed school and got high grades until she was eleven. She wrote poetry, loved music and would eventually, after getting herself out of prostitution, be accepted for a pre-college summer school which led to a university place.

Anna, with her exceptional IQ, had been put a grade ahead as soon as her school realized her potential. After leaving "the life," she too passed her high school equivalents and may now enter college. And Rachel (who we will meet presently), after being at thirteen part of a highly sophisticated stable of very young prostitutes, now teaches at one of America's greatest universities.

Did Cassie's parents ever give her a typewriter? "Oh, no," she said, and then, as often happened in her effort to be fair, she added: "If I don't have something, I want it, but once I have it—well, perhaps they thought I wouldn't make much use of it and perhaps they were right."

She enjoyed talking to people, asking them about themselves. Did she think she was good at it? And she answered characteristically, "I don't think I was good at it—but I enjoyed it!" But when she was twelve, in seventh and eighth grades, "I just stopped. I didn't do any more homework or nothing. I was too busy after school—parties."

Exactly the same thing happened with Anna and Julie, though for opposite reasons: to Anna because she was not sufficiently attractive to boys, to Julie because they paid too much attention to her.

"I was real small," said Julie, "with a big chest, you know, and that got a lot of attention in the neighbourhood." She laughed. Was that annoying, embarrassing for her? "Not really—it was sort of exciting."

Her first boyfriend, when she was twelve, was an eighteen-year-old. "I was crazy about him; he was real flash. He had his uncle's big car. We went to the movies; we drank." Did this boy work, have money? "He stole," she said indifferently. "And we smoked weed . . . and . . ." And? "Well, we played around." They had intercourse? She blushed—their fundamental shyness never ceased to amaze me. "No . . . We played with it."

Did her mother know this boy? "She saw him from afar, you know, he was at my school. I told her he was fifteen."

But didn't she insist that Julie should bring him home? "He was black," she said. "But you know"—and there was wonder in her voice—"he never, you know, he never pushed me to do anything. The grandmother he was living with was a really nice lady—she brought him up right."

Anna, too, came upon two "nice guys" to start with. "I was very involved with the Unitarians," she said. "I still am—or at least I am again now. But I used to go to camp, and that's where I'd go off into the woods with those guys." She laughed. "I mean, one at a time, you know, and we kissed and all that. But that was all." And then she said again, "I wasn't that cute—they weren't exactly rushing me. But I seemed to spend a lot of time thinking about it all, and my grades just plummeted . . . "

Did she drink, smoke pot? "With the *Unitarians*?" she exclaimed. "You must be kidding. No, all that happened a little later. By that time, these guys were out of my life."

Bud from the Hell's Angels got Cassie into drugs. "Acid, coke, speed . . . after that I wasn't interested in school any more. The six months I was with Bud we got so tight, it was like the whole chapter of the Angels revolved around us."

But at the end of the six months—a glowing period of excitement and "belonging," even now—Bud hit a rock with his bike and was thrown off into the middle of the road. "It was just beyond a curve, and this car came around real fast at sixty or seventy and hit him, and dragged him about fifty feet and it literally tore him up and he died almost immediately. Just for a moment he opened his eyes and he told me to be cool and said, 'I love you.' "

Bud's friends took her home and told her parents what had

happened, because she was four hours late getting back. "They thought it was a cover story for me coming in so late, and that hurt me more. . . ."

"I was sort of in shock for three weeks after Bud was killed," Cassie said. "Couldn't talk, cried all the time, didn't want to eat or go out of the house." The president of the Hell's Angels chapter—"His name was Normie, he was old, about thirty-five"—came around and told her she had to get herself together. "He told me I had to get up onto my feet and forget what had happened. He talked to me for a couple of hours. He really made me think and realize there was nothing I could do about it.

"So I went to a party they had the next day, and after a couple of days I started getting used to Bud not being around. . . ." And after a few more days, she fell for another boy, Craig. "He's got this long blond hair, blue eyes, he's really nice looking."

Did she like him as much as Bud? "In a different way. Bud was really wild—he was like a free thing." She still thinks about him a lot. "When I compare that relationship with every other I've had since, there's nothing to compare with it."

Pressure and pain which go beyond what one might call the norm: that is what causes children to break right away. A great many children run away from home—a million a year in the United States, approximately 20,000 in both Great Britain and West Germany. But most of them go home again after a brief taste of freedom and want. The roughly estimated ten per cent who don't go home are the children who have had to suffer more than they can bear, for one reason or another.

Cassie, in the final analysis, was more deeply hurt by her parents' lack of sympathy and faith than she was by the loss of Bud. Julie, too, received a deeper wound from her mother than she did from the man who pulled her into a car and raped her at knife-point when she was fourteen.

"I called my mom to come and get me," she said, "and she took me down to the hospital and they examined me. I had a bruise on my leg, and they took a picture of that, and then I had all kinds of tests as a rape victim. The police—they were nice, you know, and the people at the hospital were, too. But I was real upset. It was —you know—too private; I couldn't say anything, I just couldn't."

Julie was no longer a virgin then; she had had her first "real" boyfriend for several months. "What upset me so, I guess, was the thing of a man pulling me off the street and telling me he could do anything he wanted to me. He said that. He said that 'he had the right.' And he got away with it, too. That was another real shock, later—they did everything they could, but they never found him. What upset me, too, was that he had a knife and that he might have used it on me."

Knowing the sequence of events in Julie's life, I said that it seemed extraordinary that, having had such a dreadful sexual experience, she should follow it up almost immediately by turning to prostitution.

"Well, what happened was," she said, "my mom told me that I wasn't supposed to tell anybody, anybody at all: if I did, she said, they'd think I was a whore. The police, you know, they were kind, and sorry for me. But my mom, she was angry; she was angry at me and ashamed of me. It made me feel real bad. It made me feel I was dirty, and it was my fault it happened, that I had worn provocative clothes and stuff. But I hadn't—I was all bundled up because it was cold outside. I don't think she ever understood that it wasn't anything to do with me, with anything I did. For days afterwards she kept reiterating I was a whore, and she started calling me 'bitch'—you know, 'bitch' instead of 'Julie.' "

Her mother's voice is as light, as well modulated and charming as Julie's. There is no way one can imagine her calling her exquisite fourteen-year-old daughter a whore, or even pronouncing the word "bitch." "But she did," said a social worker. "It's not Julie she worries about so much as herself and the neighbours; I've seen her rage."

"We just worry so about her," Julie's mother said to me—and it could have been me or any of our friends talking about our children. "It's always with us, this worry. And the days, the hours really, when she seems happy and content . . . it's like a rock coming off my heart. I want to sing."

"Finally I just couldn't stand it any more," said Julie, and cried. "So I went away."

She went downtown, "and there was this guy, he was tall, you know, about twenty-seven. His name was Irving. I liked him, he said he'd take care of me. So I went to stay with him at this hotel, and he turned me out. Yes, I was real scared, but I figured it was better than home. You know, like I was feeling so bad about myself that I felt anything was better than that. Anyway, now I was just what my mother always said I was: a bitch and a whore."

In Anna, the build-up of pain was much slower and more complex, originating in damage done to her when she was very young. In her case there was no lack of love and understanding on the part of her mother, and her step-father too—although an authoritarian sort of man—was unusually understanding and long-suffering. It is difficult to see how they could have done more than they did to help. And Anna recognizes this by now: she knows not only that her mother always loved her, but also that perhaps she loved her mother too much.

Her mother married John, a politician, when Anna was twelve. "We were very careful. We were perfectly aware that it might not be easy for the children, especially for Anna." And indeed, a child so much at odds about her natural father, and so loaded with unexpressed guilt feelings, was bound to react problematically to the prospect of a step-father.

"Yes, they were careful," Anna agreed, "But I guess not careful enough."

She was doing a Sunday paper-round at the time, getting up at three in the morning to collect the papers when they arrived at the shop, delivering them, and then going back to bed. (The work young middle-class Americans are allowed to take on by their parents often seems surprising to those in other countries. Julie too, at eleven, had a baby-sitting job starting at five in the morning every day, then went back to bed for an hour before going to school.) "I remember coming in after finishing the paper-round, that day," Anna said. "It was the fall of seventy-six. They were both out on the couch in the living-room—the front door led right in there. They were asleep or something. I don't remember seeing their bodies or anything, but I must have said something to my mother, and then going into my room and crying. It just hurt me so much! It just killed me to see my mother living in sin. Really, it seemed very filthy to me, for my mother to be having sex. . . ."\

But when she had kissed the boys in the woods, at the camp, I said she didn't think that was filthy, did she?

"I can't explain now why it seemed dirty for my mother to be having sex," she said. "Perhaps I'd never thought of her being a sexual being. There was another time, too. We had gotten back from a late night affair at the church, a Las Vegas night where they had raffles. I had eaten a lot and drunk a lot of Coca-Cola, and when we got home, my mother and John came up to me and my mother said that John had forgotten his glasses at his apartment, so they were going over there to sleep.

"I screeched! I just screeched! I said I just wouldn't stand for it. It made me sick to think about it and I didn't want them going over there and sleeping together."

Did she really say that to them? "Yes, I finally got it all out, and then I walked away."

(Anna's mother told me, "First it had been *my* mother trying to run my life. She was so unrelentingly Catholic, remarriage to a non-Catholic was a deadly sin. And now it was Anna, on whom I knew my mother had worked.")

"They talked for a while," Anna said, "and then they came up to me and said that it was my decision. 'You decide,' my mother said, 'whether we stay here or whether we go over to his apartment.' And I said, 'Go then, I don't want to be the one with the decision on my shoulders.' So they went, and that night I got violently ill. Really, considering what I had eaten, it was no surprise. But I was awfully sick and we were alone, and it was very scary and I was sick for the next few days."

Did she think now that she might have been very jealous of the relationship her mother was starting with John? "It could have been jealousy underneath," she said. "Of course, I'd never seen parents in this situation."

What she had also never before faced was the fact of her mother's separate identity: her mother didn't belong to her, she belonged to herself. To the sexual confusion she had already encountered with her father was now added the prospect of a strange man there forever as her mother's husband. Anna's reaction—extreme but not surprising—was to take her revenge by finding a strange man of her own.

"There was this twenty-two-year-old man," she said. "I had met him because I was baby-sitting Vietnamese children while their parents were taking English classes at the Junior High. I did that as a volunteer, you know, on Tuesday and Thursday nights. He helped there, that's how I met him, and he really seemed interested in me."

She used to spend those nights at her grandparents' house, which was very near the school. Conveniently, the Vietnamese boy turned out to have an efficiency apartment—bed-sitter, kitchen and bath—right next door.

Did the young man know she was thirteen years old, and a virgin? "He knew all right," she said.

Did she establish a relationship, a friendship with him? "Kind of," she said. "We couldn't communicate too much because of the language barrier, but he did say he loved me. And—" she laughed—"he knew enough English to ask me after we had sex the first time, if I had the pill. So after another time, I went out and bought some rubbers for him."

She bought them? "Well, I looked very much older than I was."

How did she ask for them, this thirteen-year-old novice at sex? "I would like some prophylactics, please, that's what I said." Anna enunciates very clearly, and her use of vocabulary reminds one continually of her intelligence and reading. "The salesman said, 'What kind do you want, lubricated or unlubricated?' I couldn't think what that meant but I said, 'Lubricated, please'—I figured we'd try those first."

But why didn't she just ask the young Vietnamese to get the condoms for himself? She had read a book by the Boston Women's Collective, *Our Bodies*, *Our Selves*, she said, "and I just didn't feel comfortable asking him to do it, so I would take the matter into my own hands. But I think we only used them once or twice, and after that we didn't use anything. I didn't have the nerve to go again, and *he* didn't do it."

As far as she remembered, they never spoke. "I was really not aware enough of what having sex or making love was," she said. "I didn't know what to expect or what to give."

But was he kind? Was he tender? "He was embarrassed," she said. "But he *did* say he loved me," she repeated.

Of course he was alone in America, probably lonely. Did she think he had found something in her that he needed? "Maybe just a receptacle," she said, just as brutally as it sounds. "Like the GIs who took even younger children in Vietnam; I don't know."

The affair stopped after a few months as suddenly as it had begun. "One night, the last night of those language meetings," she said, "he left before me, and I had to walk home in the rain five miles, and I never saw him again."

All of Cassie's relationships, after her brief rebound affair following Bud's death, were with black pimps. Had she ever had any feelings against blacks? "My parents are very prejudiced, but I've never had no reason to be," she told me.

Are those—*were* those—relationships real ones? "In a sense, yes. I think . . . Big Daddy . . . I had a relationship with him. I was with him for a year and a half." (Later she thought about it again, and it was nearer six months.)

Did he ever beat her, as some of her later pimps had? "He never laid a hand on me, no. He looked after me—he was worried about me. He was concerned about me going on the streets."

But it was he who *put* her there? "Yes," she said factually, "that's his job."

And she never got any indication that he felt there might be something wrong in sending a twelve-year-old girl out on the street? "He was concerned for me," she repeated, still steadfast in her loyalty to the thirty-two-year-old man who had started her in prostitution.

Did she herself feel anything wrong with it? "At first, before I was doing it, of course I didn't know anything much about it; it was something I thought I wouldn't like to do. But then, after I got myself into it, it didn't seem so bad. It was kinda fun."

There is real honesty in a child who, perfectly aware of the stigma attached to her situation, can admit that it was "kinda fun." Most of the girls I talked to demonstrated what amounted to almost a craving for honesty, and many of them had a sense of humour—albeit rather a grim one.

Both these traits were particularly strong in Anna. When she finally ran away from home, taking with her nothing except a back-pack containing her favourite old patched jeans, tee-shirts, a vest and a harmonica her father had given her, she went to Sonny, the "popcorn pimp" who had approached her at the bus-stop, recognizing her potential on sight.

"Where the hell else would I have gone?" she asked. Sonny "turned her out" within twenty-four hours.

Had he given her any kind of advice or instructions? "I said to him, 'What the hell am I supposed to do?' He was really vague about it. 'Hang around the bars,' he said. 'Look for somebody who's likely. Walk up to him and say, "Hey, want to have some fun? Hey, want to go out on a date? Hey, take me somewhere, let's do something." ' And to get as much money as I possibly could, and charge extra for every additional sex act after the first one."

This crudely indifferent initiation—like Julie's—was a clear indica-tion of Sonny's standing as a pimp. The Sonnys and Irvings of the pimp world are crude operators, who are likely to lose their "ladies" within weeks or even days. A "player" like Big Daddy, a professional who in the language of the life is "qualified" to keep a "stable," although potentially more ruthless and cruel, will take the time, as Big Daddy took time with Cassie, to teach and reassure the girl he is recruiting.

So where did Anna find her first trick? "In MacDonald's, wouldn't you know?" she said. "I took a bus with him out to . . . God, I don't even know where it was. I was really unsuspecting. Because the first thing Sonny *had* told me was, 'Never turn any tricks with black men.' Makes sense, of course, because they probably turn out to be pimps in disguise—competition, you know. But this was an older black man, he was a reformed alcoholic and he was living with his AA sponsors. He was very sweet, and when I got in his bed with him, he held me and said, 'Please stay with me and be my lady—please.' But I said I couldn't. . . ."

Later, he gave her $15. "So I took the bus back with my fifteen dollars— and I forgot my watch," which she had carefully taken off. "As you can see, I was fated to be a great hooker." Later that day—this is the kind of behaviour Anna provokes—the old man came looking for her, to bring back her watch.

By the time Cassie and I met in New York, she was fifteen and a half, and on her sixth pimp. "But the only one I ever trusted was Big Daddy." (Only much later would she amend that statement.) "When I first met him, he came right out and said, 'I'm not going to tell you how great I am, and I'm not going to tell you I'm not going to pimp your drawers off. I'm going to tell you that you can trust me, that you've just got to have a bit of blind faith in me and believe me.' "

He told her that out of the money she'd bring in, he'd put so much aside for her to save. "Now, of course, I know they all say that. It's the spiel, the method, the technique. Some are better at it than others. He was very good. I believed him."

Cassie had learned to drive very early. "But my parents never let me; even now they won't let me. Big Daddy, he had a big shiny black car. It was beautiful. He let me drive it all the time. He always said—" she laughed— "it was more class to let the lady drive the man around, so he could relax. He said when he saved up enough money to get another car, he'd give me this one. It was all a game, I know that now, but he played it cleverly."

In their efforts to justify the lie they are living, to themselves, more than to others, these children often spin a web of fantasies. Cassie's, as I have said, was of golden California: her family home, she said at first, was in San Diego, her father was a big business man with homes in various parts of the country, and her childhood had been one of privilege and material ease, with yachting, skiing, water sports and riding.

"My bedroom in San Diego is *me*—I'll probably stay there for Christmas, my stuff's there. I love peacock feathers and I went to the San Diego Zoo and I've got these tall vases in each corner of my room and I've peacock feathers coming out of them. So pretty, and I have a colonial love-seat, and a water-bed—I *love* water-beds. Big stereo, I got a tiger floor rug, a big dresser and a desk. Posters all over the walls."

Such a background could just about have been true. On the surface at least, the young in America are more egalitarian than elsewhere. Nothing in Cassie's looks, manners, and—when she wished—even her language, negated the possibility of a moneyed background. But of course it wasn't true. When I talked to her mother and mentioned these wish-dreams, she was almost speechless. "Oh my God," she said, "she never had . . . San Diego? . . . She never was . . . Well," she finally added as an afterthought, "sometimes on a Sunday or holidays we'd take her to one of these rent-a-horse places and she'd ride. She liked riding."

Most of the children need to glamorize their lives as prostitutes. Cassie decribed in detail the luxurious apartment she and a girlfriend had in Los Angeles, and the extravagant clothes that Big Daddy got for her. "He bought me fancy shoes—I couldn't even walk in them, they had such high heels. He bought me satin pants, so pretty, they tied down around the ankle and this halter-collared shirt that went with it. And he put make-up on me, really good—I can't even do it as good as he did it. He bought me jewellery, he tied my hair back, put a wave in it and he said, 'There's the street.' He took me out and showed me around, what corners would be good and what bars, and then he left after saying to remember that if I didn't want to do something a man wanted me to do, that was my choice. I didn't have to do it."

She sounded full of energy as she told this tale. Later, when she had abandoned the golden fantasy of California and was telling the truth, her voice was sad and tired, and her face drawn with fatigue.

The place where he actually started her off (wearing her "faded jeans, rips and patches all over . . . mountain boots," and a Billy Jack hat) was in the slums of B——. "Really the worst street in town," she said, "all junky and run-down." Later, she described it in detail, in a letter:

[It was] the deepest and darkest ghetto of all. The neighborhood is 97% black, 2% Puerto Rican, and 1% white. The gas station at the corner was boarded up like most of the buildings in that area. In the dead-end street next to the Health Clinic, the buildings were all burnt-out and windowless. ["I used to go to the Clinic every once in a while," she had told me. Why, I asked; did she think she was sick? "No, I just went in sometimes for a check-up."]

She was still only twelve when she began to work for Big Daddy. That went on "for a while, off and on." The astonishing thing is that at the same time she was living at home and going to school, although not regularly. "It was a totally different arrangement," she said, "from anything . . ." she paused . . . "you've got to be in prostitution to understand it. It's just totally different, living at home and working."

She skipped school a lot, to go into town to see Big Daddy. She didn't always have sex with him, "but a lot." Then, as so often, intent on being scrupulously honest, she corrected herself. "Not a lot, but occasionally, at the apartment. He called it *my* apartment, but I didn't live there—I lived at home."

Later, in another letter, she described Big Daddy's apartment.

It's on X Street, looking out over a park. It's a five-story brownstone, he lived on the second floor. As you walk up the stairs, with the dim lighting you can barely see the plaster peeling off the walls. On the top of the staircase, as you bear to the right you see a shellacked brown wooden door with the letters "B.D." typed neatly and pasted up under plastic. . . .

Big Daddy's apartment would shock you as you walk in. The first room is known as a lounge, with a cream-color soft fur studio couch against the far wall. In the corner is a spiral stairs leading from the floor to the ceiling, but nothing at the top. The rug is a soft black shag, and two other chairs in the room match the couch. . . . The wall behind the couch was tiled with mirrors, and in the corner opposite the stairs was a large rubber plant, growing slowly but strong. The remaining three walls were the color of champaigne [sic] with very artistic and well done drawings of naked ladies. . . One with her long black hair hanging below her breasts was reaching over her head. The second one was stretched out on her side, leaning on her elbow drinking a glass of bubbly champaigne and the third one was of a beautiful woman about to make love to a man. They were very artistic and impressive.

The kitchen was off to the left, but hardly used—it was locked up and used for storage.

The beads hanging from the doorway separated the lounge from the bedroom. The bedroom was something else. As you entered the room, ahead of you was a big brass bed, big enough for four people to sleep comfortably. On the right was two double closets filled with his velvet suits and sun shirts. The blue light on the ceiling gave the room a nice glow and showed off the powder blue walls and again champaigne rugs, with a bearskin rug on the floor at the end of the bed. The ceiling had the same mirror tiles as the lounge.

A fish-net hung in the left-hand corner from the ceiling and climbed down the wall with starfish clinging to it. The shades were black velvet and the drapes a navy blue. Bean bags were piled up next to the bed under the fish-net. Vases with feathers and cat-tails were on both ends of the long, low dresser with a mirror. His cologne, shaving cream and odds and ends were lined up neatly on the dresser. On the left of the closets was a small bathroom with toilet, double sink and shower. The bath was gold tile with gold trim, gold shower curtains and velvetty soft personnel towels with B.D. sewn in on them. . . .

His sheets were of black satin and his bedspread of black, with a white man and woman making love in a tree position in the center. His pillowcases were of satin, but matched the description on the spread. He had pictures of himself, near his silver Continental when he first bought it. . .

Did Big Daddy tell her—as most pimps do—not to "trick" with blacks? "Yes, because he wants to be the only black man I have any relations with. They all say this," she added out of her wide experience. "There are a lot of reasons for it. One is that they don't want you to have any real sexual relationship, even if it's only a ten-minute deal—they know that black men and white men are very different in bed. I can't explain the difference. You can become attached to a black man even without realizing it; it's just the way they are, masculine. They make you feel like a woman."

This response to what is seen as the special masculinity of black men emerges particularly vividly from Rachel's extraordinary story. Rachel, now twenty-eight, married and the mother of a baby, became a lecturer at her university upon graduation. She is Jewish, the elder daughter of busy, socialite parents, and at the beginning of the flower-power period of the sixties was attending both an exclusive private school and the local conservatory. She was particularly gifted at music.

"I don't want to blame my parents," Rachel said. "In fact, I have an extraordinary good relationship with them now. But I did have what I remember as a great shock when I was thirteen and found out that my father had a mistress. I knew by mistake, because I walked into a restaurant and there they were, and my father lied to me, and I found out that he lied. I just couldn't understand that—it really blew my mind."

What happened—though no doubt it had already begun to happen before this shock—was that Rachel fell into "bad company" and started to use pot and acid, and eventually heroin. At fourteen she became a runaway and the "main lady" of Lucky, a twenty-nine-year-old player. He dealt in drugs as well, and had set up a particularly efficiently run "stable" of seven prostitutes, all between the ages of thirteen and sixteen.

"I met Lucky in the street," she said. "He was with someone I knew vaguely. It was love at first sight, what can I say? I don't know what he felt about me—I don't know to this day. Except he must have felt something because in the end it was because of him that I finally gave up drugs, and"—even now there is pride in her voice—"he never let me prostitute myself."

While she lived with him, on a strictly controlled ration of heroin which he supplied, her function was to be in charge of his household. She estimated his income from his stable at about $14,000 a week, and he was also in "partnership" with other stables in other cities. "He gave me about three or four thousand dollars a week in cash, for food and clothes for the girls." Rachel had always been dressed at Saks Fifth Avenue, and had acquired excellent taste. "He liked me to shop with the girls, and tell them how to put outfits together, and help with hair, make-up and accessories."

Had she herself never worked the streets? "In a sense I wanted to," she said. "I wanted to go out and do something for him. I only didn't because it seemed important to him that I shouldn't. He was always so *proud* of me. He was very lower-class, you know—but very street-savvy and really bright. And," she added, "he was very much a *man*."

Cassie's first trick was "an old guy, about forty. I can't remember what he looked like. I think he was a foreigner, from Brazil or something."

After Bud and Craig and several days with Big Daddy she was comparatively experienced. "Yeah, but this was different," she said.

"Other girls— I learned afterwards—knew how to make them come real fast: that's what it's all about. But I was taking my time, you know, and he couldn't come."

She laughed—the innocence of her and other children's laughter, when it was genuine, never ceased to amaze me. "I thought I had to be doing something wrong, which I was, I wasn't getting him there! So he says, 'Do you know how to do it?' and I didn't really know what he meant. And he said, 'Look, don't take your time about it—it shouldn't take more than two seconds.' " She laughed again: "I guess he had a sense of humour. He said, 'How long have you been at it?' And I said, 'You're my first trick.' And then he explained it to me, and then he gave me double the money—twenty dollars first, and then, as I was getting out of the car, he gave me another twenty, saying, 'Here, that's for your time. I hope things work out for you.' "

She didn't remember much about her other tricks that first week, but she said she got used to it pretty quickly. "The money was excellent—I had $275 dollars after a few hours that first night. But I wanted to get another twenty-five."

So Big Daddy *had* given her a quota, $300? "No," she said quickly, too quickly. Almost every girl denies the quota and almost every girl lies when she does. "He never put a quota on me, never. But I wanted to make it look good. Two seventy-five doesn't sound as good as three hundred. . ."

By this time, she said, it was four-thirty in the morning, and she had been out since seven in the evening. Did Big Daddy check on her? "Not really. He had all those ladies, nine then. He's always had between seven and twelve. I was tired, but I wanted that twenty-five so bad that I didn't let it bother me. This guy comes along and says he'll give me seventy-five dollars. He was black and he wanted oral sex. I knew I shouldn't do it. But I wanted that money so bad, so I did. He did it twice and I was frightened and sick, but I went home with 350 dollars that first night."

But since the place where Big Daddy had put her down was essentially a black ghetto, how could he have expected her not to get involved with black men? "Because there's a lot of politicians there, you know," she said. "It's a state capital, after all. Most of them are white and they show up a lot."

Did she think that a lot of the tricks she had at that age were politicians? "I know they were. There are different reasons, like you can recognize them, or they have government cars with a special number plate. And a few of them might say what they did, but most of them didn't have to. It wasn't important."

Did any of them ask her age? Even now, at fifteen, she looked pretty young, so at twelve she must have looked like a baby. "Oh, they knew I was young, all right, but of course I didn't say *how* young. If they asked—some did—I said I was sixteen or seventeen."

It didn't only happen in cars. She went to hotels, specific hotels in the neighbourhood, and the man always paid the bill. It cost $8. And how much did they usually give her? "Depended on what they wanted. For normal sex, anything between thirty and seventy-five dollars, depending on how rich they were, how much money they had on them, how drunk they were—just how much they wanted to spend."

Did she ever rob them, when they were drunk? "You don't mean 'rob' "—the word troubled her—"you mean bump them. No, I never did."

Some of the men were weird, she said. "They asked for weird things: 'dominating' them, and talking to them really nasty. And of course, you know, sex the other way around, from the back, you know. But I told them to go find somebody else then, because I'm definitely not into that. But most of them, especially the politicians," she added earnestly, "were really sophisticated. You know what I mean by sophisticated? They just wanted straight sex. . . ."

No, they didn't generally talk to her about their wives, or in fact talk at all. "I remember there was this one guy, though, who was about sixty-five or seventy. He just wanted to talk about life in general, about his life, how he was in school, how was his childhood and all this bullshit, you know—and I just had to sit there and listen. He didn't even want sex." Her tone was not that of the schoolgirl who had loved "talking to people, finding out about them."

During those first months, how many men did she see a night? "Let's see now," she mused. "Anywhere between five and ten, depending on what sort of a night it was." The smallest amount she would earn a night would be $200. "On a good night it would come up, but I'd be really lucky if I could get three fifty."

Again she showed her honesty, for most girls lay claim to much more than their real earnings. But—she repeated religiously—Big Daddy never gave her a quota. "See, he didn't because he knew I could do good; so anything I came in with was all right with him, because he knew if I didn't do good that night, the next night I'd do better— because it was always *pretty* good."

She would have liked to stay at "her" apartment, as he called it, "but I was always scared to stay there, because if I stayed away from home they'd definitely have had the police looking for me." She didn't know if Big Daddy always stayed there—he had his clothes and things there, but of course he had a lot of other ladies, so he was "real busy. But when I was working, he was there; he made sure he was, because I was so young."

Was he a clean sort of person? "Yes, definitely." Took showers, clean underclothes, smelled nice? She giggled. They made love—she thought about it,—"two or three times a week, regular."

And how many times a week did she in fact go out to work? "Every night that I could get away by telling my parents I was going to a party, or going to a girlfriend's house, or going to the movies."

And her parents believed her, and allowed her to go out that often on school nights?

"You get to a point," said her mother wearily, "when you just can't take any more confrontations. I think we knew that she was doing wrong—you know, smoking that stuff and . . . wrong people, she was always with wrong people. But when she stayed out, she said she was staying with Jane, and she was a nice girl, so. . . ."

Anna's mother had not even this dubious reassurance. When she talks about Anna's departure, this intelligent, attractive woman freezes up, her hands and body visibly stiffen and her mouth becomes tense.

"Can you wonder?" she says. "Do you think anyone to whom it hasn't happened knows what it's like when a child runs away? Can anyone visualize it? The days, becoming weeks and months of sleepless nights, of imagining one's child's life, of feeling in one's bones and sinews every single terrible eventuality? Is there anything like this pervading, this destructive fear? I can only too easily recall it right now. The constant waiting for a phone call, at the same time the dread of what it would bring and the cold panic—it really *is* a feeling of your heart icing up—when the police do ring, just to say, 'Sorry, nothing yet.' And then in a way the terrible relief that there is 'nothing yet.' Because yes, after a few weeks"—her forehead was wet and she buried her face in her arms for an instant—"after a few weeks, I did think she was dead."

*

"I chose Jane to cover for me," said Cassie, "because she was a deaf girl and she doesn't really know what's going on, and I said, 'If my parents call, tell them I'm down at the store or taking a bath or something.' And when we moved again, I found somebody else to front for me and they never caught on. Big Daddy used to come by and pick me up." She laughed.

From the *house?* "Not quite." She giggled. "I'd call him up and tell him when I was ready and then I'd go around the corner. . . . "

Did she actually believe at that time that he was in love with her? She laughed again. "I did—I admit I did. I thought I was in love with him—I didn't look at it as prostitution, you know. I looked at it as doing him a favour because he took care of me, and gave me so much attention and so much affection, you know. I'd do anything for him, you know. . . . "

This pretence of normality is very much a feature of the life. Anna, describing the things she took with her when she ran away from home, called them her "hippie things." For a long time—"really until that day when I realized I was sick of it all," she said—it was as a "hippie" that she saw herself: a hippie with her boyfriend, not a prostitute with her pimp. And all of her descriptions of Sonny and her feelings about him, even now when he has been sent to prison as a result of her testifying against him, reflect this illusion of pseudo-normality.

She worked for him in her home town "until I'd made enough for us to go to Chicago." And she worked for him in Chicago "until I'd made enough for us to go by Greyhound to New York." Other girls' pimps bring them to the city by plane or in Cadillacs, but Anna, true to type, didn't know anything about pimps in Cadillacs. "But at least I was Sonny's one lady," she said, "and it was almost like being married. We travelled as wife and husband." And in Chicago, on Mother's Day, "We went out to see some of Sonny's people. He had an aunt and uncle living on the West Side."

Rachel's life with Lucky and his stable was, in a bizarre way, even more "normal." What was her daily routine, I asked her.

"Oh, I don't know—I sat around and I helped the girls get dressed, and I went grocery shopping, and I went to the conservatory and practised. I sat in on concerts, and on Saturday when the girls didn't work—after breakfast which we all took together—Lucky and I would take them to Saks to buy what they wanted. He wanted them to look really sophisticated, so he wanted me to dress them."

And what about meals? "Ordinarily we took turns cooking," she said, "though I did most of it, but only because Lucky liked my food best. I knew how to cook because my mother taught me—she'd give dinner parties, and I'd always help. I never forget, one of the funniest things I thought ever happened was when Lucky came back one time from meeting with some of his friends, and said, 'Will you make some of your apple pies?' I said sure I would, but why? And he said, 'Because I promised them I'd get you to make apple pie, because they didn't believe that you could cook'."

For meals, did they usually just sit around or did they eat at the table? "Not always, because the girls weren't all there at the same time, except weekends. Sometimes that was really funny, you know— they'd dress up and go, three or four of them together, to eat in the best hotels. But if there were four around, we'd set the table and sit down together to eat. It's funny," she added, apparently just recalling it, "we had this big round table and I always sat directly opposite Lucky. Never next to him—you know, like mother and father, with the children between us. We played family."

4

"Parents don't want to know"

As Cassie and I talked, the tone of her voice when she spoke of Big Daddy was still affectionate, amused, almost protective—quite different from her attitude when she discussed her later pimps. And this in spite of the fact that by then, two and a half years after he had put her on the streets in her home town, she knew quite well that he had lied to her and betrayed her and used her in the worst possible way.

"Because . . . then I met Joe . . . it was January. I'd been with Big Daddy for four or five months." She paused. "Well, what I think—I'm not sure, but I really think Big Daddy and Joe were together in the whole scene. Although they denied knowing each other, I think that they were involved. Joe, he put heroin in me and beat me up."

She had gone to a weekend party at the house of a friend. Cassie couldn't remember what the occasion was, maybe a birthday, anyway her friend had been given a dog as a present and around one o'clock in the morning, with the party in full swing, she asked Cassie to take it out. "So I took it and went across to the park. It was cold, with snow all over the ground, but I love parks and it was a lovely night . . . and these three niggers are walking towards me. They just jumped me and that was all there was to it. They raped me."

Two of them raped her, right there on the ground, in the snow. She'd never seen them before, and when they finished, they left. "And I thought maybe I was imagining it because I was really drunk. I went back to the party and I went on thinking it had been a nightmare—that I'd dreamt it all, you know.

"I slept there—everybody did. And next morning, eleven or twelve o'clock, I again take the dog out and I just come out the door and this Cadillac pulls up with Joe and the other two guys and they grabbed me. They kidnapped me. It hadn't been a dream, you see."

They took her down to the ghetto, "a really filthy apartment, and they held me down on a bed and they injected heroin into my arm . . . Joe did it."

They kept her there for a week and a half of horror. "It was really weird. They had tricks set up for me, black men and white men, and they kept me on heroin all the time until near the end."

Did it make her sleepy, or what did it do? "It does make you feel sleepy, but it makes you—like everything is different, everything is like unreal, everything changes colours, everything . . . it doesn't really do anything in the sense of making you feel sexy, or able to ignore the sex, either. It makes you feel like you are speeding and floating at the same time. You can't get to sleep, and yet your eyes get really heavy and they start burning and you have to close them but you can't sleep. . . ."

How many men did they bring to her? "A lot . . . I can't really remember exactly because I'd always be so high. I'd say maybe seven or eight a day. They would constantly come in and beat me."

When she said they beat her, what did they actually do? "They just slapped me around; they jerked off on me. It was really disgusting." She'd been in jeans and a shirt when they took her: at the apartment they undressed her and left her naked on the bed. "All the time—it was absolutely *disgusting*," she repeated, her moral judgment in retrospect somehow focussed on the nudity. The rest, too awful to face, is buried deep in her mind.

But during that week and a half, had they fed her, had they taken her to the bathroom? Were they themselves clean? "I don't know about them. I wouldn't have noticed. But I had showers, and they fed me—like they were always feeding me, making sure I had food. Not cold sandwiches or junk but real, hot meals . . . "

They provided each of the tricks with rubbers, she said, an odd detail to remember. Did she wash after each trick? "Oh no. After everything was over, in the night. . . . "

After a week or so, "I think they got scared that the police were getting down on them. My parents had called the police and they were getting hot and I think that was why they let me go. Because all of a sudden, just like that, they took me off the heroin, really fast-like. They refused to give it to me . . . they refused and I got sick, and I went through all the withdrawal for, I think, two or three days, and then I was sort of all right."

When they were ready to let her go, they just unlocked the door. "My clothes were there in the room," but she only realized that when she came down off the heroin and was over the withdrawal sickness. "Before that, every time I'd start to come down, they'd come in with another needle. But then they just said, 'You can leave now—we're through with you.' "

She went over to a friend, a fifteen-year-old who lived on her own. "Her mother didn't care, she was an alcoholic or something, and her father was dead. My friend had a job 'under the table,' she looked much older than her age." She stayed there for about five days "to get myself together, and then I just went to the school I was going to."

She just went back to class, as if she'd never been absent? "But they called my name over the PA system. They said, 'If Cassie S---- is in the building, please come to the office.' So I went, and there were two police officers there, and they brought me home. My mother had been going crazy."

Did the officers question her, ask her where she had been, with whom, and doing what? "No, they just talked to me and my mother. They didn't even ask where I was."

Wasn't that pretty extraordinary? "Well, I knew these police officers pretty well. They'd helped me out a lot of times. He said he didn't want to know where I was, they just didn't want to hear of me doing it no more and all this . . . you know, running away and all that."

"Of course they knew she'd been hustling," said a police officer in New York. "Equally certainly though, they wouldn't have known of these particular horrendous circumstances—and if she had told them, they would have arrested the men in a hurry. Their problem, I'm sure, was that no doubt she was already known as a prostitute. In fact, she as much as told you that herself. At the same time it would be obvious that not only did the parents not know, but that they didn't *want* to know. So for the right or wrong reasons, a right or wrong judgment, the police officers didn't want to give her away to her parents. It is a dilemma: the only alternatives we have to offer—the courts, institutions, foster-care—which is better, which is more likely to succeed? Or should the family be given another chance? In the final analysis, each case is a matter of personal judgment."

Cassie confirmed his diagnosis. "If they had asked me, I'd just tell them I was at a friend's house or something." And the friend who, quite aside from the strong teenage loyalty convention, was herself living an unconventional and illegal life, would certainly have backed her up.

Even so, why didn't she tell them about Joe, I asked. She could have seen the officers on her own. Did she think these men should be allowed to get away with it, to go on doing the same sort of thing to other young girls? They had hurt her badly—didn't she understand how much they had hurt her? "Yes, I did, I did. That's why I didn't say nothing. I was scared of them. I was *real* scared, more scared of them than wanting them to be caught. Maybe—very likely, because they were smart—they *wouldn't* get caught and they'd get me."

And how did Cassie's mother react to what she had heard when the police brought her back? "I don't remember in detail," said Cassie, "but I do remember that she tried to be nice to me. But after a few days, or maybe it was longer, she got caught up in her old ways and just started the same shit all over again."

I asked her mother whether she had realized that Cassie had been through something very terrible? She shied away from the question; indeed, she was so obviously horrified, so totally incapable of hearing any of this pronounced in so many words that I myself shied away from forcing it upon her.

"I asked her where she'd been," she said, primly. "She said she'd been at a friend's house. I asked, 'Well, who's your friend?' And she said I didn't know her, and when she said the name, I *didn't* know her. I tried to press her a little further, but it was no use."

Didn't Cassie *look* bad—didn't it make her wonder why she looked like that? Her mother looked down at her hands, rubbed them against each other, and then, with great concentration, examined each of her fingernails. "She never looked very well, those days," she said finally, and then looked up with tears running down her cheeks. "I guess I thought it was"—she squirmed—"you know, marijuana and all that. I thought perhaps this would be the end of it—the police had told her off in front of me. She'd said to them she wouldn't do it again. I guess I hoped she'd change now. . . ."

As my police officer friend in New York had said, the parents "didn't *want* to know." It is one of the phenomena of this whole situation that, generally speaking, adults don't want to know, and parents least of all. It applies to drugs as well as to prostitution, and they can go to enormous trouble to avoid knowing.

When Rachel went seriously into drugs, her younger sister took the drugs and showed them to her parents, "but all they did was yell and scream at me and finally flush them down the toilet, and pretend that it wasn't happening." By this time Rachel was injecting about four or five "sets" (bags) of heroin a day. "I'd learned to cover my arms—it's the first thing you learn, to protect yourself from the police," she said.

But her parents must have noticed her changes of mood? "Of course they did," she said. "They just didn't want to see it."

Finally—the clearest cry for help one can imagine—Rachel brought Lucky home with her. She had told her sister that he supplied her with heroin. Her parents knew she was on heroin. The black man she brought home *had* to raise their suspicions; however "classy" he could be, he was different. "They were scared to death to know, so they said hello, and let it go."

Although fourteen-year-old Rachel left home after this, she was never technically a runaway because she remained in touch. "I phoned them from time to time and I saw them off and on—I'd drop in."

But how could they have put up with that situation? How could they bear not to notify the authorities, the police, detectives? They had money, connections, they were in a position to get help. What did they think they were doing?

Rachel shrugged: that shrug I saw so often. "They were awfully busy," she said. "Perhaps they thought I had to get it out of my system; perhaps they thought I had to fight it out on my own. Maybe they thought I could cope." She shrugged again. "Or perhaps they just couldn't bear to think."

Julie, too, tried to fight what was happening to her, and tried to get her mother's help, both in vain. After a fortnight at the hotel with "the bummy old men," she told a girlfriend, and this girl's mother persuaded her to go back home. "I made up some story for my mom that this nice man had been good to me and let me stay in his house—I mean, nobody, but nobody could have believed it. But she said, 'Oh, fantastic. What a nice man.' "

What Julie wanted was to be stopped. They all want to be stopped. "I went back to school and I felt rotten, really rotten about myself, with myself. . . ." She burst into tears and cried for a long time, with my arm around her. "I started drinking in bars, meeting different pimps, working off and on for them. Once I was in it, you know, it just didn't matter any more."

The way she did it, for about a year, was by going to school and getting after-school jobs, first in a nursing home, later in a fish and chips bar. "I did that three days a week, and the other days I'd go downtown and hustle until about two o'clock in the morning. But finally it got too hard, so I quit the jobs. My parents didn't have to know—they saw I had money, I guess they thought from the jobs, and they asked no questions. But I hated it," she said. "I hated myself."

Finally she ran away again, again ended up at her girlfriend's. And again the girl's mother tried to help, this time taking her to a runaway agency. "But I hated them, too," she said, "because I begged them to send me to a foster-home or a group home—anything but back home. But that's what they did, and I got raped again," now she sounded tired and indifferent, "much worse than the first time."

"They were two brothers. They kept me there a whole night, then they let me go." She stopped a car and was taken to the police. "The police took me to hospital, and then they called up my mom and she dragged me all around the town because she didn't want me at home. She wouldn't let me get cleaned up or anything, she just dragged me around trying to get rid of me."

But because Julie's parents were available to take care of her, no agency would take her. "So finally my mom took me home and then I ran away again because all they wanted was to get rid of me my dad too he only does what she says and then she tried to commit suicide she cut her wrists and it was all my fault. . . ." It was a litany of misery told without a comma or a full stop.

Given different conditions, Cassie's mother might have been justified in hoping that, as she put it to me, "she'd change now." The awful scare and physical abuse Cassie had suffered could not fail to have consequences. If her family could have given her love and support, and she could have had caring counselling from outside, it just might have produced a turnabout. But these circumstances did not exist. Furthermore, perhaps more destructive to her fragile ego than the physical violence she had been subjected to was the loss of her blind faith in Big Daddy. Her trust in him, however grotesque it seems in retrospect or to an outsider, was probably her most—or only—positive emotion at the time. His betrayal, which she had never put into words until two and a half years later when she finally told me, was quite probably the most traumatic shock she had to suffer.

If she was to survive—and some youngsters do not survive similar experiences—she would have to find somewhere the kind of support that would replace what she had lost by losing Big Daddy. She didn't have the maturity or the inner resources to find it within herself. To save herself, she had to seek it elsewhere. As there was no miraculous change in her parents, a return to conventional teenage life was out of the question.

They had moved—again—and sent Cassie to a Catholic school. "I got watched over there," she said, "because I was the only girl in my class that smoked cigarettes, smoked pot—I was like alone, you know." So she ran again. And again. And again. "We went so often to get her from somewhere," said her mother, "or sent money for her fare home, I can hardly remember exactly. I think altogether she ran fifteen times."

One of these times she got into real trouble. "I was with two guys and somebody offered me a joint. I thought it was regular pot and it wasn't, it was angel dust. . . . I didn't know what it was and I smoked it, and it makes you real violent. We broke into this house and we tore the place apart. We did fifteen thousand dollars' worth of damage and we stole five thousand. These two guys I was with, they're nineteen and twenty and they went to gaol, and they put me in reform school."

Cassie was still only fourteen, a child with a lively imagination and a warmly responsive nature. Some aspects of this school—a Catholic institution run by nuns—appealed to her, and her reaction indicates that wisely handled, the core of religious feeling within her could have been used to strengthen rather than to confuse her. "I liked the quiet in chapel, the music, the smell . . . and the litany. I'd close my eyes and see trees in the wind."

Did she think there was a God? "No, not now I don't. I think there's something good beyond us—peace. Your soul is there. Your body's in the ground, a material thing that you have used, but your soul is somewhere else. I think it stays in the place where you were happy. At the reform school there was this field that I used to go to all the time, and a pond, and I used to sit against this big tree, for hours. You could hear all the sounds of nature, bullfrogs and everything, and I used to sit up against this tree and make up poetry. I used to be really happy and feel really calm and everything. I think that when I die, that would be where my soul would be."

(Anna, too, had a feeling for religion. "I believe in the Unitarians," she said. "I think it's good, it's humanitarian, it says that helping people or enriching people's minds and spirits *is* a religion and a homage to God.")

But in spite of Cassie's moments of peace, and in spite of doing well in the school ("She did very well there," said her mother, "She got good grades."), she could not endure the fact that the place was to all intents and purposes a prison. "I hated hated hated being locked in, hated taking orders. I"— she searched in vain for another word—"I hated it," she concluded wanly. So she ran to North Carolina and she ran to Virginia, and time and again she ran to the Hell's Angels' clubhouse in the mountains near her home town. And finally, "They couldn't hold me, so the judge put me back in my parents' custody. And I wasn't out even ten minutes, and I knew it was all going to be the same. We had two phones in the house. I'd be talking to a friend and Mom would be on the other phone listening . . . and she'd say right into the phone, 'Who are you talking to?' And I'd say who it was, and if she didn't like that person, she'd say, 'Don't phone here any more,' and hang up. She always said they were all 'bad company.' "

But didn't she realize that her mother must have been very afraid for her and was trying to protect her? She shrugged, then nodded and began to cry. "Yes . . . yes . . . but it just wasn't the way." She stopped, for she didn't know, any more than her parents had known, or the nuns or the police or the judge had known, what the right way could have been to deal with her, to help her.

"When we got home," she said then, "you know my room was totally changed around. My posters were down, my drawers were empty. My bed used to be against the window: they just changed my whole room around. I had big piles of notebooks, and a big pile of letters I got while I was in the reform school, from different people. They were all gone and I still don't know what happened to them."

Had she asked her mother? Had she looked in the cellar? "They wouldn't be there. She just changed it the way she wanted to, and took all my letters to take away all my friends, and if I bitch about it she'll say, 'Well, it's my house and I'll do what I want with it.' "

I had heard of this "cleaning out of rooms" from several of the children, but the only parent who was aware of her own motives was Anna's mother.

Anna had kept what she called "really strange and bizarre journals" in which she recorded her own tumultuous feelings, particularly about her step-father. "And my mother rummaged through my things and found them and read them," she said. "I think that was one of the cataclysms, you know. She confronted me one night, and asked me what she could do, what was going to happen. She even asked me if I wanted to go into a foster-home. She was crying and she felt really bad. And I blew the whole thing out of proportion in my mind. At that time I was lying to myself about a lot of things, and I told myself that she was threatening to put me away. And the next day, while she was working, I woke up and hitch-hiked out to the drugstore and bought a whole bottle of over-the-counter sleeping pills and took them all—seventy-two of them.

"And then I waited and waited and my head would start ringing more and more but nothing happened. They were the wrong kind of pills"—she laughed—"just relaxants, to help you sleep. I wasn't too bright, was I? Still, my hands were cold, I could feel my fingers turning blue, I could feel my heart slowing down, and I just got so scared . . . I cried, and I tried to get up the courage to call my boyfriend. Instead, at the last minute, I called up my mother at the lab, and she just got hysterical. When she got back, she threw her hospital newspapers at me and said, 'You read about people who are having cancer and trying to live, and then you do this to yourself.' I said I was sorry and I didn't want to die, please don't let me die, and so she called a friend at the pharmacy and he looked up the pills and said it probably wasn't enough to kill me. And then she called a doctor friend, and he said I should be put in a crisis ward, and she said no, she wouldn't do that to me. Then she got some stuff that makes you throw up and she took care of me. She stayed home and had me sleep upstairs, right next to their bedroom. . . ."

Her mother—an intelligent woman—had done everything right, except for the words she spoke a little later—if only parents could catch words before they emerge: "You don't behave like you've been doing in *our* house," she said. "This is the end of it. If you do anything like this again, out!"

It wasn't long after this that Anna ran away, to Sonny. "When I ran away," she said, "they cleaned out my room—they ransacked it from top to bottom."

"It's true," said her mother, her voice now sounding drained, "there is anger, too. It's partly anger, partly self-protection that leads one to almost dismantle the child's room, I think. Of course, that doesn't happen all at once. The first time we went through Anna's things was to find a clue, a lead, *some* indication where we could start looking for her. She . . . " she hesitated, "she hadn't taken any of her snapshots, you know. None of her cuddly animals—there were two she'd never been without, before. Yes, I realized it was an attack on me. I mean, later I realized that. For the first days, even weeks, one didn't think of that. One only thought of her and the terrible, terrible danger she was in. . . ."

Cassie's mother proudly showed me the whole house. The younger child, Sally, wasn't there on any of my visits. I never met her, and well understood that my visit would be impossible to explain to a nine-year-old. But I saw her room: a charming little-girl's room with rose-sprigged wallpaper, full of coloured cushions, toys and small, decorated lamps. It was warm and pleasant—and very, very tidy.

I asked Cassie, was that what *her* room used to be like? "I had tons of animals," she said. "I don't know what happened to them. I had a lot of pillows that I made myself." Did she ever ask what happened to her things? "Why ask?" she said. "There was nothing there—can you imagine? Nothing. She'd thrown out the lot. I had a leather jacket, it was two years old but I kept it in really good condition. I was looking for it one day, because it wasn't that cold but it wasn't that warm, and she told me that she threw it out because she didn't like it. She's like that. . ."

"Oh, that jacket," said her mother. "I gave it to a church sale. It was awful," She opened a closet door in the entryway. "That's hers," she said, pointing to a classic wool coat. "I didn't throw *that* away. It's nice. I got it for her." She laughed, briefly. "I wear it sometimes; she doesn't want it."

"And you know those poems I wrote, I told you about?" Cassie said. "She threw those away, too." If her life had been thrown away, discarded—now she is able to express this in words—then there was no reason for her not to throw away her life, too. Of course, she didn't see it that way when she finally ran off to New York.

5

"Everything will be smooth"

The Port Authority Building in New York—the giant bus terminal where cheap transport arrives from all over the country, day and night—is a world in itself. It has its own police force, clinics, shops, restaurants—and miles of corridors and escalators. The building takes up one whole long area between 39th and 42nd Streets at Eighth Avenue, and stands at the edge of New York's vice district. Within a perimeter of three blocks around the terminal are a dozen hotels which serve only passing trade, and four which, while available to ordinary tourists, make their main living off pimps and their ladies. It was at one of these that Cassie landed within hours of her arrival in New York, in spite of Dan's effort to send her home. She was picked up by Slim, her first New York pimp, within minutes of her return to 42nd Street.

"When Cleo first came into New York," Slim said, "*I* was her first man." He sounded proud of it, and repeated, "I was her first man."

She was very young then, wasn't she?

"Yeah. I didn't know, y'understand? Well, I had an idea, but you know what I mean, how it was. I don't . . . you know, if she shows me identification of an eighteen-year-old, hey then, that's what I go by. Know what I mean? She shows me an eighteen-year-old ID, no way . . . " (This was fairly early in my conversations with Slim. Later, when he realized that I *knew* Cleo and her history, he would temporize, lie, and finally get angry.)

The question of age identification is important in New York, it is illegal to sell alcohol to anyone under eighteen, and bartenders routinely ask for IDs for their own protection. But it's no problem. A few days before, I had followed a bright young friend of mine, a girl of fourteen, into one of countless souvenir shops on 42nd Street. I busied myself over some trinkets while she approached one of the two salesmen about an ID card. "It was amazing," she said outside, as we compared her genuine card and the fake one. The difference was hardly visible. "I just said, 'Have you got ID cards?' and he didn't say anything. He just brought one out, asked whether I knew how to make it out—I said yes—and he said, 'Twenty dollars.' Gee, I don't *believe* this!"

What made Cassie go with Slim that night? Was he attractive to her? Were there others, did she make a deliberate choice?

"He was the first one came up to me," she said. "He looked nice, you know—" she laughed. "He smelled nice, and you know, the way they come on to you is so sweet, the way they sweet-talk you, it's pathetic. I know now that it's pathetic, but then . . . they can make things look so good. You're so down, you know. You're alone and it's the big city and you don't have any money, you know. They make things look good and you feel like hanging onto them."

"It didn't take me long to find out about Cleo," Slim said. "Pressure. Pressure is Cleo's biggest problem, she can't handle it, you follow me? Cleo by nature is a very good girl. She's not dirty, she's not sassy . . . She's got problems with her womanhood, you know what I mean? Stuff like that, which I think costs her. . . ."

Slim is a player, along the lines of Big Daddy; not a popcorn pimp like Sonny. "He was very gentle with me that night, you know," Cassie said. "He took me out to eat and he talked to me and said I looked tired. Anybody notices anything about me, anybody cares—at least at that time," she hesitated, "you know—it just melted me. He said I looked tired and he'd get me a hotel room in the same place where he had an apartment, and I'd rest and you know, we'd talk the next day. . . ."

Did Cassie make love with all her pimps? Really make love, kissing them and all that? Because few of the girls ever kiss clients. "In a way, yes. It's kind of strange," she said.

Strange in what way? Was it strange in the extent to which it was by her choice? "There's not much choice," she said, and laughed.

Did she hope for a lasting relationship with Slim, or any of the others? "That's kind of what I'm looking for, right."

But does she think that *they* feel something? "No, I know now they don't."

But then, does *she* feel something? "Sure I do—every girl out there does. Maybe, deep down inside, one knows that one is the only one that feels something. Maybe one feels so *much*, that whoever you're with, you imagine. . . . " She stopped, then went on: "At first, I think I feel something."

Like what? It isn't just sex, is it? "No, I guess it's more the protection that they give you. They feel so strong around you . . . I think I'd rather be with a black man than a white one. There's a big difference: they carry themselves about different, they are more masculine, stronger."

Is that what makes her feel more protected, or does it just turn her on more? "I don't know, I think it's both. But definitely it makes me feel more protected. . . ."

New York in August, often 100° fahrenheit and 95 percent humidity, can be pure hell, and Cassie's first stay was brief. "I went to California in mid-August. . . . nobody can tell me what to do. . ." Clearly her departure for California after just two weeks with Slim had not taken place without some objection. "I don't feel anybody has the right to put a limit on my life, what I can do and what I can't do . . ." But the pimps were telling her what to do, weren't they? "But if I don't want to do it, I'm not going to do it—he can't force me."

She was in fact comparatively lucky on this first New York foray: it isn't that Slim is a gentle person, but rather—one gets the feeling—that he can't very often be bothered to be rough. "I didn't force her to go out," he said. "Some macks say, 'You *gotta* go out there,' you understand? I didn't, and she had it good with me. I stayed on 43rd Street in a hotel that cost forty dollars a day each room, and I had four ladies. That averaged out, with phone-calls and everything, three hundred dollars a week just for me and my main lady, and that times four—that's twelve hundred a week, just for the rooms."

But surely, not everybody stays in places as expensive as that? "I put mine in the best, because mine *are* the best," he replied.

And how did Cassie make her way to California? "Chuckers," she said. She hitched on trucks.

And no doubt she "paid" for her rides? "Yeah, I did as a matter of fact," and then she reversed herself. "No, they paid me. Chuckers have a lot of money. I ended up with close to eight hundred dollars. I couldn't believe it. I got a really nice hotel room in Long Beach. . . . "

Sometime during that first week in Long Beach, however, she was picked up by three Puerto Ricans who brutally raped her on the beach one night. She managed to get to a hospital where she had to have stiches, but after two days discharged herself. Later, back in New York, this resulted in a severe and horribly painful ovarian infection.

Why didn't she stay in hospital? Were they unkind to her? "Not really, it was just that they were all—doctors and nurses too—Puerto Ricans, and I just had to get away from them. I felt like they were going to hurt me or something, so I left and went back to the hotel in Long Beach."

At the hospital she had been given antibiotics, "but I was stupid, I felt okay and I just left the pills and never took any again. And then, back on the beach, it was really good. I made a lot of friends and had a lot of good parties, beach-parties, you know? Just fun, food, and beer—I had a really good time. . . ." Yet, showing once again the ambivalence of her feelings: "But at the end of that second week, I felt so far away, you know, and so I came back."

Back to New York? "No, back to B——, back home." And then she added: "Nothing was changed." And because nothing had changed, "I rang one of my girlfriends in New York, just to talk to her."

The girlfriend she rang was Slim's "bottom-lady," Gina. "That's how Slim found out I was home," she said ingenuously, "and he came up to get me. . . ."

She could have said no to Slim, couldn't she? She was in her own house: surely he wouldn't have carried her out kicking and screaming? "Yes, I could have said no, but it wouldn't have had any effect on him. And yes,"—she laughed, without mirth—"I think he would have carried me out, if that's what it took."

("I know Cleo's mother," said Slim. "I called and talked to her. Cleo came back to me because . . . well . . . she likes the excitement of it. But she doesn't like the working part of it, going down, stuff like that. She doesn't like what she has to do to bring the men on, to bring the money in.")

"Slim sent me to work at Thirty-second and Madison," said Cassie. At a coffee-shop nearby one can find the girls any day of the week, almost any hour of the evening. Their pimps let them have $5 or $10 spending money each day. Except for a taxi home if their man doesn't pick them up, this is where they spend the money, sitting in groups of two or three, on coffee, Cokes and junk food.

"But we never stay in there for more than couple of minutes," said Cassie. "We're supposed to be out hustling, not gabbing away. You can't really relax, you got to keep one eye out for the cops, the other for the pimp."

Just a few days after she got back from California, all brown and pretty, a trick picked her up at the corner and tried to kill her.

"What happened was, I had six hundred and fifty dollars on me," she said. "I had worked all that day, and besides, I had for the first time in my life bumped somebody for two hundred dollars—" she laughed. "I was real proud of myself, you know? So I had this money and I got in the car with this trick—it was about eleven at night—and he grabbed me around the neck and he put heroin in me.

"He took me to New Jersey and he beat the shit out of me. There were two others, too, and in the end I was unconscious, and they rammed something up me. When I came to I was lying there in a pool of blood, and I looked around and the ashtray said the name of the motel. So I picked up the phone and called the manager. Later I heard—I don't remember it myself—that I told him to call the police. They came and they said they couldn't do nothing about it."

But why? Why should the police say that? The men must have been seen when they registered, motels usually note car registrations. "I don't know," she said. "They just said they couldn't do nothing about it. . . ."

("I'm afraid that's quite possible," said a police friend in New York City. "Whichever way you look at it, girls like her to most police officers spell TROUBLE in big letters. She'll have a false ID—she told you that herself—you can be sure she didn't say one true word to the officers, except that a guy beat her up and robbed her. You can bet your sweet life that she'll have spun some mighty tale about who she was and where she came from. What interest is there for the police to spend their time on girls like this? You can't win.")

"Oh, she got hurt all right," confirmed Slim. "I got a call one night—I'm lying on the bed and got a call from a hotel manager in Jersey, that she's overdosed on pills. I had to send one of my ladies out there to get her and bring her home." Overdosed? He ignored my question and didn't mention her injuries. "Somebody give it to her—understand where I'm coming from? I know about it, it was true."

"I got back with Gina," said Cassie. "Slim asked me where my money was. I said I didn't have it, that the guys took it off me. So he beat the shit out of me, he kicked my ass."

"Kicking ass" is a phrase that comes up time and again in the life. It appears that almost any violence against the girls—who themselves see it, with a disconcerting kind of pride, as discipline— comes under that heading. "I remember one thing: he grabbed me around the neck and threw me on the bed and started choking me, slapping me, punching me, kicking me around. Gina brought me up to my room and she stayed with me, and I passed out like for two days."

Her two days of "rest" over, Slim sent Cassie back to work. "I was standing at the street-corner feeling lousy and I thought, to hell with this, I'm leaving, and I went to Earl . . . "

Slim's analysis of her is perceptive, though I hope that his prediction for her future turns out to be wrong. "Earl had a Cadillac," Slim said. "That's what she really dug, y'understand? I had Cleo when she was new—*I* had to teach her. She got away from me because I copped so many ladies and she couldn't stand it, her position being lost, y'understand what I'm talking about? Each lady likes to have a position, that's only natural, to want to be the number one lady. I liked Cleo, she's all right, but she's not my style, she's not my type of lady. No, I would never take her back. She'd come back to me again if I gave her enough—you know—*talk*. But I wouldn't have her back. She's not worth it to me, she's nothing but headaches. Trouble. If she could just go out there and stand there and look pretty and be a professional hooker that way, she'd love it. But she doesn't like doing what she's got to do, to get the men, to get the money. Even so," he added, "she won't stay out of it, because her lifestyle became part of it and she's fascinated by the life."

"I'd heard Earl's name a lot," Cassie said, "and I'd seen him driving around—he was always trying to get me in the car with him. So one night he drove by and stopped for a red light, and I went over and knocked on the window. He rolled it down and I said, 'Do you have a minute? I'd like to talk to you.' And he said, 'Sure, come on in,' and I got in and we rode around for two hours, talking."

Every girl describing her first meetings with a pimp will emphasize the non-sexual side of the relationship: the pimp's interest in her as a person, his understanding, his protectiveness and finally his affection—not to say love—for her. Making a girl feel valued is the art of the pimp.

("Do I feel something for the girls?" said Slim. "Yes, I do feel something. Not love"; though later he claimed to have loved one, just one, of his ladies. "But I'll take care of them, I'll give them their needs, I will protect them, I will do what I have to do for them. I will not let anybody take advantage of them. They *know* that I like them: they also know that I don't love them.")

What did Cassie and Earl talk about, riding around that night? "Just about everything that had happened. And he said, 'Well, if you want, I'll be happy for you to work for me. I'll teach you good, and everything will be smooth'— you know, all that bullshit, except then I didn't think it was bullshit." So Earl said he'd give her a try-out, and he put her down on Eighth Avenue, away from her previous stand at Madison and 32nd.

There are countless flea-bag hotels on or near Eighth Avenue which exist by renting rooms for half an hour: no bathrooms, no change of bed-linen; a wash-basin "if you're lucky. I was coming out of one of those hotels that same night," said Cassie, "and some guy was getting killed right outside the hotel, not more than six feet from where I stood. It was really something!"

She is fascinated by events such as this; her voice changes, her whole body comes alive when she relates such stories. "There was two guys and three black guys jumped them, right? This one guy was wearing all white: white jacket, white pants, and the first thing I knew he was just covered with blood. I couldn't *believe* it—people stood and looked and everything, and I just wanted to get out of it before the police came. So I went up the street and found Earl. I guess he'd been sticking close to me because it was my first night with him. Anyway, he was in his car and I jumped in and said, 'Earl, take me home—you're not going to believe what happened! You know, it could have been me, they had a knife, I saw it—it was amazing—I was so scared.' And he said, 'If you don't want to, you don't have to work no more tonight.' "

The point of her story was not the scare she had had— she had so often been threatened or hurt herself—but to convey to me how valuable she was to Earl, to justify her having gone to him, to point out his concern for her and protectiveness of her.

Earl was twenty-four, much younger than Slim, and he had one other girl, a fifteen-year-old named Brandy who, when Cassie joined him, was living with him in his apartment on 45th Street. Cassie's description of Brandy made it very clear that she was determined from the start to oust the other girl from her position. As Slim had said, the jostling for top lady is constant and can be vicious.

"She hated me," said Cassie, "because she didn't want him to have any other lady. She was really ugly, though, and she was only making a hundred dollars a night—*if* she was lucky."

After Cassie had been working for Earl a week or two, back on the more lucrative East Side, he took his two ladies to Atlantic City. "We stayed on Kentucky Avenue, right on the front," she said, "it was really nice. But Brandy was getting on my nerves all week, and she and me got into a big fight. In the end he didn't want her no more, and we left her in Atlantic City and went back to New York."

To Cassie, Brandy had no importance—almost no existence—except as a minor incident in her own life. I would have known nothing more of her if I had not by chance come across her on Riker's Island, the prison where prostitutes are sent when they are sentenced in New York for soliciting or petty crimes.

Brandy was not very pretty when I saw her, but she had been in prison for ten days—devastating for any girl's looks. I noticed her because of her hair: it was the colour of new chestnuts, or of brandy, red-brown and fine, curly but voluminous, the dominant impression one had of her. She was so small, her body so thin, her face so tiny that one only noticed that extraordinary hair.

She was sitting on the floor in a corner of the cell, leaning forward, hugging her legs with both arms (which were covered with blue spots). Her face was buried in her lap, her hair spread over her knees. "That's Brandy," said the prison officer when he saw me looking at her. "She's a hard case." Her body looked like that of an eleven-year-old, her ID said she was nineteen, and her face could have been anything up to forty. "How can one tell?" said the officer. "She'd just as soon spit at you as tell the truth."

Her brief interlude with Earl as his main lady, with its illusion of security, the excursion to Atlantic City and her abandonment there had all been many months before; for her it must have seemed light-years away. This was her sixth time at Riker's Island in eight months, I was told. The officer leafed through her file. "She's had VD every time she came in. They go out with pills, but—" he shrugged. "What's the use?" He shook his head. "A hard case," he said again. "I've never heard her say a word yet."

I told them she was only fifteen. They said they'd pass it on. They were kind men, as kindness goes in these short-term prisons. But they looked at me pityingly when I said something must—could—be done.

Cassie, too, had her experiences of gaol, but the longest she'd been in was for three days. "It stinks. One of my friends who went for two weeks, I couldn't believe she was the same person when she came out. It isn't so much the food and all that, even—I think it's what you are put through, you know. They are so hard on you, there are so many black girls there, twenty black to one white."

"Yeah," said Polly, a tall, slim fourteen-year-old black girl, who I met through social workers in the Bronx. She'd been in prostitution for two years but the agency, by separating her from her family, fostering her in the home of one of the agency workers, and organising a carefully structured life for her which included tutoring in subjects she was interested in, was now feeling a guarded optimism about her future.

"Sure, I was in gaol," she said. "One month they picked me up five times, would you believe it? There's an unwritten rule that nobody gets picked up more than once a month or every six weeks. Jesus, if they don't at least stick to that, they'd have nothing *but* hustlers in their prisons." She roared with laughter. "The hell with robbers and murderers—what harm do they do compared with us dangerous chicks? Anyway, they picked me up five times. I spent fourteen days inside that month, and seven the next. It was grisly . . ." she said, and repeated, "GRISLY! And yeah, it's true what that chick told you—it's about twenty black girls to one white. You know why? Because us black girls, we is uptown, not downtown. And uptown crawls with pigs, about the same ratio." The word sounded odd, until I heard later that one of her tutored courses was algebra.

"Twenty cops uptown hassling the girls, against one—well, I guess two, as they always go in pairs—in midtown." And was it true that the black girls are hard on the white ones in prison? Polly became very serious. "Yeah," she said, "I guess that's not untrue. It's because of the n acks, see: there's a lot of the girls who's real angry because so many black boys, by preference, are choosing white ladies. . . ."

Cassie stayed with Earl for almost two months altogether, the longest she was with anybody except Big Daddy. "I was living with him in the apartment," she said, "but about a week after we got back from Atlantic City, he got another girl—her name was Barbie. She was nineteen, pretty, young-looking but stupid as hell. Like she gave the police his licence plates, her welfare card with her real name and everything on it. She told them everything about Earl.

"I tried to tell Earl, but he wouldn't believe me. In the end I had to leave because if he didn't believe me, there was no kind of relationship there."

Cassie took a room in an East Side hotel she'd used on other occasions, and for two weeks she worked for herself, without a pimp. "I never went to gaol during those two weeks," she said, which emphasizes how often she had been arrested before. "I made enough money to pay my rent and eat, and if I wanted anything, I'd just make more money."

Did she feel unsafe? "Not really—I was having the time of my life. I went out, I didn't have to work, you know. I didn't have to stay out there all night, and if I wanted to spend time with one person and get to know him better, I would do it." But her next sentence revealed the real state of her feelings: "I had a good time talking to all kinds of pimps, playing with them, making them think I was going to come to them, and then stringing them along."

How much money did she make every day, spending more time with people and working fewer hours? "About seventy-five dollars a day. My room was twenty, I used up about ten for eating, so I ended up with maybe forty-five dollars a day. Until I met Lovell, and he more or less talked me into going with him."

Lovell was the pimp she liked best, after Big Daddy. Even so, again she only stayed with him for about three weeks. "He'd just gotten out of gaol for promoting prostitution, and they—the court—had taken everything from him: he had a laundromat, and two boutiques, and a car and two apartments, and they took it all. Debbie was his other girl. She was twenty-seven and Lovell was twenty-eight, and we got along really good. They had a suite upstairs, and I had a room. Lovell was really nice to me—he spoke to me as an equal," she added, with no apparent awareness of the irony of the remark. "But Lovell, too, he played games. They all do, it's as if they have to. . . . Deb and me, you know, we got on really well. But when he was with me in my room, he'd have me call Debbie and say, 'Deb, do you know where Lovell is?' And I noticed when he was with her, Debbie would call me once in a while, and ask the same question."

Why did he do it? Since he obviously wanted them both to work for him, did he do it just to play with feelings? Was that his need? "Girls get jealous," said Cassie. "The whole scene is very emotional, you know." She reflected, then went on: "Of course now I know it's not *real* emotions. You know what I mean, the pimps make them up . . . Debbie was very jealous and I've walked in on them fighting about me, and she'd say, 'I'm going to leave you unless you get rid of her.'

"He didn't know that I wasn't the kind of person to get jealous. He'd just do that to make me feel like he wanted me more than her, and to make her feel the same thing. And I didn't like that, because if you can't be real about feelings, then what is there? Feelings are nothing to play with. But they all do it."

Cassie was saying this at a time when she was getting close to giving up the life. She was beginning to see through the pimps and their games, and to find words and courage to express her new understanding. For it isn't the pimps' "need"—their emotional requirements—that makes them play these games; it is part of their technique in handling the girls, an awareness of psychological manipulation many a psychiatrist might envy. The pimps know very well that what these lost youngsters primarily seek is a personal, human contact.

Cassie left Lovell the moment she found a more real relationship. "There was this girl Sherry; she and me, we became real tight." She didn't like Sherry's man, Andy, but went to him for the sake of her friendship with the girl. After only a few days, however, she was walking down Madison Avenue when a cab pulled up and she heard someone calling her name. "I turned around and just went like crazy! I couldn't believe it, you know? It was Big Daddy! He *took* me and *put* me in the car and we went to the airport, and when we got to B——, we went to his apartment and stayed a whole week and talked and talked, and ate and made love and talked."

The seemingly idyllic reunion led to a crucial act on Cassie's part. She was not specific about what happened between them, but gradually her suppressed knowledge that Big Daddy had sold her to Joe came to the surface. Her manner when she spoke of it became hesitant. "He . . . he would have got a cut for each of the guys they brought that week . . . and he would have known about the heroin, too. So you see . . ."

When she could no longer ignore that realization, she performed a deliberate act of retaliation. She stole money from him, and left for New York.

"A girl will never steal from her pimp," said a police officer I talked to in Minnesota. "Not only because they are—let's never forget it—

amoral and violent men, and it is therefore very dangerous. The more important reason is because the pimp–whore relationship is a very precise one, with rigorously defined and mutually accepted conventions. The primary one—a fundamental part of the game—is that she denies even to herself that he cheats her; and at the same time, she never cheats him. If she does, he punishes her, and in this morbid and pathological relationship she expects and even provokes the punishment. When they call it a 'game,' this dishonesty—which he imposes and which she colludes in (although she may fool herself, if she is very young)—is not just part of, it *is* the relationship. It is this emotional corruption which the young girls find almost impossible to erase or reverse, even if they manage to break away from the life. Unless they are brutally honest with themselves and receive really effective help, it is this—much more than the physical damage they suffer—which more often than not may ruin their lives."

"There was an envelope in a drawer," Cassie said, "the same drawer where I had seen he kept his bankbooks. When I was with him when I was twelve he had two big accounts. I remember looking at them and he had something like eighteen thousand dollars saved. But this envelope I took only had about a hundred dollars in it and I took the money and I got a bus back to New York."

By openly stealing Big Daddy's money, Cassie was performing a major act both of courage and of moral revolt. She was serving notice on him that she knew of his betrayal and that she was prepared to fight him. He was unlikely to underrate the danger: if she gave him away to the police and testified against him in court, his sentence for putting an under-age child into prostitution could be seven or even ten years. In fact, Cassie—although she did subsequently cooperate with the police on various cases—never gave Big Daddy away. She gave a very precise description of him to a New York district attorney, but misled them by placing him in Los Angeles where naturally enough the police were unable to find him. Nor did Big Daddy pursue her, as might have been expected, to persuade or threaten her.

"I didn't want to give him away," she told me later. "I just wanted to let him know how I felt and then never see him again."

He represented her beginning in prostitution and had provided her with her most important emotional experience—and her greatest disillusionment. Her gesture of defiance, when she broke the rule and stole from him, was vitally important to her for what it represented in relation to herself, even more than what it represented in relation to him. It marked the beginning of the end. She was rejecting the silent collusion. In her own way she was saying—to herself more than to anyone else—"I will not go on playing the game."

But to implement such a decision is desperately hard: more often than not it is achieved only as a result of injury, illness, a particularly traumatic event, or some combination of all three. It is possible that if Cassie's home circumstances had been different, if some warm place of refuge, with concerned and sympathetic adults, had been available, she might have been able to make her break at that point. But these prerequisites did not exist. Inside herself she had briefly admitted that it was, or soon would be over; but it was not over yet. Very, very rarely can children escape from the life on their own.

6

"I don't let myself think . . ."

When Cassie got back to New York, she looked for Lovell, who had talked to her "as an equal." "I looked for him high and low. But I remembered him telling me once, 'If you ever leave me, you're not going to see me again.' Well, he meant it. I didn't."

So her next search was for Sherry. "I went to Thirty-second Street. She wasn't around, but Andy was. I told him I'd been taken away by Big Daddy, and [her second break with convention] I lied to him and said I hadn't had any money when Big Daddy took me. I wasn't going to give him that hundred and fifty dollars," she added. "Anyway, he didn't believe me and threatened me and I got very scared of him, so when later that night I met Cal, I said I'd work for him." And she revealed again the need to lend human qualities to a pimp in order to retain some feeling of self-value: "Cal was funny. He was nice, though, really nice. I told him all about how scared I was of Andy, and he told me he'd have a talk with Andy and that I had nothing to worry about from now on."

I met Cassie just after she began working for Cal, when she was still very frightened of Andy. She had changed her name and was avoiding the East Side—Andy's territory—by hiding in the squalid hotels of the worst street on New York's West Side. These were to be her last weeks in prostitution, but oddly enough she was working harder than ever: seven days a week, between seven and fourteen hours a day. It was almost as if she needed to prove to herself that she wasn't giving it up because she wasn't good at it, or because she wasn't considered good enough at it as Slim had implied, but because, in spite of succeeding, she herself rejected it.

On average, how many men was she seeing a day? "I'd say between eight and ten," she said.

Had it always been like that, with all of the pimps, never a day off?

("My ladies never work on Sundays," Slim had said. "Mine rest, dress, count money and read the Sunday funnies, that's all they do.")

"Not really," Cassie said. "I've had days off, but I get bored." If she went to a movie, she got bored after the movie. If she went out to dinner, "I just get bored too, so I end up out there. I guess it's like an addiction: I just get so used to going out there." Later she would say, "It's a good way to stop yourself from thinking."

What percentage of these seventy or so men a week did she go to a hotel with? "About two-thirds."

And how long did she spend with each? She laughed. "About ten minutes."

And what happened after the ten minutes—did she wash? "Oh yeah . . . There's one hotel I use, it's got like a sink in the room, so I use that."

Did she look at the man to see if he was clean? "Sure I do," but no, she didn't make them use disinfectant, as some girls do. She gave them rubbers and yes, some of them objected to it, "but it's either that or no deal," she said. "I tell them."

Did she tell them that in advance? Again she laughed. "No, once I get them up there they've got no choice; take it or leave it. They certainly don't get no money back."

She always got her money first, and most of the tricks, she said, were pretty good. "Most of them are gentle," the word sounded oddly touching, "except for the lunatics." Again that strident laugh. "There are some lunatics."

Did she ever get scared of them? "No, I have a knife, just in case."

Did she ever say no to anybody? "Yeah, if I think he's a cop, or if he doesn't just look right." How can she tell? "You can tell by the eyes."

What she didn't tell me until later, when we were better friends, was that if the girls suspect a man of being a police officer, they ask him to unzip his fly. American police officers are prohibited by law from undressing to get evidence against prostitutes. "If they refuse, they're cops," she said.

"If a trick can't look you dead in the eye and talk to you," she said, "I'm not going with them, because there's something wrong."

But what about physical things: would she say yes to any man, even if he was physically repulsive to her? "If he was going to pay me, I'd say yes," her tone challenging me to argue. "If I say no, some other girl out there is going to take him, so I might as well get him first."

I had noticed that whenever Cassie and I talked, she'd get a cab back to her hotel. "I never take buses or subways," she said, and added, "They're not for me." Other girls had said almost the same and it had taken me some time to understand. Their rejection of public transport was only partly because taxis are still a status symbol for them. It is also because they feel out of place in close contact with "ordinary" people.

What did she do when she got back to the hotel after work? "Nothing . . . well, I come in, turn on the TV, lie down and watch, and when I get bored watching, I write some, or wash my hair. Then I watch more TV and then I get tired and close my eyes for a while and hope to have a sleep, and then I get back to TV."

When did she eat? "When I get in," she said. "But I don't eat much; I'm not that hungry." This, too, is something many of the girls appear to have in common. "Eating," said a psychiatrist in Madison, Wisconsin, who specializes in research into child prostitution, "is a confirmation of life and a self-fulfilling pleasure. These children finally don't allow themselves—don't think themselves worthy of —pleasure, or in many cases, life."

A letter Cassie wrote me two years after we met is of interest here. She was now living with a boy she hoped to marry, and was planning to go to college.

> I remember that one time you said to me that you were really into food and all, enjoyed tasting all different kinds of food. It didn't mean anything to me then, but now I know exactly what you meant. Don't get me wrong—I'm not getting fat or anything but . . . now I know what you mean. Food is real good, isn't it?

When she was still in the life, and I asked her whether she ate in restaurants after work, she answered, "No, there is this coffee-shop downstairs, and I have stuff sent up, hamburgers and stuff." And did that go on the hotel bill? "Oh no," she said, "I pay when they bring it up." From the $10 a day Cal gave her as pocket-money? I asked incredulously. She shrugged. "Yeah. Anyway, my main meal is breakfast and—" she sounded proud, "Cal usually pays for that."

Cal had three girls in addition to Cassie, but he came to see her at about four or five o'clock most mornings, and when he felt like it, made love to her.

Did he make love to all his girls? Would they all expect it? She shrugged. "I guess so." Did she make love to him in return, I asked again, really make love, kiss him and hold him? "Yes," she said.

Yes, because that "real" lovemaking, a make-believe on both sides and, strange as it may seem, the most corrupting part of the life for the girls, is part of the deal, the bargain, the unwritten contract.

"Other times," she said, "he just lies down next to me and sleeps." And in the morning, he ordered breakfast for both of them, big meals of eggs and bacon and sausages and loads of toast. "Usually he even gives it to me in bed," she said. "We have it together, and then we get dressed, and around eleven he drives me to work."

And while she works, what is he doing? She shrugged again. "Sitting in pimp-bars, drinking, showing off about his ladies. Driving around in his Caddy, checking on his hoes." ("Hoes" is street pronunciation for whores.) "You never know when a pimp is going to show up. They're regular but irregular—" her laughter this time was a bitter guffaw—"so that you never know when they might come or from what direction, but you sure know they are coming. The only one, except Big Daddy, who I knew wouldn't mind if I knocked off for coffee when I was tired, was Lovell. With the others—even Cal—I wouldn't dare. Just once or twice a day, that's all. Now I go into one of the diners on Eleventh Avenue. I reckon I'm pretty safe there—he can't look through all of them."

By the time I met Cassie, the ovarian infection from which she had been suffering since her trip to California in August, which had been gravely worsened by the rape in New Jersey, had become agonizing. For months she had hidden her condition from her pimps and suppressed the pain with aspirins, taking as many as fifteen a day. During the three weeks since we began talking, I had watched her become paler and more listless. Her face was now covered with spots and no longer pretty.

She was working entirely on Eleventh Avenue, the cheapest pick-up site in Manhattan, justly known as "the sink." Because her illness incapacitated her, all she could do was oral sex in cars, for $10. Her daily quota for Cal was $150 so she had to do a minimum of fifteen men a day. (The days she spent talking to me, I gave her the money.)

By now I was in regular consultation with police officers, and we had got in touch with officials in the Department of Family and Children in Cassie's home town. All of us thought that the time—which has to be judged carefully—was almost ripe for an attempt to help her leave the life.

Cassie's brother Bob, a hard-working salesman, had agreed to work with us. He had suspected for some time what Cassie was doing, but knowing his parents—especially his mother—he considered it pointless to tell them. Cassie had told them that what she was doing in New York was modelling; she even sent them some photographs of herself taken by one of her tricks, to substantiate the story, and they continued to believe it, or to pretend to believe it, through thick and thin.

Bob wanted to help Cassie. "I feel bad about her, real bad," he said. "I should have spent more time on her, been a real brother to her, and I wasn't." He was very reluctant to tangle with his parents: "I really just don't want to get involved in family hassles. To be brutally frank, I don't think I can take it. Perhaps I'm weak, at least not strong enough for that. I can't afford it." Yet in spite of this, he decided to try. A year before I met Cassie, her mother had sworn she would never allow her back in the house, and it was Bob who finally persuaded her to change her mind.

At my urging, Cassie called them one day on my office phone, to say hello, and her mother invited her to come home for Christmas. "Oh," I heard her say, "How's Sally? . . . How's Dad? . . . How are you, Mom? Oh—you sure? . . . Okay then . . . yeah, I will . . . Okay . . ." And when she had hung up she put her head down on the desk and cried.

But it was clear to everyone that Cassie's parents were not the answer in the long run. Possibly, we thought, she and her brother could become closer (she seemed to want that) and she could, at least for a start, make her life with him. This didn't prove workable for long, but Bob agreed that she should go to him after Christmas and that he would take responsibility for her, while a distinguished social worker in her home town promised to mobilize whatever facilities existed there, to help her in her return to normal life. None of this was known to Cassie—we intended to tell her only when she was ready for it, when we had the last of our New York conversations. She needed to take, so it seemed to us, just one further step towards readiness.

What had to be done now was to mobilize her own residual capacity for rational thinking. The essential thing would be to choose the precise moment for a direct approach—a very risky matter with children like Cassie, who will almost automatically reject anything that duplicates or even resembles the attitudes of their parents.

*

We were sitting in the famous Oyster Bar in Grand Central Station: sea food, she had told me, was the only thing she had some liking for, and glamour has its uses. She had ordered lobster, but hardly touched it. She was sweating; there were pearls of sweat on her forehead but her face was grey, with deep shadows under her eyes, and her usually shiny blond hair was stringy. Her obvious physical deterioration made it imperative to act.

Didn't she think, I asked, that it was time to stop? She looked ill—would she come to a doctor with me? She shook her head, her eyes on her plate.

Did Cal know she was ill? "He don't care," she said listlessly, "as long as I bring in the money."

Three weeks earlier she had told me that when she had started with Big Daddy, she had found hustling "kinda fun." Was it still "kinda fun" on Eleventh Avenue—blow-jobs in commuters' cars, hours of standing on freezing corners, hidden moments of refuge in diners? Continual fear and now continual pain? Was that really better, as she had also said when we began to talk, than an office job?

"Well, in an office job you don't make the same money," she murmured.

But she *wasn't* making any money, was she? "No," she answered. "I'm making money, but it's not mine."

But if she got herself into a position of holding a job, any ordinary job, the money she earned would be hers, wouldn't it? "Yeah," she said, "but it wouldn't be the same amount."

But what was the difference *what* the amount was, if it wasn't her's? She giggled nervously. "Isn't it extraordinary," I went on, "to do what you're doing, for free?"

She looked up, "Is it . . . is it because I *like* to do it?" she asked. "Oh God . . . I just don't know."

Well, *did* she like it? And did she think the other young girls did it because they enjoyed it? "I think it's . . . perhaps because it gets one a place to stay?" she said, questioningly.

It got her a flea-hole to stay in, I said. Yes, she knew it was a flea-hole, but it was better than being out in the street wasn't it?

But if she had a normal job, or went back to school, the choice wouldn't be between a flea-hole and the street, but between a flea-hole and a nice room or apartment, with friends or foster-parents.

The mere mention of foster-parents put her back up. "I could have a nice apartment now," she said summoning up her low reserves. "All

I have to do is ask Cal for it." I waited. "He'd give me an apartment if I wanted one," she went on. "This is just temporary for right now, until we decide where we're going to go. See, I don't like to think about tomorrow. I take every day as it comes."

What did she think was most important about herself as a person: That she was a female? That she was pretty? That she was young, and bright? "I don't know. I'm not that conceited."

What *did* she think of herself? "That's a hard question," she said. "I can't answer that. I really don't know. I'm surviving." She was wiping her wet face on her sleeve, leaning her other elbow on the table.

"I don't let myself think about the future," she said, "because it scares me, because what *am* I going to do?"

I ordered tea with lemon and poured four spoons of sugar into her cup. It was after four by now and the huge restaurant was empty. The sugared tea gave her a new spurt of energy.

"Whatever I'm doing now," she said, "it's I who am making the decision, even if the decision is whether I want to be hustling on Madison or on Eleventh Avenue."

But looking at it another way, I said, it was the pimps who were telling her to bring $150 or whatever every night and she *had* to do it. If she didn't then they "kicked her ass," wasn't that right?

"Some of them would," she said, "but there again, it's my decision. If they do and I don't like it, I can leave them, I can go to somebody else . . ."

And would that somebody else be any better? Would he take less from her, give her more—not just in money, but in feelings? Would any of them be honest?

She thought for a long time, drank tea, looked around the room. "It's getting late," she said, and pointed at the waiters sitting at a corner table. "They must be furious at us for still being here." And then she said suddenly, as if there had been nothing between my question and her answer, "No. No, there is no honesty in it at all." She laughed, a laugh so bitter, so old, that I covered her hand with mine to stop it. "A game, that's all it is," she said. "A game."

"A game," I said, holding onto her hand, "at which the pimps are clever. But what about you? What are you getting out of it?"

Her answer was very quick, coldly factual and firm: "I'm away from my parents, and they've got to believe that I don't need them to survive. I'm making it on my own."

*

I put her in a taxi then, and sent her to her hotel, to rest. For the next day—my planned next step in normalizing her life—we had arranged that she would meet us—my husband and me—at the Algonquin Hotel for a drink and we would than take her out to dinner.

We were there a quarter of an hour before the arranged time, 5pm, and sat down at a table in the hall from where we could immediately see her as she entered. She didn't come.

We waited for an hour before I phoned her hotel, remembering only as they answered that I had deliberately not asked what name she was registered under. My fumbling description of her failed to convince the seedy desk clerk, though he no doubt knew her. We waited another hour before going round to the hotel. I had no better success face to face with the man; there was no such young lady registered there, he said.

It was freezing outside. We walked down 42nd Street to Eleventh Avenue—the sink. We stood at the corners of this windy street, waiting for an hour—a salutary lesson for us, for she had been doing this for months. Now we knew what it felt like. We then walked down the avenue, from one diner to another in the hope she might have dropped in at one of them to have a coffee or get warm.

At 11 pm we gave up, took a taxi to a restaurant a bit further uptown and telephoned Karen, one of the pimp squad officers who had helped—or tried to help—Cassie for months. Karen, herself a beautiful young blonde, lived on Long Island.

She called back at 11:45. "Panic is over," she said, happily. "Took a little longer than we thought, but it's okay. She's just arrived at home. She left New York this morning. She sends you her love and says please forgive her for standing you up, and thanks."

Four days later it was Christmas. Now, as I write this, it's three years afterwards. Cassie has not returned to New York.

Cassie, predictably, has had a very hard time finding her way, so hard, indeed, it is astonishing and a mark of her basic strength that she has not fallen by the wayside as so many do. She was, it turned out, pregnant when she left New York that cold winter night. She steadfastly refused to have an abortion, and after the baby came insisted on keeping and nursing it for six weeks. Then, her heart breaking, she told me, she gave it up for adoption. "They told me they found a very nice young couple," she said, crying over the telephone. "I *am* too young,

Gitta. I'm too much of a mess still; I have no right to keep it."

After two years of living with two boyfriends, each one for about a year, she finally took a refresher course in accountancy and almost immediately landed in a job she loved and held for nearly a year. "I'd still be in it," she told me, "if the boss hadn't finally said either I went to bed with him or out. So out I went." But she knows that a successful work experience with good references ("He couldn't very well not give me those," she said) will help her in the search for a new job in which she is engaged at this writing.

What happened to Julie also demonstrates how help can and does come effectively from often denigrated official sources.

"What it is," said Julie, "you have to get to the breaking point. You get so tired of all the bullshit and the things you go through. But it takes—you know—something like a crisis to get you out." Her own crisis came after an arrest. "It was the ninth time they had taken me in, so I guess it just happened at the right moment."

This time she had the immeasurable luck to come up before a wise judge, experienced with juveniles, instead of in a police court, where alas, prostitutes of any age are no more than shadowy numbers to be dealt with as swiftly as possible. ("To be got rid of, you mean," one of them said to me.)

"He sent me to Juvenile Detention," Julie said. "It's a nice, clean, modern building with quite pleasant single rooms. There are bars on the windows, but there are flowers outside. The food is good, the people looking after it are social workers, not guards. It's warm and clean but not sterile"—she smiled—"and my bed had flower-sprigged sheets and pillow cases, little roses with green leaves, I couldn't believe it. We had to go for walks every day, but that was the only 'must.' Otherwise all they wanted of me was to sit and think. And I did."

It is impressive evidence of Julie's capacity to think constructively, that she was able to take and use the help she needed from this institution; for her mother was unlikely to be able to change. She could not find support by going home, any more than Cassie could.

Unlike Cassie and Julie, Anna had the good fortune to be loved by an intelligent, stable mother. She was less desperate for love than the other two, and therefore able to command it more easily. Even popcorn Sonny had loved her in his own way, and when she had been in New York with him for four months—boring months rather than violent ones—one of her tricks fell genuinely in love with her.

This was Anwar, a small, shy Indian, twenty-four years old, who had come to America as an immigrant four years earlier and had graduated from dish-washing to cooking, which he enjoys. He lives in a dingy midtown hotel and his clothes have obviously seen years of wear.

Was he receiving a proper wage, I asked him. "My boss is very generous, very good. In Bengal I have eleven brothers and sisters, all younger, and now I am fine, very fine. I can help them." He earns $200 a week, his boss pays for his room, he eats on the job—and he is, indeed, "very fine."

"I love Anna," he said, smiling his shy but peculiarly sweet smile. When he first picked her up he did not realize how young she was, because "she is . . . you see . . . " and he indicated with his hand how tall she is. But "when I began to love her, she was young, and I loved her more. In India it is not bad to love a very young girl. I wanted to marry her."

This kindly relationship contributed, no doubt, to Anna's decision to stop. She could—and should—have walked out on Sonny, telephoned home collect, and got on a plane. But she felt that she owed it to him to do it openly.

"He'd gone to get me a kitten. I thought he'd give it me, say good luck and good-bye. I was really getting deluded."

What Sonny actually did was beat her up and break her jaw, then send her straight out to work. "I was babbling insanely and crying, and for the next twenty-four hours I couldn't look at him without fear, without tears coming in my eyes." She was in horrifying pain, but it was two days before he let her go to one of the City hospitals. Six days later, when she returned to Sonny with her jaw wired shut, he again sent her straight out to work.

"And that was the end," she said. She went to Anwar for help, and he paid to get her—under his name—into a first-class hospital in the Bronx where she had to have a second operation because the first one had been appallingly badly done.

Even then she could not quite accept that her relationship with Sonny was not a real one. Her confusion and misery is vividly demonstrated by a page from a diary which she kept in hospital:

So, this is the 1st page of a new book, of a new life, or maybe returning to my old one, well, anyway, I haven't met with this much mental confusion, uncertainty etc since i left home. i don't know. i'll call sherry tomorrow. its a big decision, but now, i'm so alone, i can't see how without going back to sonny i could be as happy and fulfilled as i was, i guess i'll call him too. . .

so, ah, i know sonny isn't coming. i just wish i could be able to get in touch

(an' he walks on in)

So, ah . . . later, no feelings. no thoughts. NOT HIM.

Three days after leaving hospital—and after seeing Sonny yet again—she finally called her mother. Two FBI officers picked her up and flew her home with an FBI nurse. "Within two hours of arrival they stuck me in a mental hospital," she said, where at first she was "angry and shocked as hell." But after a long while, "it made me realize that this was where the lie ended."

Anwar telephoned her home. "I wanted to marry her. I spoke to her mother and later I also spoke to Anna." His sweet smile was now sad. "I knew then—no. They are different people. I shall love her to the end of my life."

7

Slim, the Player: "Why should a woman give you her money?"

The pimp squad wanted to do what they could to help me write this book because all of them—naturally enough—deplore child prostitution. It was frankly as a quid pro quo that they obtained a pimp's agreement to talk to me. "There are times when it is useful to help some of them, and other times when it is useful to some of them to help us," said Sergeant Trapp.

"They've been very fair, downright truthful with me," Slim admitted. "One thing about them, they tell you up front what they can do and what they can't do. Now, if they can help you out, they tell you. If they can't . . . ." he stopped.

What did he mean by "helping out"? Was it a matter of "If you help us, we'll help you?"

"Okay," he said. "Say they have a case—a prosecution case, know what I mean? They need help in a case where a girl's been beat up by a so-called pimp, player, mack, hustler or what you want, and me being in the life as long as I have been, I can—you know—sometimes I can get the word about what's happened. To help them out, same time help myself out. Like if I'm going back into court on a certain date, you know, or one of my young ladies is, they'll see to it that we don't have to hang about, lose time—you see where I'm coming from? Anyway I don't—I repeat—I don't like b.r.u.t.a.l.i.t.y!" He had this habit of spelling out a word he wanted to emphasize. "I don't approve of it and it is not necessary."

In this instance his lady, Gina, had to go to see a district attorney at ten o'clock that morning, about a charge "on somebody else," as he put it, which meant that Gina was summoned to corroborate another prostitute's testimony against her pimp.

"My lady was very sceptical, very drawn-in about giving this information," he said. "But it is very important—a big case. And I convinced her that the people she was dealing with were all right, and that if we helped 'the man' [the whites in authority], we'd get help in return when we needed it."

To show his lady that he too was prepared to "help," he had agreed to talk to me while she was downtown giving evidence, which he very firmly expected to take no more than an hour or two. Later, when he discovered that his lady's presence was in fact needed for much longer—indeed, on another occasion, for a whole day—he was to get very angry.

The small room where Slim and I talked the first time was off the main pimp squad office, a huge bare space on the fourth floor of a hideous old police building on West 40th Street. It was in fact the interrogation room, where pimps are brought after arrest and handcuffed to a chair while being questioned: Slim had no doubt been there before. There was little to recommend it as a setting for soul-searching or confidences; but while the squad were willing to find me a suitable person to talk to from among the 1,700 pimps on their files, they would not allow at least the first meetings to take place except under their supervision. "Even the best of them—and that's a manner of speaking—can be dangerous," said George Trapp. "They've got to know that our eyes are going to be on them from the word go. That's the only way we can be sure nothing happens to you."

I never felt myself in danger from any of these men, wherever I saw them—sometimes in strange places. What I did feel was an awful distance between them and me. Theirs really is another world: a world of amorality and unreality so isolated from that of most other people, whether black or white, that bridging the chasm between the two is hardly possible.

Whatever the room's past associations for Slim, the present situation was quite different. Tipping his chair back until it touched the wall behind him, crossing his legs in their immaculately creased trousers, and gesturing with a cigarette in a long holder, he made obvious to one and all his amusement at his change of role.

He had thought, to start with, that this meeting for an hour or so was all I would want from him. His intention, of course, was to shoot a line. He was quite worldly-wise as well as street-smart: he thought he knew exactly what I wanted and how I would go about it, and he had ready all the stock answers to the questions he was sure I would ask.

Slim is slight in stature, appearing a little taller than he is by walking (or so at least it seems) on his toes. His gait—a kind of skip—is very light, very graceful, very conspicuous. He is not handsome. He has a small face, small as if compressed. His features are small, too: a small, rather elegant nose, small deep-brown eyes with lids that seem too wide for them—when he thinks deeply, or is depressed, they hood his eyes, and his face, suddenly without expression, looks drugged and dead. His lips are thin and his colour is comparatively light. He was to betray pride during our talks at the evident fact that there had been some mixture in his family.

Did he know what I was doing? I asked.

"Yes, I do," he said. "It's not the first time I've heard of young ladies," he corrected himself with realistic gallantry and a meaningful look at my face, "of ladies trying to get reports on players, pimps, prostitutes, hoes and all that."

That wasn't quite what I was doing, I said, and explained that I was mainly interested in very young girls (and boys), that I was talking to them, to their parents, and also to their men—people like himself.

"Well," he said, in a gently condescending, explanatory tone, "you can't really get too much outlook, background on a young lady's parents, because first of all a young girl who's under age is not going to *confide* in her parents what she's doing, about selling her body . . ."

Did he think that some of these girls are taking a sort of revenge on their parents? "Yeah, sure, a lot of them."

Surely they must talk to him about their folks, don't they? "Yeah, some."

Did he get the feeling that they actively wanted to hurt their parents? "Uh, definitely," he said. "Even though they don't tell them, they know their parents will find out, and I'm sure they *want* them to find out. And anyway," he added, "most of the parents know—they make as if they don't know, but they know. Many of the girls, you know, don't like white boys. . . ."

I mentioned that several of the men I had already met, and now he too, seemed like bright guys. "Yes, I am," he agreed. So why on earth, I asked, were they in this miserable life?

"Well, in the first place," he said, settling back even more comfortably, "to go back a little bit, I'm not a kid. I'm not eighteen or even in my early twenties. I was born in 1946, so I'm in my thirties, so I've been in it . . . um . . . fifteen years."

So what made him go into it? "Money, clothes, fascination, challenge. The excitement. The glamour. The Rolls-Royces, the Bentleys, the Cadillacs, all that shit. Money . . . what I'm saying is that being a black man, it's money I'd never have, never get the experience to hold—not the amount of money I am able to hold."

I asked if he had ever thought of making himself a different kind of life.

"Yes, I have," he said. "I did and I could. But first of all, I used drugs when I was young, started when I was about sixteen." His family, originally from Brooklyn, moved to Long Island when he was a boy. "We moved to the suburbs," he said, "because it was supposed to be a better neighbourhood, where we'd be supposed to be dealing with a more different kind of people. But anywhere you go today, you find drugs, people who sell you drugs. Okay, I started off at a young age using drugs, at sixteen." (This would have been in 1962, nearly the beginning of the drug era.)

Slim was in high school at the time. "And I met a girl, from the next town to ours, that was, uh, Jewish. She had her own Coupé de Ville with a record player built inside. She was a year older than me, eighteen. She had all these things, and she liked me, you know what I mean?"

Was she the first white girl he'd known? "She was what I considered the first white girl," meaning the first white girl that he had developed a relationship with.

"They liked me," he said, "but it wasn't . . . you know what I mean? Coming from the town where I come from, it was more or less white was on one side and black was on the other, y'know what I mean? I'm not trying to be . . . " he hesitated. "I don't want to seem like conceited, or anything like that, but I know that for a black person I am a nice-looking person. You can strike that any way you like, how you feel, how you look at me. But I know how another woman looks at me. I know what comes out of my mouth. I know the way I can look, dress, the finesse I have, that *makes* me."

And this was a rich girl, was she? "She was *extremely* rich! I never met her parents, because it was one of these things like black and white. She was a Jewish girl, too. Her father *owned* a hospital—it was named after him."

He'd met her through a friend. "She dropped him and began to like me." And they became friends? "Well yes, friends . . . I'd cop a smoke for her." She didn't take drugs, he added quickly, "she smoked reefers, that's all. I'd get her a half a pound or a pound—she had the money for anything."

"She liked me," he repeated, "you know, sexually, because I was . . . well, you see me now but then I was . . . at the time I was a cutie-pie type," he laughed, "know what I mean? And she sexually befriended me and she came with gifts."

At that time, he said, he wasn't even aware of the pimping game, the mack game, and anyway she didn't need to be a prostitute. "She didn't have to," he said, "she had all the money in the world. Her parents gave her anything she wanted. And she gave me anything I wanted . . . you know, like I said I wanted some of those Italian sandals guys were wearing then—they cost like sixty, eighty dollars—she just got them for me. And you know, she liked the Village scene and we would go there. . . ."

He was at school all that time. "I finished high school," he said. "I graduated; I even qualified for college and went to NYU. I took an introduction course in computer programming." His first job was on the Stock Exchange, for a broker who ended up in bankruptcy. "But the little money I was getting just didn't seem to meet up with my situation. Plus I was using drugs, so really, you know, it didn't take care of what I needed, you know what I mean?"

Up to this point my questions had more or less followed the expected line. My next question—so he told me much later—took him "unawares" and "upset his schedule." I asked him if he could tell me about his family, his father and mother, and he was slightly disconcerted.

"I can give you that in short plain English," he replied. "My mother I loved until she died, in 1973. She was my heart," he said. "I loved . . ." he stopped, and then repeated: "She was my heart. My father, I never had any type of relationship with. My mother got separated when I was, oh, fourteen, fifteen years old."

He had one brother, who is a correction officer. "He's straight all the way, cool, y'know? He does his thing." Did he see him, I asked, and, as would happen repeatedly, he couldn't understand my English accent. "Excuse me?" he asked, as always impeccably polite, and then replied, "I see him occasionally. He knows what I'm doing. He's not happy about it but, uh, what can he do? I'm a grown man. What can he do?

"Me and my mother had a family life. My father was off the set a lot. We moved, like I said, in fifty-seven. He was a general contractor then. My brother and myself, we knew that my mother and father wasn't getting along too good, and we were both getting hung up. Me more than him, because I was the youngest and the baby of the family. I seemed to go more toward my mother."

Did his father look after them financially? "As far as I'm concerned," he answered, "no, he didn't. He had—he's always had the money. Right now he's the head electrician of one of the man's big institutions, and he makes plenty of money and he keeps his money."

Did his father beat him? Slim took his cigarette out of its holder and elaborately extinguished it. He put the holder away in his pocket. All this took time, and was done in silence.

"I've had . . . I remember . . . " he finally began slowly, "there were times I had beatings from him that was . . . ", he paused, "sadistic." The word sounded dry, not histrionic.

Did his father beat his brother, too? "No, never." Did this happen when he was small? "You see," he said, and now his voice had changed: this was new for him, he was thinking back rather than glibly describing events. "You see, my brother is more or less on my father's side of the family, because he's a little darker. I always seem to have been on my mother's side, because I was a little lighter. My mother's family was all a little light, you know?"

Did that really make a difference? "It made a difference in our family, yes. One Christmas my mother was at my aunt's house—my father's sister—and both my brother and I sat in our aunt's lap doing Christmas decorations. I couldn't have been more than four or five years old, and you know, she pushed me off her lap, y'know what I mean, and cuddled my brother. That's the sort of thing you remember as long as you live. Forever. To treat one of two kids different. You have a family yourself, you know what that's got to mean."

When talking to people who lead such chaotic lives, one has to approach every story with a degree of scepticism. But equally one learns quite quickly to distinguish between lies and truth, between fantasy and reality. There is almost always a point of decision: not reached suddenly, sharply, perhaps not even consciously. It manifests itself less in words than in the tone of voice, and in a curious change of pace and energy. Fantasy often equals energy, and truth fatigue.

Slim too changed, as soon as he began to speak of his parents and childhood. His clear and articulate way of expressing himself became more fluid, words and sentences began to run into one another, his voice became so low it was at times unintelligible. And his movements changed. Where before he had smoked pensively and deeply, creating and playing with artful smoke rings, now he smoked without the holder in quick puffs, his hands never still. His legs were uncrossed, his knees shuffled rhythmically to and fro. And his face, which at the beginning or our conversation had looked young and smooth, almost boyish, had slacked and paled.

Was there mixed blood in his mother's family? "We're light," he said. "We are all light. We are Indian—Cherokee Indian. My father's dark, and my brother's dark—and when I say dark, I mean *black*."

Was his father Indian too? "No, no," he sounded impatient. "My *mother*, my *mother's* side was light . . . You understand, if you look at my complexion, I'm not a dark black person."

"No," I agreed, "you are brown."

"Well, this is the darkest we get on my mother's side. We don't get any darker than this. My father . . . " He started again, with a conscious decision to go further. "When I was young," he said, "I stole out of a five-and-ten cent drug store and I was brought home by the police. That night I was taken down to the basement by my father, tied up in the basement by my hands and beaten. Understand? I remember this . . . I couldn't have been more than seven, eight years old. That happened to me two or three times, by my father."

After stealing something? "Stole, or whatever I did wrong, riding on the back of a bus with skates or whatever. I'd get these terrible beatings from my father that still stick today. Sure, my mother would chastise me when I spoke out of turn or something. But she wouldn't *beat* me, not so I'd faint."

What did his father beat him with? "Whatever he could get his hands on, a belt, a cord. Nothing made of iron, you know, nothing like that, but leather, he'd always beat me with something made of leather. And I was, well, not a baby but . . . you know, *seven*, or *eight*."

And his brother? "No—my brother was —it's funny. My brother wasn't timid but he just never seemed to get into the trouble I got into, y'know what I mean? I can't remember him ever getting beat like me, ever. I got it so bad, so terrible, I ran away. Said good-bye to my mother and ran away when I was about eight." He laughed, without mirth. "We lived two doors away from my grandmother and I ran away to there. I stayed in the basement for a day and then the man [the white owner] found me. He didn't molest me or anything like that, he just told me to git and let me go. My brother saw me come out and he chased me a block, caught me and took me home.

"And there my father did the only thing that I could say was ever like a father. It was during the World Series, y'know what I mean, and he gave me and my brother tickets—yeah, he did do that." He thought for a minute. "But what the hell. It wasn't nothing for him."

I suggested that, on the contrary, his father probably thought it was a lot to do, after Slim had no doubt caused his parents a great deal of worry by running away. "Well, yes, I suppose so, for him. Yeah. But then y'know"—he wasn't going to give an inch in his father's favour—"I was busted back in seventy-two for armed robbery." (He would have been twenty-six years old.) "By this time my mother and father had been divorced for years, and she'd remarried twice. Her second husband died of a heart attack, and her third came from Chicago, so she relocated to Chicago.

"When I got busted, she flew in very frequently, working on my father to bail me out. But he wouldn't give up the money—$4,600 cash bail, no collateral, nothing—$4,600 cash, that's what the man wanted.

"It took her *three months* to talk him into it. I went in from July 11 to October 11."

But he did finally pay it? "Yeah, after three months he coughed it up, but you know—hell, he didn't do no more than he was *supposed* to do. I did wrong, but he didn't do nothing for me when I did right. And do you know what it's *like*, three months in the man's prison?"

He paused. "He's doing fine, my father, fine. But you know, if he croaked tomorrow—he's my father, yeah, and he gave me life, but if he croaked tomorrow, a tear wouldn't drop. When my mother passed away . . . " again he paused. "Well, she's dead now. My family brought her back to New York to die here; she had cancer of the throat. . . . She left my brother and me each seven thousand dollars."

Did his mother know what he was doing? "At the end, before she died, yes. She didn't approve of it, but"—his voice changed, becoming much higher and smoother—"but she said, 'whatever you do, be the best at whatever you do.' "

"Really?" I said. "She didn't try to talk you out of it?"

"She said, 'Be the best at whatever you do.' " It sounded like a recitation. "She didn't try—there's no point to try and talk me out of it—I'm a grown man."

But he wasn't a grown man when he started, I said. "Then, she didn't know. I was a grown man when she died, and she said to be the best at what you do: and I *am* the best at what I do!

"What brought me into this life? I was in gaol. I was seventeen and

I was square, but *square*. And I was using drugs and I was locked up
with a player, a pimp. And he was pacing the cell one night when we
first got locked up, and we were talking, and he says, 'You don't know
shit, you know that?' And I said, 'Shit, I know I don't.' " Slim looked
at me. "You don't mind me talking the way I am, do you? I'm just
giving it to you straight. 'You don't know shit,' he says again. And he
says, 'I'm going to ask you a question and I want you to answer this
question: Why—*why* should a woman give you her money?' That's
what he said.

"And do you know, all night, part of the next day, by not being in
it, not knowing, I couldn't give him no reason. I just simply didn't
know. I couldn't give him no reason why a woman should give it to me.
Y'know what I mean? But when I got my first woman, then I knew. It's
because I'm *qualified to have it*, first of all.

"And second of all, I can take care of her needs. If she could take
care of her own needs, she wouldn't be doing what she is doing. She
needs that image of someone stronger, more powerful, someone that is
able to manage her. Now . . . " he smiled, really quite wisely, "I didn't
say her money—I said manage *her*. Do you understand what I'm
saying? I'm capable of managing any lady that's with me. But only a
chosen few can be with me. I do not have just any girl that wants to
come with me. First of all, I do *not* have black girls with me,
understand?"

Why didn't he have black girls? "Because it's too much trouble. I
don't like the knock-down, drag-out beat-up battle that you have to
have with a black girl. She doesn't have the respect for her man that she
should have; she doesn't give you your property that you deserve."

"The reason why black pimps prefer to have white girls," said one of
the wisest social workers that I met (she was black herself, and was
talking about prostitution generally, not about children), "is because
the black girl is just as street-wise as he is. Yes, she too will give him
money. But many, if not most, of them will insist on a real percentage
of their earnings. They don't even pretend to believe all this bullshit
about saving up for her and all that. They say, 'Up front, buddy. That's
when I put out and no sooner.'

"So the pimp who has black girls is likely to be a very different kind
of man—quite possibly, I dare say often—a *man*. Living illegally of
course, in a conventional sense living wrongly, on her earnings. But

he'll more than likely make a home for her, let her have his kids, be their father—all the things the pimps will never do for their white ladies.

"And finally, there is one more thing. The black girl—because, like him, she's grown up in this rotten white society and because, like him, she has so far survived—she will, like him, have a sense of humour. Perhaps it's that, almost more than any other of their shared qualities or characteristics, that makes their relationship into something mutual, something shared . . . quite often, something real."

But Slim, living his life of unreality, would either never see this or—even at his most honest—be able to admit it. "A white girl," he maintained, "seems to have potential understanding of knowing a man, what his qualifications are, and what his desires and needs are."

The essential turbulence of Slim's personality manifested itself at the merest pretext, above all if he felt himself slighted, looked down upon, or even underrated or misunderstood. And when that happened, he could turn within seconds from gentle philosophical charm to vicious anger.

At one moment during that first long talk in the police building, we were interrupted by an officer from the vice squad, who shared office space with the pimp squad. He came in to look for a file. Later I would learn that this man had what the others called a "pathological loathing" for pimps. "They are vermin," he would tell me bitterly. "They should be stamped out like this"—and he ground his heel into the floor.

He displayed these sentiments clearly when he thundered into the little office where we were sitting. His disgust at even minimal contact with the pimp was conveyed by pushing Slim's legs—which were marginally in his way—aside with his foot, and he almost as cavalierly brushed by me without a word.

We had just been discussing how Slim and his brother had paid off "fifty-fifty" the mortgage on the house their mother owned on Long Island. My tape then vividly records the wordless but noisy intrusion, and Slim saying to me with icy dignity, "Would you please turn off the tape recorder?"

His dignity evaporated the moment the officer had left the room. "This is the type of shit—" he burst out, "excuse the expression, but this is the type of shit that *burns me up*! Because my lady goes down there, helps out—she didn't have to, she's doing it because I asked her to, she's on my side. Sure, she might get a few fucking marks knocked off for her own case, if one comes up—excuse my language again, but man, hey, they're cutting my fucking bread and butter down. I can get two fifty, three hundred dollars, man, her sitting in the fucking courthouse, man, you know what I mean?"

All this was his burning anger at the contempt the vice squad officer had shown for him. "You come in here, with a suit on, tie on, like you been busy all day. Hey man, you been busy—but you didn't voluntarily blow two, three hundred dollars, man, understand where I'm coming from? Three, four hundred dollars, today being Friday it could have been *five* hundred dollars for me just this morning. Know what I mean?

"The case she's helping on, you know, I can't go into it, it's confidential. But I'm just saying, hey man, you know I ain't getting reimbursed for doing that. And then he comes in like what you call the 'lo-o-rd of the-e mano-or,' " he stretched the phrase sarcastically, "Yeah, I know that expression. Well, I ain't getting reimbursed. I don't mind helping out, but when I help out, let *nobody* give me this kind of shit. Fuck that—push comes to shove, I don't *need* any favours—I don't *need* them. I'll get a private lawyer. I've got the money, all I have to do is reach in my pocket and get a private lawyer. Don't let *him* give me shit because he thinks I'm being done favours. You're down here from England, doing what you need to do, but I'm down here too, trying to help out and be for real. But don't let them jam me: I know how to play the game from both sides. I can give it to you nice—I can give it to you for what you want to hear—and I can give it to you for what you *don't* want to hear, understand where I'm coming from?

"I can play the rough side and tell you really what the game is about. Let me tell you something about this game: I don't *camp* here in New York, I *live* here. You get people that come in here from Memphis, you get people from California . . . but I'm a native New Yorker. With me, it's not a game. This is my lifestyle . . . this is how I live." He looked me full in the face. "You keep saying you want 'to go back,' to know about my childhood and all that. . . ."

(He had been deeply involved and touched when talking about his childhood. Some days later he said that he had never in his life spoken about his childhood, to anyone. "Who cares?" But the gross intrusion at the wrong moment had broken the mood, and in order to save face, to regain the respect he felt he had lost by letting me see his humiliation, he had to denigrate what he had already said.)

"Hey, listen, let me tell you something. Being beaten by my father and all that—you can get that story from every kid down there in New York. But if you get down to the point, 'Man, what are you about?', then you are getting to the problem where you're *doing* it, where you're perfecting it, where you're *living* it—THAT's the part *you* want to know about."

"Not everybody is *qualified* for this life, but I am. I know every player who is *someone* in New York. Now, I don't know about these Johnny-come-latelies that just come in New York and get twos and fews [a couple of girls] and stuff like that, but those that are *about* something—I know, because I've been there, and I know. I've had it and I know. Hey, I'm being as serious as possible with you: What I'm saying, the Fleetwoods, the Broughams, the Rolls, stuff like that—I've had it, so it's nothing big to me, no big thing. It's like I've had it and I'll have it again, if that's what I continue to want, understand where I'm coming from? I lead the life I love"—I tried to interrupt—"No, let me say one thing. I lead the life I love, and I love the life I lead . . . Now, you can say what you want to say."

It took him a long time to regain his equanimity. I went out to get us coffee, from the pimp squad's coffee pot. We smoked my English cigarettes, both of us using almost identical long black holders. We discussed the comparative virtues of English and American tobacco (a subject I know very little about) and he slowly recovered his cool by telling me about his triumphs with a pretty English girl.

"She was a real lady," he said. "She talked like you do, that's why I know that English accent. She taught me a lot . . . I have a lot to thank her for, how I learned to talk and, you know, conduct myself in public."

8

"I *am* their daddy . . ."

Our second talk took place two weeks later, in an Italian restaurant in New York's East 70s. I had arranged a quiet corner table and our date was for seven-thirty. He came at 8:25, full of apologies. He was wearing a black made-to-measure suit in matt Italian silk—I had priced a similar outfit in Rome for my husband, not long before, at $480. His shirt was of white silk with a discreet silk cravat. The only slightly jarring note in his appearance was his shoes—black with white stitching—which he casually pointed out were hand-made.

He was manifestly nervous and admitted it frankly. "I'm sorry I'm late," he said. "I know it's rude to keep you waiting but I had a tough time making up my mind what to wear." He laughed. "I changed three times."

I never forgot with Slim, or with the other pimps I spoke with, that they are pastmasters at manipulation, but there comes a point in these relationships when, within the limitations of one's instinct, one must be willing to accept the other at face value. I was taking Slim to dinner because I wanted his story: one might say that his usual role was reversed and he was being used. But our conversation at dinner, though certainly one-sided, was no more or less intimate or intrusive than many others I have had with friends—or other strangers.

He was aware of the pretty women in the room, looked them over with an expert eye and made perceptive comments. ("She's wearing too much make-up," or, "That dress cost a few hundred, but it's too young for her," and about one lovely slim blonde, "That's one beautiful girl," and he smiled openly at her.)

Did he like women, I asked. "I like intelligent, witty, strong women," he answered. "I like a challenge, strong girls. If the moment is right, I don't think there is a woman alive that can resist me. Like the other day, I was in the World Trade Center and there was a young lady: she had on a satin suit, hair very fine, long black silky hair. Beautiful blue eyes. And I was following her into this large department store and got up close to her, and she turned around and said, 'Are you following me?' But she didn't say it, you know, angrily—'*Are* you following *me*?' She said it and smiled. So I knew—well, I *knew*, and we went and had a drink."

Meeting a girl like that, well dressed and obviously well bred—meeting her by chance and having a drink together, would he feel that this was a girl that he could turn on, and use? He nodded. "Yes, eventually yes. Because if she is open enough to me to start a conversation . . . " But even so, she wouldn't know what he is, what he does? "No, not unless I tell her." Well, he could just be a nice guy, somebody who wants to know her, nowadays meeting people this way is no big thing. "Well, yeah," he said, "but it's just a feeling I get. A professional like me sees, can tell what she feels—or might feel," he added. "I can tell very quickly."

Had he ever thought, did he ever still think, of changing, of doing something else?

Rachel told me that she had asked Lucky that same question "lots of times—he was the sort of man that could have done anything. But his point was always, he got a kick . . . this was what he wanted to do, it was exciting, he enjoyed it, he made money fast—and he didn't have to work."

She illustrated this by describing conversations she'd had with Lucky. "Once we were talking about Dostoievski and *The Idiot*, and he understood it very well. I remember listening to a professor here at the university a couple of weeks ago, and he didn't do half as good a job as Lucky did. Looking back on it, Lucky was a very bright guy and he must have felt so frustrated, because he felt he wasn't really good enough to go and do the things he could have done. The thing is, among the pimps, that they don't feel that they *can* get out of it.

"I remember thinking this with a lot of the pimps I met, my God, if they went to college—you could have the best bunch of black lawyers! Of course there's a terrific inferiority complex, and a real need to compensate with material things, and the only way they can get material things *fast* is to do this. . . . And there's a terrific need to manipulate, and the easiest people to manipulate are girls. And of course, for the blacks, there's a terrific need to have power over the white girls. . . ."

I had also discussed this waste of talent among the pimps with a police friend. "These guys could do anything," he said. "They could be anything. In a different society, those would be the teachers, lawyers, politicians."

. . .When I asked Slim that question—did he ever think of doing something else—he replied, "Sometimes, yeah, but not very often now. At my age you've got to do what you are good at and stick with it. As I've said to you before, very few men can do this correctly."

He really believed, did he, that he was doing something for these girls that justified taking their money? "I do, I do," he said. "I give them something they can't get from their fathers and mothers and that they *have* to have."

But they could get it from a husband, couldn't they? "They can get something from a husband, some of what they get from me. But they get something from me they *can't* get from a husband. It takes a special woman to be successful in this work," he said, "to take it day after day, night after night, week after week, month after month, year after year—and still get a charge out of it."

But the very young ones, I said, surely their main qualification, if that was how one could put it, was their youth, wasn't it? It wasn't that they had experience, or knew how to handle themselves.

"That's true," he said. "But you'd be surprised how eager they are to learn. I don't mean to be . . . " he hesitated ". . . you know, coarse, but it is surprising—it surprises even me sometimes."

Does he try them out?

"Some. Some I do, some I don't. Some I'd look at and say, 'Wow, I want her.' Some leave me sexually cold."

Would that mean that they wouldn't be any good at it?

"Not necessarily. It just means they don't turn me on."

And if they don't turn him on, does he not make love to them? Isn't the physical relationship between a pimp and his lady a must?

"Not entirely," he said (the professor again, and he wasn't faking it). "There are other things she needs from me, perhaps more than sex. That's what I mean when I say I'm qualified, you understand what I'm saying?"

How many ladies did he have now, I asked.

"How many ladies?" he repeated. "I have three ladies right now."

I knew that in fact he had only one. "Three?" I asked.

"I have one main lady, one that I can count on: one that I know is taking care of my business, that can handle *all* my business, y'understand where I'm coming from? She *means* something to me, know what I mean? That's Gina. She's twenty years old, but her birthday was just two days ago. She means that much to me, hey listen to me, she's in my corner, I'm in her corner."

How long had he known this girl? "How long? Long enough. Enough to know her. Because this is my lifestyle, my business."

But did he really feel something for this girl? "Do I feel—yes, I do feel something for this girl. Her birthday was the fourth, two days ago. I bought her—I was in a position to buy her a *mink*, a diamond ring, an opal, and a Sony Trinitron colour TV, y'understand what I mean? You add that up in your mind and you can't come within less than a thousand dollars on that. She's for real, that's why. You get people that's for real, you get people that's not for real."

This girl, Gina—was she from New York, I asked.

"No, she's not. She's from out—from Massachusetts." Did he know her parents? "I don't know her that long, just long enough for me to know her." I found out later he had known her for only two or three weeks.

Had Gina told him about her childhood, and how she got into prostitution when she was twelve (information I had from the pimp squad)?

"Of course," he said. "I've had Gina break down and cry, have a nervous breakdown, nearly everything—know what I mean? But I take care of her; she needs to be treated like a baby when she gets home. I know what Gina's about, y'know what I mean? I know what makes her tick."

Did he know what makes Gina tick, because he knows about girls who get into prostitution when they are still children? He was usually very careful about admitting any dealing with young girls, but he missed this one.

"Yes, I know about them," he said.

"Because you've had a couple of real young ones, haven't you?" I knew he had.

"Not *kids*," he said quickly. "I don't have *kids*. I deal with ladies. You see, first I deal with women and then I make them into ladies. . . ."

Did Gina have a quota? "No, I don't put a quota on my ladies. She knows what my hand deserves—what I'm qualified for. So like I says, on a bad night I get two hundred. Okay? If I have my three ladies, a bad night from three, that's six hundred, that's *bad* nights. And six times six, counting only on bad nights, that's 3,600 dollars a week."

How many men would they have to be with to earn that? "I don't know, I don't count them," he said. "I don't even care. I don't even want to hear their stories when they come home"—a very different picture from the one he had painted of Gina "needing to be treated like a baby" when she came home.

How much money did he give them each day? "I give them what they want, what they need. I give them their front money, which gets them to work, which they need for cigarettes, stuff like that. I give them twenty, thirty dollars a day pocket-money. [Cassie said he gave her five or ten.] Now she comes to me that evening, says she wants to go shopping, I give her two, three hundred dollars, y'understand?" Cassie and another of Slim's ladies confirmed this easy generosity—with their money.

"I tell them you can buy whatever you want. If you want to spend it all on your mother, spend it all on your mother. Do whatever you want. You ask me for money, you got it, y'understand where I'm coming from? It's that simple. Okay—getting back to what I was saying, average six hundred a day times seven [he had forgotten that he had previously said that his girls had a day off a week] that's 4,200 a week. My expenses, of course, are very high—the hotel alone costs about 1,200 dollars."

Did he give his girls drugs? "No. No-o, not at all. A woman can't be with me that uses drugs. She can't support a habit with me."

But it is true, isn't it, that most pimps are using? "Cocaine, sure. Some use hard drugs—I did, but I don't no more."

He said he enjoyed eating well: "Like a king! To start the morning off, I have an extremely large orange juice, two eggs over light, home fries, crisp bacon, ham and sausage, English muffins, and very sweet tea with milk."

And would his lady be having breakfast with him? "If she's home, yeah. If she wants a Danish, or whatever, that's okay, but that's what I eat. Then when I'm full I feel good, and I buy a bottle of blackberry brandy, have a walk and if my nerves are kinda high, take a Valium . . . I get nervous, because I always have a lot of things on my mind."

Had he taken some Valium before coming to have dinner with me tonight? He laughed. "Sure, course I did."

How did Gina feel about the life? "She doesn't like it," he said. "She's not happy with it; she's threatened every day by tricks, by other macks. Right now—that's the thing that I can't really talk about, but it's the big thing that's going on now—she has a lot of pressure on her." (Evidently from the pimp against whom she had given the supporting evidence downtown, that first day Slim and I talked.)

And then, as happened repeatedly—I suspected as a result of the cocaine he took—his mood suddenly changed. His face tightened, his hands began to fidget and his voice became sharp, almost vicious. "She went down there again today," he said. "There was no mandatory provision that she had to. She said she wanted to go down to the precinct to get warrants taken care of. And when I get home, she'll want to go out—but I'm going to say *NO*, she can't go *NOWHERE*! She wanted to go down there today but it means my money is fucked up—I won't get a fucking dime today!"

But if there are warrants out against her, surely she was right to take care of them rather than wait to be arrested? "Tough," he said.

Well, didn't she have to do that? "She had to do that *or* get my money, one or the other. Anyhow, *all* the day didn't have to be spent on that—do you know, she only got back just before I came up here to meet you? As far as I'm concerned, she didn't do what she was supposed to do. If she took care of business right she'd have been in there, out, and back to work, taking care of business and taking care of my money. She wasn't, and that's why I left her sitting there." (I had suggested that Gina join us in the restaurant, later in the evening.)

So what did he think she would do?

"What she'll probably do is look in her little book and make phone-calls . . . " His mood had now changed back to gentleness and philosophising, which he loved to do. "That's the kind of woman I have. 'Daddy,' she'll say, 'I didn't get you any work today, so I called up my sugar daddy and he's going to give me a hundred and fifty dollars.' " (Most of the girls keep a trick book, with phone numbers they can ring if work is slack.)

"Understand? She's getting my money. I don't mean this from the point of, 'Git it or I'll hurt you.' I mean it like, 'Hey, you took time off from work to do what you had to do, now make mine because I have expenses.' "

But he wouldn't hit her?

"Why? Why should I hit her? If I have a girl I have to hit, I don't want her around—y'understand where I'm coming from? That's why I don't have black girls, that's the point we go back to. You asked me why: that's why."

Because black girls expect to be hit? "Yeah—they like that fight back with you. A white girl, she understands what you want, she goes out and gets the cash. . . ."

I had asked Rachel if Lucky had any black girls. "No," she said, and it sounded as if it was the first time she had realized it. "I knew a lot of black and white girls—both runaways and others who lived at home—who were in child prostitution in my city and in New York, but it's true—Lucky's girls were all white.

"I know one thing about him. I know that he never touched, never beat up any of his girls ever, and this was because he was beaten when he was a boy. He always thought that that was the worst, most awful thing. . . . As a matter of fact, I never knew any pimp, of all the ten or eleven I knew, who beat up. It's not in their interest, you know, and if they're bright they know it. Lucky, his whole thing was, you know, that his girls should look *nice*. He'd say, 'I don't want them to look eighteen—these men don't want eighteen-year-olds. If they did, they'd look for them,' He wanted them to look young and healthy . . . and he never never beat up on them, he never touched them. . . ."

George Trapp remained unconvinced by Rachel's account of Lucky, and her interpretation of his motives for looking after his girls. "The ability to persuade, to manipulate, is their greatest asset," he said. "What they all have in common is a perversion of almost all human emotions and ethics. However intelligent Rachel was," Trapp went on, "she was a child. The understanding, the evaluation of a girl's vulnerability is their stock in trade. He would know that if he disillusioned her, or—being the kind of person she obviously was and is—if she thought him venal, his hold on her would weaken. So he got her to believe that he felt real concern for the girls. He didn't, of course. No man who pimps thirteen-year-old girls is concerned for them, except as she quite rightly said to keep them in good condition for his own benefit. His motives—and this applies to all of them—were entirely mercenary. He was a pimp."

George Trapp, who has any number of degrees in sociology, psychology and criminology, was the most knowledgeable and the most enlightened man I met in the field. But by the time we met, he too had perhaps seen too many horrors and met too many despicable men.

I believe there *is* a difference between pimps, sometimes a very marked one, and it is impossible to disregard a witness such as Rachel.

"Lucky *did* have a conscience," she said. "Somehow for him, thirteen was an all-right age to be a prostitute. It's wrong, of course, and I don't know why he thought it all-right. We talked a lot and about many things, but some things we just never mentioned: that was one of them. But you must remember the number of runaways there were at that time, with nowhere to go. There were an awful lot of eleven- and twelve-year-olds and other pimps used them, but Lucky, never. It was absolutely out of the question for him. At that age he would say, 'You are too young,' and he would try to find a place for them, a refuge. I remember two runaway centres we went to, to take girls to—one belonging to a church, and the other a project. He sent several girls there who he said were too young."

I don't doubt the truth of this, or of Rachel's testimony that this particular man never beat girls, looked after them when they fell ill, and even paid for them to go back home if that was what they chose to do. It is true too, no doubt, that this was a superior kind of operation, much of it a high-class call-girl business, with girls being sent on dates in luxury hotels. Nonetheless, "he didn't like 'older women,' " she said. "His oldest was seventeen, and the ones who brought in the most money were the thirteen-, fourteen- and fifteen-year-olds." There was in Rachel, as well as in a few of the other girls I spoke with, a curious remnant of loyalty and affection towards her pimp, which may have clouded her judgment. She credited him with saving her from drugs and the life by breaking off their relationship and sending her home. And she too, in all her security still vulnerable about this childhood experience, only mentioned in passing that this coincided with his taking a new, younger girl as his main lady.

When Slim told me that white girls did what was necessary without needing to be hit, I reminded him that in fact a lot of them do get hit—many of the young girls get badly hurt.

"Yeah, because they . . . they ain't been turned out right. Y'see, I've had white girls that come to me from other players, other pimps, other macks, stuff like that. They have so much garbage in 'em, I got to get rid of all that and then bring the refinement into it, know what I mean?" He smacked his hands together, hard. Several diners, startled, looked in our direction. "If that's how her hand calls for it, I'll do it, only because I'm then spending my time, money, effort into something that in the end it's going to click. Know what I mean?"

So when everything works okay with Slim's girls, where does he take them, what do they do when they're not working? "Oh, I might just jump on a ferry-boat and go out to the Statue of Liberty," he said. "Or I take them to movies—I do everything and anything that pleases them. If they want to go and see the ducks in Central Park, why, let's get a carriage and ride in Central Park. Or let's go jogging . . . "

What do his girls do on Sunday, do they work? "No, mine never work on Sunday. Mine rest, dress, count their money and read the Sunday funnies, that's all they do."

So his girls *do* have a day of rest? "Did you understand what I said?" he asked sternly. "Repeat back to me what I just said."

"Rest, dress, and count their money," I repeated.

"And read the Sunday funnies. Or they go shopping. I tell 'em, I give 'em what they want. I say, 'What do you want?' She says, 'I want this much.' I say, 'Fine, what makes you happy, sweetheart. You want Daddy to take you to so-and-so?' "

Do they all call him Daddy? "I *am* their daddy," he said. "I'm their mother, their father, their sister, their brother, their lover. I'm everything."

As for Gina, said Slim, "For her age"—thereby confirming what I had heard elsewhere, that she was very young—"for her age, she's very strong, and despite the pressures has put up a very good front for whoever she's had to put up with. But *I* have to see her when she comes home from work; *I* have to deal with her at home; *I* have to call the dude that's putting the pressure on her. Outside the house" (his hotel room) "she's the strongest woman you ever hope to meet. But inside, with me—I told you before, she's a baby and I know what she needs."

Did he think she minded giving him all her money?

"No, she doesn't mind it. Being what I am, and respecting me for what I am, she goes along. She gives me my respect, that I deserve for being what I am."

"But—and forgive me for putting it so bluntly—" I said, "what do you consider your part in this work?"

"To teach," he said. "You have turn-outs that you have to teach. Popcorn pimps," he said scornfully, "know nothing about this. I've had girls come to me and they know nothing—*nothing*."

*

When Julie had told me about her first pimp "turning her out," I asked how he did it. What did he tell her?

"He said that later he'd take me to California and that he had more of his ladies in Hollywood and that he'd give me a penthouse there, and all that shit." She laughed. "I was really very, very innocent. He had a room and he got me a room on the floor below, and he said we needed some money to get out there, so I was going to have to earn it. He explained a few things to me, like you know, how a trick would come up to me and what he'd do, but mostly I just had to learn for myself. And I knew nothing . . ."

Did he tell her about birth control, or hygiene, or give her condoms?

"No, no."

Did she have any feeling for this man?

"Yeah, just then . . . he . . . you know, he made me feel more secure. He said he'd take care of me, and I just had no place to go."

She had sex with him first, did she?

"Unh-huh."

Was he good at this, was he kind?

"Yeah . . . Mm-hm . . . I really hadn't had much experience of sex." (She had had one "relationship", furtive episodes with a sixteen-year-old boy in a basement near her house.)

The pimp hadn't given her a quota, she said, but told her not to take anything under $20. "But he said I had to do anything they asked for."

Did she know what that meant—or could mean?

"Not then."

Talking with Slim, I reverted to his rejection of black girls, and he answered with rare brutality: "The best money is in white girls."

He knew, didn't he, that there is a much more complex side of this black and white thing? Another pimp had expressed it bluntly: "Can you think of a better way to get back at whitey than to deal in his kids?"

"I don't *want* a black girl," Slim repeated, and tried to rationalize it. "There's more demand for white girls."

"But aside from that," I said, "isn't there a reason in *you*?"

He interrupted, "Because it takes a special man to be able to cop a white girl, y'understand? Just an ordinary black man can't go and cop a white girl."

Does he hate white girls? "No-o-o! I *like* white girls." If he likes white girls, does he like white people? "Do I like white people? Some, yes."

"Please be honest," I said.

"Some, yes. On the whole, no."

"Let me put it another way," I said. "On the whole, do you dislike whites?"

"On the whole," he said, "I don't trust . . . it's not that I don't like—I don't trust them. I don't dislike individuals. I don't dislike *you*," he said. "And I don't hate or anything like that, because I have white friends."

White male friends? "Yeah, I have white dudes that I affiliate with, that I do business with."

What sort of business did he do with white men? "Oh, if I want to get rid of some merchandise. There's possibilities just opening up," he fantasized, "that will prove *very* beneficial to me. I'm not going into it now, no disrespect to you, but it's not the moment."

Did he think the Mafia was involved with the young girls?

"Shit," he said, "the Mafia is infiltrating so much, it's beginning to be pathetic. Let that be put in there: *It's beginning to be pathetic*! They want their piece."

Does he have to pay them? "I don't pay them shit."

But do most people in the life? "Houses pay them."

"Father Ritter [the head of the New York crisis centre, Covenant House] told me that all of the pimps are paying them," I said.

"Father Ritter doesn't know what he's talking about . . . Yes, I know who he is, but he still doesn't know what he's talking about, because the Mafia hits the houses, the show world, places like that, know what I mean? That's where they get their money. From individual players, pimps, macks they get nothing. Nothing."

Did Slim intend to stay in the pimping business forever? Could he?

"I don't want to do it forever. I'm getting older, I would like to get my money, get my lady, get out of this, get her a boutique, whatever she likes, that makes *her* happy."

Every single one of the men like himself I had talked with, I said, had brought up the "boutique" idea. Could this be a myth, I suggested, something they tell the girls to keep them docile?

"Well, I don't care if she wants to keep a fucking wig shop," he said vehemently. "Whatever she wants, we'll get out of here. You say you've talked to nine, ten pimps?" This made him really angry. "I'll bet you one thing: I bet you *never* met one like me! I'm something *very* unique."

"You are very articulate," I said.

"Very—excuse me? I'm articulate because—uh—I'm street-wise, but educationally I'm not that educated."

"Well, your lack of coarseness is certainly unexpected for me, if you see what I mean," I said.

"Thank you very much—I appreciate that, very much. But I'm saying this much, you will never meet another person like me as long as you live, because for the simple reason that I have *such* a belief in myself, of knowing what I'm doing."

I knew a good deal about Slim: from the pimp squad, from district attorneys I had talked to, from other pimps (who of course lied about him as much as he lied about them), and also from a number of young girls, and older prostitutes as well, who were helping me. To some extent I was provoking him into answering questions with lies—questions to which I knew the true answers. As it was, becoming honestly interested in the project at a very early stage, and more than capable of understanding its purpose, he admitted a great deal much sooner than I had expected or hoped. One might say that he held on only to enough make-believe to retain the artificial self-respect he made up as a substitute for the real thing. In this he was like the girls, to whom the abandonment of fantasy felt like the abandonment of self-value.

Didn't he agree that much of the life was very brutal, indeed depended on the threat of brutality?

"I don't like nobody that beats up on young girls, stuff like that," he said.

(Rachel said, "Pimps *may* be respected. It depends on how they treat their women. The pimps I've known that have been the most despised ones, have been the ones that let their women get into bad shape, who have let their women go down. Because you're not supposed to: you've got to take *pride* in your women. You've got to make sure that they're clean and that they look good. And that they feel good—because then they can bring in the money. That's just good business sense; dead women don't make good hustlers.")

But, I asked Slim, didn't most pimps beat up? "I dunno—first of all, I'm a loner. I don't get into what Joe, Mike or Bill get into. I know what Slim gets into, you know what I mean? I know how *I* treat my ladies. . . ."

No doubt this was how he saw himself. But I remembered Cassie telling me about being heroin-drugged, gang-banged and cut up in New Jersey, and being brought back to Slim in New York. "He asked me where my money was. I said I didn't have it, that the guys took it off me. So he beat the shit out of me . . . He grabbed me around the neck and threw me on the bed and started choking me, slapping me, punching me, kicking me around. I passed out like for two days."

" . . . I know why my ladies stay with me for years, not for one, two months. I know why mine stays for years—five, six, seven, eight, nine *years*," he said, lost in fantasy again. As I knew from Cassie and his own admissions, his ladies stayed with him as briefly as with any of the other pimps.

Did he *feel* anything for them? "Gina I love," he said.

This, too, turned out to be untrue. The Gina he now had working for him was, as I said, a girl he had known for only a few weeks. But there had been another Gina in his life, a middle-class Boston girl of fourteen whom he called Sparkles. This girl, materially spoiled but largely ignored by her parents, was in a way a replica of the young Jewish girl he had met as a boy: both of them came from a world he craved to be part of, and they were really important to him. Sparkles, it would appear, did develop a real feeling for him. In a movie, or in a different world, it could have had a happy ending.

But the others he didn't really feel anything for, was that what he was saying? "I wouldn't say I don't feel nothing for them, I'll take care of them. I'll give them their needs, I'll protect them, I'll do what I have to do for them. I won't let anybody take advantage of them. . ."

They think that he likes them, though? "They *know* that I like them, but they know I don't *love* them."

Do they think he wants them, sexually? He laughed. "Sexually? Quite naturally, at times. Variety is the spice of life. When my ladies leave me," he said, "there's only two things they can do: either go to the nut-house or back to their mother, y'understand? Because that's literally how I have them mentally steadied. Either they are so blown up by losing Slim—'Oh my God, I'm losing Slim!' " he cried in a falsetto voice, "that they crack up, or I've got them fairly squared and they go back to their mother, know what I mean?

"I have kids from my ladies," he went on. "I have two that are pregnant right now—one is in Philadelphia, one is in Boston."

How old are they? "Seventeen, eighteen. No, both eighteen, excuse me." (Both girls were in fact under age.)

And both girls were pregnant by him? "Both." What did he intend to do about them? "When they drop the baby, they'll be back here like *that*!" and he snapped his fingers. "Quicker than you can get back to England."

What was he going to do about the babies? "Well, my anticipation was . . . I didn't *want* them to *have* the kids, y'understand?"

Why didn't they have abortions, then? "Because they feel that it draws them closer to me."

But he didn't share that feeling? "No, hell no, I don't feel it."

So again, what was he going to do with the babies? "What do you mean, what am *I* going to do? *I'm* not having the kids, you know. They had ample time to arrange an abortion, or do what they decided. *They* want them—when the time comes to give them up, they'll give them up."

Was Cleo one of the girls, I asked, knowing that she wasn't (he knew Cassie only by her street name, Cleo, and I always used that in talking to him). "Excuse me?" he said, caught unaware.

"Is Cleo one of those girls?" I repeated.

"Cleo? You know Cleo? Cleo was with me first—she loved me," he said. "I'm going to tell you something. She was with me, she was with Earl, and after Earl she was with another cat. Cleo was—I'm going to tell you something—it didn't take me long to find out about Cleo."

It was the first time I had shown him that I already knew certain facts about him, and he was suddenly frightened. If I really knew Cleo—and it was obvious that I did—then I knew that he had had an under-age girl. Knowing was different from suspecting, or asking questions. He became suspicious and very cautious, and immediately mentioned that Cleo had represented herself as eighteen years old. "Anyway," he lied, "I put her on a bus and sent her home. See, one thing you'll find out about me, I don't have to lie."

And then, looking at my tape-recorder, he panicked for a moment. "Fuck it," he said, "if this tape goes in there [to the pimp squad] and I get busted," his tone was slightly threatening, "and they take me away . . ."

"This tape," I said quickly, "is only for me and for my book. And neither your real name, nor Cleo's nor anybody else's will be in it."

"I'm just saying, push comes to shove, it goes in and I get busted . . . and I know what down is, understand what I'm saying? But as long as I have my convictions inside of me, what *I* know, I didn't do wrong. I didn't *force* her to go out—not like some macks."

He knew Cleo quite a while before Gina, didn't he?

"Gina wasn't even with the system," Slim said, meaning she wasn't in his stable. "But there was another Gina, from Boston—the best girl I've ever had in my life. If you take them *all* together, all of them I've ever had, y'add them up, come to thirty, forty, something like that. You get down to it, Sparkles (Gina was her name, but I called her Sparkles), she was the only one," his voice grew low and husky, "that I ever loved. She was seventeen" [I knew she was fifteen]. "She's home now, having my baby."

But if he loved her, why didn't he take the baby? "I would—I'd take her, the baby, I'd take anything that goes along with her, when she comes back. The baby will be born around my birthday, May, June, latest July. I would take them back damned quick. I loved her. She was one of the prettiest girls you've ever seen in your life."

Does Sparkles want to come back? "She's *got* to come back."

Does she want to bring the baby back? "I don't know her plans about the baby, but *she'll* be back." She had stayed with him, he said, from March to October.

And how long had she been in the life?

"From when I copped her," he said, thus admitting that it was he who had turned out this child in New York, just as he had the fourteen-year-old Cassie. "If they didn't deport her from Philly and send her back to Boston," he said (he had sent her on a date to Philadelphia, where she was caught by the Youth Squad and returned to her parents), "she'd be back with me right now."

But, I asked, would he have her in the life if she's having a baby?. . .

"They don't care a damn," said one of my police friends. "There are perverts who WANT pregnant girls, that's how they get their kicks. And the pimps, they make them go on, sometimes until the day they give birth." Two days after he told me this, Dr Judianne Densen-Gerber and I talked to a sixteen-year-old girl on Eighth Avenue who was quite obviously within weeks or days of having her baby. She told us proudly that because of her condition, her guy was not putting a quota on her. "But yesterday I got one hundred and fifty dollars," she said, and seemed pleased.

"Well, no," said Slim, when I asked if he would send the pregnant Sparkles out. "I wouldn't want her to work right up to the time. I told you, I steer a point, a point as far as I go. She's one beautiful woman," he repeated huskily. "And it isn't even because she's beautiful, it's because she came to me *wholeheartedly*. They sent her back, the police. They find out, the Youth Squad. They find out she's under age and sent her back."

Only minutes before he had claimed that she was seventeen or eighteen. But, I said, at seventeen she's no longer under age in New York State. "Oh yes," he answered (wrongly), "until they are eighteen. Anyway, I don't know," he said impatiently. He was not going to admit that he had sent her on a job to another state, as that becomes a federal offence. "Whatever age it is, they sent her back eight times. *Eight*. Eight times she ran away and came back to me."

If Sparkles came back tomorrow, would he drop Gina? "Whew," he said. "It would be *so* hard—I don't know what I would do, to tell you the God's honest truth. I would try to keep the peace between them, and try to have them both with me. It would be the hardest thing I ever tried, the hardest challenge I've ever had. Because Sparkles wants me to herself. Gina *definitely* wants me to herself, too."

Sparkles kept in touch with him "occasionally," he said. She phoned him at a special number nobody else had. "You asked me a question," he said, "and I have to think about it, really think, because it's strong as acid, your question. Y'know, I mean, it's very strong. I don't know what I would do. I just feel like this: Sparkles gave me something no other woman ever gave me. Not just the money. Like a lot of people she gave me the money, and I accept the money because I put her in the position to *make* the money.

"But she is just *beautiful*. When the police—the p.o.l.i.c.e.—when they see her, they tell her, 'You're one of the *finest* young ladies that we've ever seen in our *lives*. If you come back to New York, we'll *bury* you!' That's what they said, it's an expression they use. Because they don't want nobody like that here, because she's just so . . . so-o . . . "

They probably want her out of the life, I said. "She's coming to an age to make her own decision," he said. "When she does, she's coming to her man."

But how does Sparkles feel about the life? "She loves the life she lives and she lives the life she loves—" he recited his little ditty, and then added, spacing out his words, "And . . . she . . . loves . . . Slim's . . . last . . . year's . . . dirty . . . socks!"

But does she love sleeping with men all day long? "She doesn't mind," he said, "because she doesn't look at it like sleeping with men. She looks up at the ceiling and counts the cracks in the wall-paper, y'understand? He's busy getting his thing off, taking care of his business. She's clever: she's counting."

("They expect you to be an expert at sex," said Julie. "How can you be an expert at sex at fifteen? I mean, *really*, they're expecting this big amazing thing to happen, and they're let down because it's the same as with their wives. Of course you can pretend. I'm a great actor. I've had experience!" So in fact, she made them feel that they were terrific? "Not all of them. Some of them I just lay there. Let them get on with it. Watch TV.")

Did Slim ever consider: for a girl like Sparkles, who he claimed to really love, would he consider *working* for her?

"Would I consider *working* for her?" he repeated. "No, I wouldn't work for nobody. The only reason she works for me is I'm a professional. I'm not someone who just got into this life. I'm not a turn-out. I know this life better than the police know fags, dope, stuff like that. I *know* this life. I live this life."

And did he think it was wrong to work like other people work? "Do I think it's wrong to work? No. . ." He was obviously incapable of a conventional association with the word "work." "No, I think it's wrong for young ladies to be abused, misused, hurt, threatened and scared out of their wits. If she decides she wants to work, and there's a trick wants to pay for her services, then I'm here to see that she can do it safely, y'understand where I'm coming from? S.a.f.e.l.y."

"What all the pimps end up having in common, even if they don't individually start out that way," said George Trapp, "is the loss of a dimension of energy innate to all human beings. Eventually this results in a real inability to work—in its real sense—and with it a deep disdain for ordinary people who do. Once this characteristic is established within a man, he has isolated himself from the mainstream of society and —one might say almost by necessity—becomes part of a destructive subculture."

Would Slim want to marry Sparkles? There was a long pause before he repeated the question. "Marry Sparkles?" He paused again. "If I knew she wanted to . . . if I knew how to get to her right now, I'd . . ." he stopped.

Did he know anything about her parents, did she say what sort of people they were? "Yeah, the kind of people that go bowling, that sit and drink beer and watch the TV. Her brother busted her cherry when she was fourteen years old." He guffawed bitterly. "Incest is the best, they used to say. Yeah, we used to sit and talk a lot—she's the only one I wanted to talk with. I loved her, loved her . . . "

Did he not think perhaps (I felt my way very carefully) that there was a measure of unreality in this idea of marrying this very young girl who was now back with her parents and probably very carefully guarded? Had he ever considered marrying a black girl?

"Never!" he said explosively. "*Never*—it would be impossible, because I have nothing in common with such a girl."

But there could be a beautiful black girl, a light black girl. . . .

"*No*, no black girl." Then once again Slim's tone changed totally, from grim determination to flippancy. "I don't want to make a life with *no* girl. There's plenty of mileage to be made, unregistered mileage with teen-agers . . . *Legal* teen-agers, of course," He grinned at my quizzical expression. "Have you *any* conception . . . " he began, and then interrupted himself. "Without being disrespectful, how much money do you make?"

"Not much," I said. "Spread over several years, because every book takes years to write, perhaps $20,000 dollars a year if I'm lucky."

"Christ!" he said. "Excuse the language, but do you know what I earn? My *minimum* is sixty thousand, in a bad year. Eighty thousand's more my average."

If he weren't having dinner with me tonight, what would he be doing? "Two things. For instance, if everything worked out I'd be home lying down watching a game or something. Or I'd be in the bar" (He mentioned two pimp bars in the West 40s) "watching my lady, make sure she's managing."

I offered him dessert and coffee. He refused both but poured himself another glass of red wine. "I like this wine very, very much." He looked around the restaurant, which was now almost empty; there were only two other tables occupied and suddenly it was very quiet. He shook his head, looking into his wine-glass. "You know," he said, "you caught me on one of my off nights today. I feel odd . . . because . . . "

Weren't things going right for him?

"Will you let me finish?" he said. "If things were the way they should have been for me, everything would have been different, know what I mean?"

Did he mean that the money was not right?

"Yeah." Suddenly there was no pretence whatever. His voice had lost both flippancy and stridency; it was just the voice of a sad and intelligent man. "I have only this one lady, now," he said. "I had gotten one other, but she was jealous so she pretended to be sick, and brought no money, and one thing led to another—I opened my big mouth too wide, you know—and next thing I knew she'd fled."

Gone home? "She went home or perhaps she didn't, perhaps she's making it on her own."

Were there many girls now on their own? "Times have changed. Women are choosy—they want more than they might have two or three years ago. They're more cautious, more by themselves. It's because there are so many people in the life now that aren't prepared for it, don't know how to deal with it. It's dangerous, you know—" he suddenly said. "If a young girl thinks she can manage on her own, she may for a bit, but then she finds it hard to be alone."

I said that one thing I'd been surprised to learn was how calmly players took it when a girl decided to leave them.

"Well, if the lady does it right," he said, "if she calls him and gives him the respect that's due to him when she tells him—yes, and the money too, but the respect, that's what really counts—then that's all right."

Has Slim ever advised young fellows, the way that player in prison advised him when he was seventeen? "Sure I have. I've had fellas that come in and tell me, 'I . . . want . . . to . . . be . . . a . . . pimp! What should I do, should I square up and stay with my job, or should I get into the life?' I can pick 'em real quick, I tell him, 'Hey, my, uh, opinion is—work, stay with your life, enjoy your life, stay the way you are. You have a better chance.' If *I* had the chance, the way it turns out—like I said, I love the life I live, I live the life I love. But hey, right now, I'm thirty-three years old. It's a little bit hard to change your lifestyle after that. You know what I mean?"

Would he change it if he could? If he thinks back how would he do it differently? "Well, put it this way: from when it started, I'd probably stay the way I am now. But if I had the money, the opportunity right now to do what I want to do correctly, I'd jump out of this life so quickly . . ."

By now we had left the restaurant and were walking down Third Avenue. "I have to apologise to you," he suddenly said, very formally, "for two things: for getting so—you know—depressed there in the restaurant, there at the end. But also, to have let you pay the check: I don't usually let a lady pay a restaurant check . . ."

Part Two

GERMANY
The Scene

9

"All anybody cares about is money"

If child prostitution is particularly visible in West Germany, this is not because the Germans are less moral than other people. On the contrary, post-Hitler West Germany has produced many of the most questioning, most principled people in the world.

Some of the reasons for the large number of wayward and isolated children in West Germany are to be found in social upheavals common to all the Western world, but some of them are peculiar to the country. Since Germany has been split into two "nations," West Germany has had no natural centre. Much has been written in the past about the dangers presented by capital cities—the way they absorb the financial and human resources of a country, and thereby create internal inequalities and bitterness. But West Germany suggests that the lack of the feeling of centrality provided by a capital city may be even more damaging. Certainly it has affected government, business, education and culture—and the nature of the country's criminality. In other countries, child prostitution centres on one, or perhaps two, major cities. In West Germany, child prostitutes, both male and female, can be found in equal numbers in Hamburg and Berlin, in Frankfurt, Düsseldorf and Munich. Even more surprisingly, they can be found in many smaller towns whose populations appear to accept the situation calmly, even when it involves youngsters well known to everyone.

In addition to being so widely disseminated, it is particularly *blatant*. But this is due less to the large number of youngsters involved than to the West German tradition of being open about sexual appetites or vices. Except, perhaps, during the secretive Hitler era, the Germans have always been much blunter—or, if one prefers to put it another way, less hypocritical—about such matters than the Anglo-Saxons.

Prostitution (by adults, not minors) is legal in West Germany, as it is in Scandinavia, Holland, and a number of other socially enlightened countries. In West Germany, every major city has its official—or unofficial—red-light district. A profusion of porno-shops offer magazines and video films of all descriptions: they cover sex between men and women, men and men, women and women, children and children, children and adults, humans and animals, sado-masochism, bondage and every other perversion.

In dimly lit sex clubs, which grant instantaneous membership on payment of a few marks, porno-movies are served with the drinks and live sex-shows are available in squalid backrooms. "Peepshows" offer naked girls gyrating to canned music, and "Eros Centres"—huge bordellos with drinks and dancing downstairs—provide cubicles upstairs for fifty to a hundred prostitutes working in shifts around the clock.

Prostitution, and Eros Centres in particular, have become the subject of considerable controversy, with political overtones, not only in West Germany but in France and Britain as well. Some city fathers, anxious to bring the growing vice problems in the streets under control, favour precisely such "Centres" as a solution to prostitution which, they admit, is here to stay. The restriction of all prostitutes to Eros Centres, they argue, would get the women off the streets, control the involvement of organised crime, protect "ordinary" women and —not to be forgotten— safeguard real-estate values.

Some prostitutes agree, if for different reasons. The Centres, they say, are safer—even safe from pimps, if they wish to dispense with that kind of "protection." Others, however—the "new" prostitutes, given a voice by the British, American and French "collectives of prostitutes," who receive considerable support from radical-political and feminist groups, and staged the recent sit-ins both in Lyons and in London—sharply reject the regimentation these Centres represent, and any proposed legislation that would limit the right of prostitutes to exercise what they consider their freely chosen profession, which many of them claim is an essential social therapy. They describe Eros Centres as "cattle pens" where the management, far from being individual entrepreneurs, is in fact almost invariably part of organised crime and is free within these closed communities to misuse or abuse anyone they wish, thereby making the woman's lot less safe, not more so. Furthermore, they suggest that pimps are as active within the Eros Centres as they are outside them. If they come in the role of clients, they cannot be kept out; and anyway (so argue the "collectives"), they ought not to be kept out, because the majority of prostitutes want and thus ought to be free to have "protectors" with whom they voluntarily share their earnings, as do women in other professions with husbands or lovers.

None of these arguments theoretically applies to child prostitutes, a problem adult prostitutes are no more willing to confront, or capable of confronting, than are the public authorities (as was demonstrated not long ago at a conference on prostitution in Nice).

While American police, on the whole, openly admit their despair and helplessness over child prostitution, the police authorities in West Germany and Great Britain tend to deny its existence.

"First of all," said one senior police official in Berlin, "the places you mention, 'Eros Centres,' 'Sex-clubs' and 'Peepshows', too—although they, incidentally, don't provide opportunities for intercourse—are regularly inspected, without prior warning.

"All of them know they'd be closed on the spot if we found anyone under age, whether as an employee or client. And don't forget, in West Germany all prostitutes must carry a health card at all times and attend clinics every two weeks. It is the law. They lose their cards if they don't go. We can't be hoodwinked," he assured me with a smile.

Three blocks from his office and one block from my exclusive hotel in Berlin's centre, the friendly manager of a large Peepshow confirmed this. Here, for 1 DM (30p or 50 cents) a minute, customers sitting on wooden chairs against a wall can watch through a peephole as naked young women in bare little cubicles, individually, or in pairs or groups, perform pseudo-dance, pseudo-sexual movements. For 10 DM, the wall comes down: the customer can sit next to the girl for five minutes while she undulates. "But no touch," said the manager. "That's forbidden." And he agreed unhesitatingly when I asked to talk to some of the girls during their break, if they consented.

"What harm does it do?" asked the stunning young blonde in a belted paisley dressing-gown and wool knee socks who was the first one I talked to half an hour later. We sat in the rickety dressing-room she shared with four others, then at work, and drank orange juice brought in by a boy, with the manager's compliments.

When I quoted the manager's assurance that there were no under-age girls there, she nodded, avoiding my eyes. Her name, she said, was Alex. She laughed. "Anyway, that'll do," and she began almost at once to turn the table on me and question me—most ably I thought—about my book and what I had so far discovered. She was fascinated by America, as are so many Germans. "We are just doing American history," she said, then blushed, realizing her blunder.

"So what year are you in at school?" I asked, and how did she combine this activity with her schooling?

It turned out that she and two others working the Peepshow were fifteen and under—the manager, she said, didn't know. "He's an okay guy," she said. They went to school all week and worked the late shift on Friday, from 5 pm to midnight, sometimes later. "And Saturday," she said, "we usually do two shifts. That gives us between three hundred and twenty and four hundred DM [about £108 or $200] for just working one and a half days a week and no harm done."

How much pocket-money did her parents give her? "Ten marks a week," she answered, and added bitterly: "It's a matter of principle." Her father owns a small factory; they could afford to give her more. "But they think I should 'learn to manage.'"

Ten marks, I knew, would just about pay for one hamburger and a Coke. Nonetheless, did she really feel that doing this work did her no harm, or was she perhaps trying to convince herself?

She thought about it for a long moment. "I'm not sure," she said finally, in her educated middle-class German. "The dancing around bare is just a giggle, really—we don't see the creeps who pay their filthy one mark." She sipped from her orange juice, and rubbed her smooth forehead. "But I don't like it when they come to sit next to me. And I really detest it when they touch me." In some Peepshows, it turns out, for 30 DM the girl can be fondled above the waist for five minutes. "There is something about them . . ." she paused "you know . . . they smell." She laughed, embarrassed. "Well . . . they don't really—it's just in my mind."

"If that is in your mind," I said, "then it *is* harming you. Why not stop?"

"The money," she said. "Once you've had it, it's very difficult to do without. I honestly don't know that I could. And it's another three years, with more and more homework coming up, before I graduate. So even when I'm sixteen, I just won't have *time* to do an ordinary part-time job. Let's face it, this is the easiest way to deal with the economic problem until I complete my education."

Two years ago in Munich, after the suicide of a beautiful young girl, a first-year medical student who, to finance her studies, had worked in several pornographic films, the mother of another member of the cast was interviewed by the press. Yes, she said—her looks and language those of a middle-class woman—her twelve-year-old daughter did pose nude, but *she* was there to keep on eye on her. Well, yes, she admitted, there had been the odd occasion when somebody had "tried something on" and yes, in fact once "it" had happened. "But I told him what I thought of him in no uncertain terms," she said, and added: "After all, it's not my fault if the permissiveness of our society permits me to offer my daughter for this work."

In a West German documentary produced as a result of this suicide and showing, with admirable honesty, the making of a porno-film, I saw 216 applicants queue up for the 15 parts. Fifteen of them were minors, all of them shown full-face in a film which was going on general release.

Before the auditions began, the candidates were informed succinctly of the conditions and requirements: they would be filmed in the nude; they would be expected to perform—not fake, but perform—sexual acts. But they would have no lines to learn, as they would be directed by voice as they went along, and the pay, for five days' work, would be 800 DM (£250 or $400) per day. Not one applicant left because of the conditions.

The fifteen were selected. The girl chosen for the lead was just sixteen years old, thus a minor under West German law. At first it was all fun and games. They danced, they kissed, they fooled around in foam-baths and chased each other round a room.

Half an hour later, the girl playing the lead burst into desperate tears when, lying on the floor with her partner and told from one take to another what she was to do next, she was instructed to perform fellatio on him. "I can't do that," she sobbed. "I didn't know I'd have to do that. I never have." The producer-director told her not to "be childish" and reminded her that she had signed a contract undertaking to "follow directions as given." She continued to weep. "This nonsense is costing money," he said, ordering a short break. "We aren't playing nursery games here.

"Are you all right now?" he asked, more gently (possibly remembering the documentary makers' cameras recording his words), after she had been talked to kindly by her partner, given a cup of coffee and time to compose herself. 'I'll be okay,' she said in a tight voice, powdered her cheeks and eyes to erase the marks of tears, crossed herself, and returned to work.

The documentary, of which I had seen a preview, was running in

Berlin at the time I interviewed Alex. Had she seen it, I asked her.

"Yes," she said. "I wouldn't do that for anything."

Not even if they offered her a large sum of money, given that she was very pretty indeed? "They have," she said. "They rope in every pretty girl they can get. But can you imagine?" she went on sounding outraged, "actually having sex on camera?"

Leaving that aside, I said, how was it actually possible for a film company or anybody else to employ quite obviously under-age children who were, after all, fully exposed to the public?

She laughed cynically. "Because nobody cares," she said. "All anybody cares about is money."

Would she or either of the two other under-age girls at the Peepshow consider expanding their activity into prostitution? Do the Peepshows sometimes lead to it, or encourage or require it?

"I won't do it," she said, "just as I won't do pornos. And this place neither encourages nor requires it—some do. The manager here is okay, you know," she said again. "Of course, here too the opportunities present themselves all the time. And yes," she added, "one of the other kids does it sometimes, but not regularly. Just when she has to have extra money," she finished defensively.

The manager had told me, I said, that the police regularly checked the establishment; how did they manage to persuade them that they were of legal age?

"The *police*," she mocked. "They couldn't distinguish between a genuine or fake ID if it was their own faked signature that stared them in the face. You know why?" she said. "They are all men; they all want the same. They wouldn't mind looking through the bloody peephole themselves—they probably do. They don't care," she repeated. "Do you *really* think," she asked me, very seriously, "that anybody in uniform, anybody in authority apart from a few do-gooders, cares about young people as people? You know what we are to them? A nuisance, a damn nuisance."

This kind of cynicism about adults and "authority" is something almost all children engaged in commercial sex of any kind (and, no doubt, many others) have in common. And Alex's argument was fair enough: no doubt there *are* police officers who go to Peepshows. Of course, there are police officers who are corrupt and who accept pay-offs in money and in women from brothels, pimps and organised crime. Equally, though, in most occidental countries it is nowadays policewomen who more often than not deal with children and young people. Oddly enough, the girls I spoke with were, on the whole, more resentful of policewomen than men, but that is no doubt a consequence of complex reactions of identification, shame and envy. Obviously, policewomen can't be bought off with offers of free sex and, interestingly, the records so far show hardly any known cases, in the United States, West Germany or Britain, of policewomen accused of corruption.

But it was never my impression, in West Germany or anywhere else, that the police—whether men or women—didn't *care*. I spoke with dozens of police officers of either sex, many of them parents themselves, and almost all of them seemed to me to care very much indeed. The real problem is that they are neither trained nor given the resources to find solutions or alternatives to the present totally negative approach. Thus, realizing their helplessness towards the extreme problems presented by these particular young, they end up by closing their eyes.

"I've been working the *Jugendschutz* [protection of minors] for nine years," said a senior inspector in Hamburg's St Pauli, the district that includes one of Europe's most famous vice streets, the Reperbahn. Manifestly uncomfortable with his assignment of dealing with this troublesome visitor from abroad, he smiled a lot and did his best to sound reassuring.

"During these nine years," he went on, "I've had to deal with perhaps four girls under sixteen. And at the railway station there are around fifteen under-age boys, always the same ones, who stand around. We know them all and chase them off from time to time to discourage them. But that's about it."

In three weeks in Hamburg, on my first trip there in the course of this research, I went seven times to the main railway station he had spoken of. It was cold and snowy, and I deliberately chose different times of day and night. Although there were some boys I saw repeatedly, I found in front of the station and inside it eighty-one different boys, obviously very young—at most fourteen, but many of them eleven or twelve—and all quite openly soliciting.

The inspector, as it happened, was a nice man. He was in his early forties and the father of three children, the oldest sixteen. "In our family," he said, "nobody goes out on school nights, my wife and me included. On weekends, the kids can go to discos, movies or the houses of friends, as long as we know where they go, and they are home by ten-thirty. And our girls are always brought home—either we pick them up or their friends' parents drop them." He sighed. "I know that in other countries you think of us as heavy authoritarian parents, and what I'm saying to you here probably sounds like that, too. But it isn't necessarily so, you know. It's less a matter of making rules than of giving one's children the feeling that one is on their side, enjoys them, does things *with* rather than for them."

It sounded good, I said. But his claim of having dealt with only four girls under sixteen in nine years? How could that be so when I, in my first five days in Hamburg, had already met more than a dozen children, boys and girls in their early teens, who were engaged in regular or part-time prostitution? What about the statistics, familiar to any social worker in this city of 1.7 million inhabitants? Out of between 5,000 and 6,000 female prostitutes, only 1,200 were registered and therefore subject to obligatory health checks; and there were between 300 and 400 *Strichkinder*—children working on the street—without counting thousands more who earned their pocket-money in the sex industry as part-timers while living at home and going to school. What about all the places where this commerce, involving children, went on quite openly? I named ten notorious bars. And what about the famous pick-up street, the Lange Reihe, and the advertisements in the large-circulation press?

I knew—I said—that it was not only in Hamburg or West Germany this happened, but in other countries as well. But was that a justification? If someone somewhere didn't call a halt, how could it ever be stopped?

There was a marked change of tone and attitude when the inspector answered. He poured me some more coffee, lit a cigarette and—almost for the first time, I felt—looked me straight in the eye. "What can we do?" he said, sounding and looking just as weary as his counterparts in the United States and London had looked when I confronted them with similar questions. "It isn't an isolated phenomenon, is it? It's something that's happened to and in society. Since the end of World War II, I think. We are obsessed," he went on, "obsessed with money, things—and sex. How can we protect our children from what we ourselves have created?

"The sex-ads in the papers? Of course they're outrageous, but how can we stop them? That would be called interfering with the freedom

of the press. The same applies to posters and magazine covers. When I
stop at my corner kiosk with my seven-year-old son, all he sees are
naked girls. How do you stop it? You can't, if they won't stop
themselves. And if children have the upper hand in their families and
parents can't control them, don't have the time or the energy . . . how
can you legislate that?

"And the places you mention . . . we do what we can to check the
obvious ones. But, after all, we can't patrol every hotel, bar or
apartment in the city. If one is to believe the media," for the first time
he sounded bitter and deliberately coarse, "the baby tarts and *Kalbfleisch* [young meat, i.e. boys] are everywhere."

That same afternoon, in a huge Eros Centre just across the street
from this very police station, I met, with the help of a young social
worker, two girls, one fourteen, the other fifteen. Both of them had
used "the facilities of the Centre," as they put it, for over a year,
conveying the impression of a kind of happy free-lance arrangement
rather than any kind of "cattle pen" organisation.

Did they have health cards? I asked. "Yes, of course." And how
could they get them, at their age? They laughed. "Listen," said
one—we'll call her Renée (many West German girls like to assume
French names)—"I can buy a card any time I want it. Want to know the
going price? One hundred and fifty-six DM. But the clinics are so glad
to have us come in, they don't care *what* age we say we are. Anyway,"
she asked, looking interested, "could you tell that I'm fourteen?"

I couldn't. My guess would have been between nineteen and
twenty-five, but Renée wouldn't have understood that that was not a
compliment.

10

Annette, from the Hamburg docks, was also fourteen when she first landed in a St Pauli Eros Centre—using it, oddly enough, to hide out from the police. When I met her, she was fifteen and looked like an expensively dressed, tired Dresden china doll. She was not made up and wore what was manifestly a boutique creation: a billowing beige skirt, a white silk shirt and a suede waistcoat. The delicacy of her appearance was matched by the tone of her voice, high, light and quick, and by her language, which was of a remarkable lucidity and purity—the result of years in children's homes in the care of university-educated social workers. The matter-of-fact coarseness with which she described her life in prostitution was in startling contrast to this and to her appearance.

"What a beautiful girl," said a friend of mine who came upon us dining at my hotel. "Is she attached?" I told him she was only fifteen. "Oh," he said, "I would have taken her for twenty-one." Before going down to dinner, Annette had spent half an hour in my bathroom, making up. She carried around an arsenal of creams, lipsticks, brushes and lacquers, and the transformation from the wan, ageless little female to a conspicuously pretty pretend nineteen- to twenty-five-year-old had been staggering.

"Where did you learn to make up like this?" I asked her. "A colleague taught me," she answered.

(Much later I was to tell her grandmother, a woman of ostentatious propriety, that Annette had dined with me at this very elegant hotel. "Good heavens, no!" she exclaimed. "How could you bear to take her there? How embarrassing for you. Does she know how to eat proper-ly?" In her concern for my dignity she appeared to forget that it was her grandchild we were talking about, whose perfectly adequate table manners one might have expected her to be familiar with.)

For days Annette's recital, a deluge of four-letter words and the names of men she had slept with when she was thirteen, streamed out in a tone of bored monotony.

"Andie fucked me Frank didn't want to fuck me but finally did Friede fucked me but I didn't like him and after three weeks left him Friede Two always wanted to fuck me and I finally let him and stayed with him. . ." Then back to Frank, one Hermie, one Arndt, again Frank, Roland, Donnie, Luis, Hennes, Siegfried, Henne, Heine, Robert, Klaus—the list was endless. Every single one of them had been on the criminal fringes, every single one of them had known she was a child. I wanted to take and shake her, or hold and hug her, but couldn't do either, because any reaction other than cool interest would have put me in the category of sermonizing, hassling "squares": the longed-for and feared enemy.

So how did she finally end up in prostitution, I asked. "Well, I was with a rocker, Arndt, and I finally thought, in the end you are only fucking for alcohol, you might just as well do it for money. One way or the other you are only being exploited, and so I started doing the streets with another girl, Dori, who was in my children's home with me—she was fourteen, too. She left after a while. She's working in Münster now, doing very well, I hear."

Was it Dori who started her out, or she Dori? "Oh no, we decided together."

And how did they start?

"Well, we went walking around in St Pauli and went into a bar and chatted with the manager and he said, 'You can go up together and you'll get four hundred.' Dori thought he said one hundred and said, 'A hundred, okay.' He must have been delighted. So we went up and she did everything—you know, sucking and fucking, and everything without rubbers—I didn't do much. I just lay there and mucked around and thought it's a pretty easy way to earn a hundred or whatever, and so we got into it first in the street. I went to St Georgi and first worked for one or two weeks on the Lange Reihe."

Was she working in cars there? "No" (impatiently). "It isn't a car pick-up, it's a *street*. I didn't do cars, anyway, that's too dirty for me, I have a mania for cleanliness and you can't wash after doing it in cars. And after that I found a bar and that's where I worked for half a year, really more as a hostess."

Really? She laughed. "Well, and a bit of the other. And after a while I went to work in a club and earned real money."

What sort of club was that? "*You* know" (impatiently). "One of those St Pauli clubs where you go up to a room with fellows and then I got ill. . . . " In her urgent need to talk, she frequently spoke without punctuation—her only sign of emotion.

"Was it VD?"

"No, the flu, so I went back to the children's home, and when I recovered I went back to it and lived in a hotel where I worked."

"What sort of hotel was that?"

"A hotel where guests went in and paid one hundred and fifty DM [she said guests, not clients]. In front there was a bar where the girls sat at tables and then they took the guests to rooms."

"Did you take them to your own room, or were there other rooms where clients were taken?"

"Other rooms," she said. "I had my own. And then after a while a girl who was jealous because I was only fourteen and she was twenty-five dropped me in the shit and informed the pigs. I got away in time, but they took the whole house apart looking for me. I knew a bloke called Bertie. I called him and he told me to wait for him in the bar of this *Puff* [a low-class brothel]. He was running three women in there and we talked, agreed on the percentage and I moved in."

What sort of *Puff* was this? Again she replied with that angry impatience at my ignorance. And she spelled out the horrible truth in her most aggressive tone to date with a disconcerting kind of flourish. "A *real* one," she said, "in the Eros Centre in St Pauli."

The strange thing was that until she was about seven, Annette's childhood had been comparatively stable. Although her parents separated when she was about a year old, "because my mother got pregnant and my father thought the baby wasn't his," her mother very soon afterwards married the lodger. "To me, it was really him I remember as my father," she said, "because he brought me up."

The step-father—we'll call him Herr Brockner—had a steady job with the post office and was kind to the two little girls, Annette and Renate, and to their baby brother, Michael (the step-father's child with Annette's mother). For six years it was a fairly normal family life. Annette's natural father, a dockworker, had remarried—his new wife was blind—and they had no contact with him. Her mother, she says, was a good mother. She remembers her as being obsessively clean around the house. "She didn't smoke because it would make the curtains smell. When there were visitors, she would wipe the clean cups before she served coffee, and after they left she'd get out the carpet-sweeper and vacuum wherever they'd stepped." But, on the other hand, she didn't bug the children, as some such mothers do. "She didn't mind how dirty we got. Every night after we took off our clothes, she washed every bit of what we'd worn and we wore clean clothes from inside out every day." Nor were they beaten. "Only if we deserved it," Annette said realistically, "like when she gave me money to get medicine from the chemist and I spent it on sweeties instead."

Everything changed one evening when Annette had just turned seven. A few weeks earlier the apartment above theirs had been taken over by a divorced woman with four children. "She and my mother became very thick, and this woman, Frau Remm, gave her all these sob-stories about how her former husband wasn't paying for this or for that, and my mother would come down and tell my step-father at supper. And she kept saying why didn't he come up with her—I guess she thought it might help the woman to talk to a man. But he always said he didn't like the sound of her.

"But then one day he did go up with her, and then my mother came down to make supper and —I remember as if it was today—a bit later she said, 'Run up and tell Papa that supper is ready,' so I went up to get him and he said, 'I'm not coming back.' And the next day he came to get his things and moved up there altogether.

"My mother just went berserk, she started to drink and tried to commit suicide. Four times she made as if she was going to jump out of the window, always when we were there—so we would stop her, you know. And then all these men came around. . . ."

The two little girls and the baby brother were moved into the bedroom and the mother slept on a couch in the living-room. "And there was that night, we were in bed and she got going with this guy—you know, her fellow—and she moaned and cried so loudly we thought he is killing her and we rushed in, both of us crying, and screamed, 'Let her go! Leave our mother alone!' and so on. And she got up and she gave each of us *such* a beating. We didn't even know why. I started to hate her from that day on."

But why? "Because she'd done things I just couldn't come to terms with; I never could. I couldn't accept that she should have made love in front of us."

It wasn't really in front of them, was it? It was in another room and making love—as she now knew—wasn't usually all that silent, was it?

"Yes," she said, "but she doesn't have to be so noisy about it that the whole house can hear it. [She still spoke of it in the present tense.] Anyway, my mother soon realized that I hated her, and from then on she always preferred my sister. You know," Annette suddenly recalled, "I can remember that exact day, the day I came home from school and she said, 'Well, we've got engaged, congratulate us.' You know what *he* said? 'Now I'm your father, I can at last let you have it.' And I went to the kitchen and picked up a frying pan and he came after me and tried to take hold of my arm and I hauled out and hit him on the head with the frying pan and he turned me over and beat my arse black and blue.

"And so I ran away to my granny and I told her what he had said and done and she said, 'Now you stay here.' She'd always wanted to have me. But then I got homesick for my sister and didn't want to leave her alone there either, so I went back and my mother screamed and yelled at my grandmother and it was so bad that our neighbour—later I found out she was a prostitute—she said, 'You come with me,' and took me to her place and I slept there that night, and she said, 'From now on, if they beat you or anything else happens that bothers you, you come over here.'"

So now there were a lot of beatings? "After the divorce, awful."

Obviously, the husband's desertion and the betrayal by the friend upstairs had destroyed Annette's mother. "She did all kinds of things—everything changed. I remember, one afternoon, we were sitting around in the living-room, my mother opens up the couch and she and this man—this 'fiancé'—they undressed and went to bed. The neighbour and her husband were there, and so were we kids, and they just went to it."

"You mean they had intercourse in front of everybody?"

"Yes, the visitors and us. And he smacked her and threw her about and they went on doing it. The neighbour finally took us away to her flat. I'd got horribly afraid of everything and had nightmares. I used to love my mother while she was with my step-father. Until he went upstairs to that woman who had claimed to be my mother's friend and even now only says bad things about my mother. I hate her."

("You can't imagine how that child can hate," said Annette's grandmother. "It makes cold shivers run down my back—*a child, hating.* Have you ever heard of such a thing?")

Annette can't remember, and her grandmother doesn't choose to recall, the precise occasion when the two little girls, Annette rising eight, and Renate six, were finally taken into care and sent to a *Kleinkinderheim*—a local authority home for small children. After six months the step-father, now married to Frau Remm upstairs, obtained parental rights over the younger sister Renate. "They'd taken Michael up almost right away, after a few weeks. Then he adopted Renate and took her to live with them upstairs." (Annette's mother was apparently still living chaotically on the ground floor of the same house—the word "upstairs," the shock of it engraved on her mind, was always appearing in Annette's stories.) "But *me* they left at the home," said Annette, her lips pale and thin.

Was the little sister perhaps the step-father's natural child, as her own father had originally suspected? "No, she was my own father's daughter, all right. I was dreadfully hurt when they took her home, because it was only for her I'd gone to the children's home. You see, I was supposed to go and live with my granny, but then they said my granny could only have me and my sister would have to go to the children's home. And so I said no, if that's how it was, then I'd go to the children's home too."

Why didn't her granny want her sister, too?

"She told me long ago that from when my sister was quite small, she was always sucking up to everybody. And then my aunt, my grandparents' youngest daughter, was jealous of her, too. She's only six years older than me—she's twenty-one now—so she was thirteen then and she was used to being everybody's pet, and she didn't want my sister around who also liked a lot of attention. *I* never cared."

She did care, desperately. She desperately wanted to be petted and cuddled; she desperately wanted her mother—her mother as she had once been, pretty, clean, even fussy, not the disorderly woman who had been so shamingly rejected by her husband and had come to be despised by everyone. This small girl despised and denied her mother even as —agonizingly—she continued, and still continues, to love her.

I was never able to discover completely why, when the smaller girl was adopted by the step-father and his new wife, Annette's grandmother did not take her older granddaughter to live with her. The grandmother's answers to this question were always evasive. But, to my surprise, she confirmed everything Annette had told me: to my surprise, because I had supposed that Annette, like many of the children I talked to, might have been led by the bitterness of her experience into fantasizing about her past.

When Annette was at the children's home, said her grandmother, "She *was* allowed to go home for weekends."

"Allowed?" I asked, pointedly.

"Not every weekend, perhaps every fortnight, or once a month. Of course, Annette was that sort of person." The words used were much stronger than the English—"*Annette war so ein Mensch*"—a most unlikely description of an eight-year-old by her grandmother. "The children had to say 'Mummy' to Frau Remm, but Annette refused. She called her 'Tante Gerta.' And after she had been there a few weekends and a holiday, Frau Remm called the children's home and said Annette wasn't to come again." (Annette herself never gave her stepfather or his new wife the courtesy of "Mr" or "Mrs." It was always "Remm" and "Brockner.")

"When Brockner came to get Renate," said Annette, "he said *Guten Tag* to me, and I just answered, '*Guten Tag*, have a good trip.' I couldn't really believe this was happening. After all, he had been *my* father, too. I just turned around and went back in. If he looked in his car mirror he would have seen I didn't even turn around. I stopped eating for a while afterwards, I couldn't get anything down—but I didn't cry."

What happened afterwards? "I got to be quite happy in the home. It was nice. The counsellors were nice; I got on all right, I made a lot of friends and managed school."

Did she see her mother? Did her mother visit her? "No, she didn't, and I didn't want her to come. I was glad to be rid of her."

Did other people visit her? Her grandmother? "She came once while my sister was still there: she brought us sweeties. But after she was gone, nobody came to see me for a year."

Eventually "they"—the Brockners—did have her "as a weekend foster-child. Of course they did it for the money. They got paid for it by the authorities. The first time I went, they played at being friends, I could choose either to say 'Mummy' to her, or 'Aunt,' they said. So I said I'd say 'Aunt.' I wouldn't call her 'Mummy.' And when I said that, she said that was all right with her, she didn't want to have me in the first place.

"And Brockner said if Michael asks after your mother, never refer to her as 'Mother'—if you have to say something, then refer to her as 'Aunt Gertrud.' Well, that shook me. After all, she *was* our mother and *she* [Remm] never stopped abusing and vilifying her. It used to make me sick on those weekends to see the beatings my little brother and sister got because they were our mother's children. It was awful. You know, Micky, he was a thin little boy—you know how kids of that age are about food? Well, she cooked very spicy: blood sausage or things like that, and he said he couldn't eat it, so she made him, and he threw it up, and she made him eat his throw-up and then she spanked him, hard, and dragged him and his plate to the lavatory and he had to eat it there. Oh God," she went on, "he was always so glad when I came. Even when we were still at home, it was always I who took him for walks and washed and dressed him. I don't think he realized any more who was his mother, because by that time our mum had fallen apart. Every time I got beaten, he cried"—for the first time, as she remembered this, Annette cried—"And now, upstairs, it was he who got beaten. It was terrible how much they beat him," she repeated. "Now they are better, I hear, since her oldest daughter died and one of the others moved out, she is nicer to him."

Frau Remm-Brockner's daughter died? "Yes, the oldest one, she was my age; she was in a car accident and died about half a year ago. I'm glad," she added in a vicious tone. "Remm murdered my mother. She deserved all she got."

When did her mother die? "I don't know exactly; a few years ago, from pills and alcohol. *She* killed her. It's called *Rufmord* [character assassination]," she said, obviously using words she had heard but didn't understand. "Psychological murder."

And Annette herself? Had she never seen or spoken to her mother again?

"Once—I was in a new home then because I had turned ten—she came there. It was horribly embarrassing. She stopped a boy in the garden and said, 'Where is my daughter? I want to see my daughter,' and she sobbed and carried on and he didn't even know who her daughter was supposed to be. Anyway, in the end they came to get me and I saw her and all I wanted was out."

Was she so changed? "Yes. She wasn't drunk. But she looked worn out, like an old *Hascher* [this can mean addict or whore]. She had a man with her, again a different one, and she said, 'Come here; I won't do anything to you,' and then she said they wanted me to come back with them and I told her what I thought of her, that I wouldn't come, because I couldn't take it. And she said she was married again and had a little girl and a baby boy. I couldn't stand the man—his face was full of scars and he wanted to put his arms around me and he said, 'Come along, daughter,' and I pushed him away. I thought I was mishearing him. *Daughter*. And I ran up to my room and when she came and sat on my bed, I jumped up and sat on another bed. I didn't want anything to do with her; I didn't want her near me. She sickened me.

"And then when she left and on the stairway going down collapsed into tears, I stood at the top and laughed. Later another girl gave me an envelope and said the man had given it to her for me. There were three Deutschmarks in it. They thought they could *buy* me for three Deutschmarks and then [no pause, no punctuation—a significant association] when I was eleven I got my period and went with boys to discos and drank beer."

Annette's grandmother, who is a good-looking woman of about fifty-five, young for her age and living in a meticulously clean, pleasant apartment in a leafy suburb, confirmed all this.

Was there nothing *she* could have done for her daughter's oldest child?

"Nothing," she said curtly. "My health is very delicate."

Did she *want* to take her? "Yes," she said. "I would have. I told her only a few weeks ago when she said she'd like to come to live with us now, go to school from here, meet new people. 'You see, child,' I said, '*now* you want to come. It's *then* you should have come, when there was still a chance we could have made something of you. . . .' "

I asked Annette whether she went to the funeral when her mother died. "Yes. But only because they said there'd be coffee and cake."

Her sister wasn't there; her grandmother was there and all kinds of relatives, most of whom she hardly knew. ("The Brockners never told Renate till it was all over," said the grandmother. "She had a nervous breakdown then. Later she told me that until then she'd always thought that one day they'd let her go back to her mother.")

Was there anyone she liked among the relatives at the funeral, I asked Annette. "Yes, my cousin. All I did during the funeral was laugh and think of the feast we'd have afterwards. I giggled and so did my cousin, and the counsellor kept stuffing sweeties in my mouth to stop me from laughing out loud. Because it was all a show. The pastor went on and on with his bullshit, everything was very quiet, and then he sneezed and somebody dropped a handbag with a bang—I nearly peed in my pants, I laughed so."

"Nervous laughter, don't you think?"

"No, I found it comical. When I threw the flowers into the grave, I asked the counsellor when we could leave, I was getting bored. I said it didn't look to me as if there was going to be any coffee and cake—that, and missing school, was all I had been interested in, otherwise I wouldn't have bothered to go because," she emphasized, "I was *not* interested."

Her claim to be uninterested—in her mother, in her step-father, in the rest of her family—was, of course, a pose. And her description of the brutality used against her little brother, her sister and herself by the Brockners was very probably exaggerated. Physical punishment is still the main form of discipline in many families, both in Europe and America. And Annette was, by her own admission, an exceptionally difficult child.

"I was pretty fresh," she acknowledged. "I got into alcohol and smoking at the home and the Remm woman said I was a bad influence on her kids. Her wonderful kids," she added bitterly.

And what about her real father? Was he completely out of her life? "Not *completely* completely. I quite liked him, you know. Now I'm on quite good terms with him, but I had too little contact with him when I was small. He'd come to visit me once a year or so in the home."

Wouldn't it have been possible for her to live with him and his wife?

"No, they didn't want me, either. He had a little boy with his new wife, the same age as Micky, and he was just as rude and difficult as I. My father thought, with his wife blind and all that, it was just impossible to have two like us. And then, too, you know, when I was eleven or twelve, he tried to pressure me—he heard that I was truanting and running away and drinking and all that, and when I called him up once, he said, 'Either you straighten up and fly right, go to school and behave, or else I don't want to see you any more.' So I thought okay, to hell with all of them: if I go to school, I do it because it's *my* decision, nobody else's. Where did he, with his measly once-a-year visits, get away with trying to put pressure on me? I decided they could all lick my arse."

"So there was never any adult relative to whom you could respond?" I asked.

"Yes," she said, bitterly, "there was that cousin, remember, the one I saw at my mother's funeral? Well, she was twenty-five and she came along one day and took me out to her place and she even let me drink beer. I thought here at last is someone I can really talk to, you know, confide in. But then she started to kiss me, you know, and it got funnier all the time. She wrapped me up in a rug and sat me on her lap, and you know I thought that was funny because, after all, I wasn't a baby—I certainly didn't want to be one, on the contrary. Anyway, later I heard she was lesbian. So you see, she too only wanted to exploit me . . . well, as I told you, in the end I just gave up and said I didn't want to see any of them any more, and then I didn't see them for a long time.

"Years later [it was two years] I met my sister in the street near the Brockners' house [the children's home was miles away from there, and again, it was significant that she had haunted her old neighbourhood]. She had greasy hair and messy clothes and I stopped her and said, 'How are you then?' and she didn't recognize me. I guess because I was well dressed—at the homes they always dress us well. Anyway, she pulled me around the corner saying she wasn't supposed to speak to me, and I said, 'Where's Micky?' and he came up then, on roller skates, and I said, 'Hello,' and he said, 'Who are you?'

"Well, that did nearly break me up. *My* Micky, looks at me with his big blue eyes and says 'Who are you?'. I said, 'I'm your sister, Annette,' and he said, 'I don't have any sisters except Renate and Tina.' It shook me. It shocked me. Well, after that I just thought the hell with all of them, with all of it . . . I think it was that evening one of the rockers raped me—my first one, he was twenty-four. Before that, a lot of them tried, but nobody got in, but this one—well he did and kept me locked in that apartment all night. Later, when I told him that he'd been the first one, he said he was sorry, he was drunk and . . . well, that's when it all started."

Annette's debut in prostitution was unusual in that she immediately fell in, not with one pimp—who might have had some interest in protecting her—but with a whole group of perverse and corrupt men who, playing on her naïveté and innocence, passed her along from one to another, all of them posing as part of an in-group—she called it a "Rocker-group"—which she longed to be part of.

"They played a sort of game with me. They'd come and sit and talk, first to me, then to each other about me, and they'd laugh and say, 'Well, she's certainly too young,' and then others would come up and sort of tousle my hair, you know, and laugh because I was so little. And because of course I didn't want to be taken for little—I wanted to be grown-up, so I'd say, 'No, no I'm quite old enough. I've done it before, often.' And so I'd end up in bed with them. I never knew they paid anybody; but of course they did, only not me. All kinds of things happened. Once one of them put something in my glass I guess, because I didn't know anything, but when I came to I had been shaved—you know what I mean—and much later I saw photographs they'd taken.

"Arndt—that first one—he also said at first, 'No, no you are too young, etc.' and then I stayed with him for two months. . . .well, he *did* on one occasion look after me, when a real fat man came up to our table and asked for me, and Arndt said, all indignant-like, 'Even I don't get on top of her, she is too young.'

"Ha!" she commented bitterly. "And as time went on, he'd bring up more and more men, introduce them as 'colleagues' and tell me to go fuck with them. Once one of them, looking at me, said, 'She's too young,' and I, mulish as ever, said, 'No, I *want* to go up with you,' and we went up and we were lying in bed you know, talking, with me still in my panties and he said, 'You don't really want to, do you? You just said that to show off. You don't have to, you know.' And then Arndt came in and saw I still had my panties on, and he said, 'What, not at it yet?' and he tore my panties off and said, '*Now, at once*,' and went out, and I cried and that other chap, Rick—now I know of course that he was a punter and had already paid—he was quite nice and gave me a cigarette you know and we did it and afterwards I said, 'I'll ask Arndt whether I can stay with you all night,' and he said, 'I already asked, you can.' And when I told Arndt the next morning that I liked Rick, he said I wasn't there to 'like' any of them . . . well, that's how I was slowly initiated into prostitution."

Annette's long periods of prostitution alternated quite consistently with returns to the children's home. The director of this home, a most exceptional social worker specializing in work with children, maintained what he admitted was an irrational—purely intuitive—kind of faith in her. "The obvious thing, of course, would have been to expel her. This applies to many of our girls," he said. "The next stop after us is a closed institution. We are supposed to be 'secure,' i.e., nobody can go out without permission and they must sign in and out. But we do allow people out. I *will not* run a children's home like a prison."

This man—we will call him Hans—had sensed in Annette a reserve of strength and integrity which sooner or later could cause her to pull herself away from the precipice her life had become. "Only the child itself can make that decision. For better or for worse, they are masters of their fate."

I found more of this strength of feeling, this courage—or determination—to take risks, in West Germany than anywhere else. Good social workers are special everywhere, but in modern West Germany they are exceptional.

To a large extent, attitudes and reactions in West Germany thirty-seven years after Hitler depend on age. First of all, there are the old, who all of them were part of Hitler's time of glory and defeat. They may have denied it and him both to others and themselves, but despite the postwar economic miracle, despite West Germany's acceptance into, and subsequent dominance of the western European alliance, Hitler's dream and the nightmare it became dominate the lives, or at least the spirits or the consciences, of those who shared in it. Some—the exceptional ones of that generation—dedicated themselves to effecting a change by teaching, or by the example of their own lives.

Their children, the next generation, who are today between thirty-eight and fifty-six years old, had the hardest and most thankless task: it is they who paid for their parents' sins or omissions, they who fought hardest, at the most difficult time, to overcome the terrible and unfair legacy of "the bad German." It is from amongst them that great German writers and academics and film-makers have arisen, a media of integrity, and statesmen of real stature who re-created in an incredibly short time rule by law and democracy. It is in some of this generation, and in some of *their* children, that one finds today the deepest commitment to national and personal freedom, deeper and more determined—or so at least it seems to me—than in the young of other nations.

For men such as Hans, experimenting with new approaches to the care of problem children is putting the principles of individual freedom into practice. This can't be done without taking personal risks.

The staff turnover in institutions such as that run by Hans—and similar ones in Britain, Holland, France, Sweden and the United States—is considerable. "Most people can only take the strain for so long," said Hans. "The point comes when they must choose between leaving, or risking marriage troubles and nervous breakdowns. All of us are subject to those."

Did Annette realize that the home, and Hans especially, were on her side? That they were trying to help her? "Yes," she said. "I like Hans a lot, really a lot; I can even tell him so, you know, and I can listen to what he says to me. But . . ." she hesitated, "if I'm *really* to talk about what's happened or is happening in my life, then I have to talk about feelings you know, real feelings. And that I can't do with a man."

But there are women counsellors. Had she never found one she could confide in?

"It's too difficult for them," she said. "They are too close to us. And there are too many girls, all of them *needing*, all competing for their *special* attention. And many of them, you know, have worse troubles than I have. Oh, I've talked, like a waterfall, when I've been drunk. But when I sober up and am reminded of what I said, then I'm so embarrassed, so ashamed, I'm apt never to see that person again. I wouldn't want to feel that about Hans. So you see, if he starts to talk to me, I try to deflect the conversation by being flippant or rude or silly. If he persists, I just stammer and blush and feel myself starting to cry, so I run out of the room.

"What I really need in a man," she said suddenly in a quite different, challenging tone of voice, with a tinge of artificial and even hysterical gaiety in it, "is someone who shows me my limits, who'll just haul out and slap me hard if I go beyond them."

"You mean you want someone who says no to you?"

"Yes, somebody who if he sees me in one of the bad boozing places, slaps me and says, 'one, two, three, march, off home with you.' You see, if he slaps me in the pub, I look a fool, and that would stop me from going back there."

"So what you want is somebody who can control you, whom you respect?"

"Yes, in a way I do, but if I find he's just a creep who *pretends* to be 'strong' because he senses that I need it and wants to use me, well then, now that I know the game, I turn the table on him, and use *him*. No," she said firmly, "it only works if he's consistent."

"You mean slaps you, consistently?"

She laughed. "Yes, I suppose so, from time to time, just to let me know I can go so far and no further, and if I don't mind him, then he ignores me . . . *that* I don't like at all. I need . . . I need . . . " she fumbled, "you know, somebody like . . . I have something like a father-complex."

Where had she heard that phrase? "Some guy once said that to me. He tore one hell of a strip off me one day and then he said, 'You don't see me as a friend, you see me as a father.' That just finished me because, yes, it was true, but I didn't want to admit it. He was a pimp, too, but he never made me do anything. There *were* some like that."

Over a period of two and a half years, Annette was beaten, raped, sodomized, bought, sold, auctioned, abused and betrayed in every possible way. This thirteen- and fourteen-year-old child "worked" on the streets, in clubs, in bars, discos, saunas, as a call-girl from two flats and —to crown it all—in an Eros Centre right smack in the middle of Hamburg's Reperbahn.

Every one of the men who used her took, if not all, then certainly most of her money; and considering the amount of "traffic" she was exposed to, her earnings must have been staggering. But it is true that she demanded and received more personal attention from her countless pimps and pseudo-pimps than any of the other children I met.

I spoke with only one of these men—we will call him Max. Max was thirty-one, and very articulate. Speaking with a broad Hamburg accent, he was also disarmingly frank about his own life on the criminal fringe, and oddly perceptive about Annette.

"Hamburg is different from other cities," he said. "People—in general—are not specifically pimps. It's usually a *Seitensprung* [slang, with a double meaning, for "having it on the side"]. Of course, it can be very lucrative."

Is it lucrative with girls like Annette? "Yes and no," he said. "She is, of course, exceedingly pretty. But she is trouble—big, big trouble. She takes up one hell of a lot of time." He laughed. "She's not made for it, you know. The *real* ones, they want money. It's a profession for them. Most of them don't really like men, or if they do, then strangely enough, they are one-man women. The punters are nothing to them, they don't even see them. Annette . . . well . . . " he hesitated.

"Annette is a *child*. Isn't that the trouble, and doesn't it mean anything to you, what is being done to her?"

"Oh, you mustn't give me that moral twaddle," he said. "She's asking for what she's getting. Her terrible mistake—I told her—is that she's looking for a man for herself amongst men who are way beyond what she wants . . . hardened sinners, you know." He smiled wickedly. "Really, in a way, if people slap her around—and they do—it's because she needs it. She needs to know where she stands. Without that, she can't function, because she tries to hide her unsureness . . . oh hell," he said suddenly, "her misery, by insolence. Actually I've seen a lot of people be much nicer to her than she deserves. Oh hell," he said again, "she should be at home, with parents, being either hugged or spanked—that's what she wants."

But wasn't that true for many of these very young prostitutes?

"Yes, it is, though her case *is* extreme and most people just want to get rid of her. The money isn't worth the hassle. As for the *Strichkinder*, as you call them, on the whole they simply provide what the market demands. If the authorities wanted to stop it, they'd have to stop the buyers, not the sellers or us—the middlemen." He shrugged. "You know, prostitution is big business: *Kalbfleisch* is very marginal in it, really. One handles it because it's asked for and it's there. I don't know about other places, but in Hamburg most of us would just as soon do without it."

Did he himself have children?

"God forbid," he said, with deep conviction.

Annette, of course, had no idea that any of the men who used her felt like this. "I never really *break* with any of them," she said, "because I don't like to break off bridges behind me, it's too dangerous. They think because I look a little naïve they can say anything in front of me, so they talk about themselves and their wives and their businesses and it taught me a lot."

"What about the clients? Do they tell you things?"

"I'm not interested in anything *they* say. It's as if I was working in a shop and sell somebody a bag of sweeties and he pays. 'Thank you, *Auf Wiedersehen*,' that's it. It has nothing to do with my life. If I lie in bed with them, I'm just thinking of what I'm going to eat later. If they insist on talking about their wives—which many of them do—I try to say something sensible until the time they paid for is over. Then I say, 'Time's up, I've got to go down or you have to pay again.' "

But the pimps' talk, that did interest her? "Yes, they talk to their colleagues while I sit with them, about their ladies, and business, and all the funny business they are in. The way they discuss everything and everybody did open my eyes to the extent to which they collude with each other."

They discuss their ladies? By name? "Oh yes. Like they will say, 'Annette, she is very good at this and that, but not good at this,' and they'd laugh, or else discuss it quite seriously, like business information, totally ignoring the fact that I was sitting there and listening to myself being discussed in the most private terms by groups of men."

Annette is aware that most of the men have several "ladies." What she is not sure of is her own place in their hierarchy. "Frank has three ladies," she said about one pimp who, supplying her with unlimited alcohol, kept her in two different flats for several months. "They earn on average four to six thousand Deutschmarks a month, never less, sometimes more. He takes each of them on holiday once a year, *real* holidays," she emphasized, "to the Bahamas and places like that where they can really relax."

She herself was obviously not in that category and not complaining.

While he was off in the Bahamas for a month at a time with each of his three ladies, I asked, what was she doing?

"I worked at the Club-hotel. He got me in there, a nice room with bath, a place in Lüneburg. The manager was a friend of his."

Did the youth police ever catch Annette? "Once. They picked me up in the street and they took me to the clinic. I got on pretty well with everybody, except some of the policewomen because they didn't like the blouse I was wearing because when I leaned over, one could see my breasts, you know, and they went on at me about it, why couldn't I dress decently and all that shit, and then, you know, they really let me have it because I told them to fuck off." She laughed stridently, and went on to describe an incident reminiscent of Julie's experience with her mother, four thousand miles away in mid-America, after having been raped. "I was wearing a sponge, you know. I had my period and that's what one does, you know, and they said take it out and I did and then I said, 'Can I go and wash my hands?' and would you believe this, they wouldn't let me? I said, 'You filthy sow, how often do *you* wash your hands a day?' and they said again, 'No, no washing,' so you know what I did? I grabbed hold of her hand with my dirty hand. Boy, did she not like that!"

What did the policewomen do then? "They took all my money off me and I was sent to a closed children's home for a while, but in the end Hans got me out."

(Now that Hans knew all the horrors Annette had been subjected to during the years he readmitted her time and again after her fugues, did he still think his had been the right way, I asked him.

"I do," he said. "There are some children who cannot learn except through experience and she is one of them. I remain convinced that nothing except what we did had even the slightest chance of helping her to find her own way out and into normal life.")

Exactly like the girls I worked with in America, the beginning of the end for Annette came as the result of a deeply wrenching emotional experience. She had fallen in love with Mario, a German-born pimp of Italian ancestry. "He gave me everything I had always missed: all the tenderness I suspected had to exist somewhere, the feeling of safety." She knew he was a pimp but no longer cared. "I cared about what I felt," she said. "It was so different."

One day, not so very long after they had met, they were lying in bed—"I was feeling wonderful." So she suggested "offhandedly" ("very offhandedly. I knew better than to let anybody know I cared for them") that perhaps they could make a go of it together, normally. She'd go back to school or learn a trade and they could be "friends." "But he said that he didn't fancy a woman who, if she stayed out with him for a night, got three days' detention in a children's home. I said I couldn't help that; I was still in care and that was my place of residence. 'Ah well, that's it then,' he said."

Pulling out all stops, Annette suggested that he should come to the home with her and meet the director. "Hans's rule is, that if he meets our boyfriends and approves of them we are allowed weekend leaves with them. And he said yes. We drank to our decision and made a date when he would come the next afternoon. I waited, but he didn't come. The next day I went looking for him and said, 'We drank to it.' 'To what?' he said. 'To your breaking with Galina' (the sixteen-year-old he'd been keeping company with) 'and becoming my boyfriend.' 'You are crazy,' he said. 'I'm not anybody's *boyfriend*.'

"And then he tried to get me to come to bed with him. I told him to go to hell and went straight back to Hermann—he owns a bar. He's one of those big blocky guys I used to imagine were like fathers. Fathers, ha!" she mocked. "He'd already heard about my stupid falling for Mario. 'Aha, so you're back, are you?' he thundered across the bar. 'Upstairs with you,' and he fucked me till I couldn't move. 'You . . . are . . . going . . . to . . . stop . . . fantasizing . . .' he said, riding me with his two hundred pounds or whatever.

"I was sad after that. I wouldn't see Mario for days, even weeks. I'd got used to some things, you know, being held, you know, and rocked and going to sleep lying on top of him with my face in his shoulder, he'd stroke me and kiss my hair . . . And we'd do all these silly things, pretend fights, you know, chase around the room and then he'd come and hold me like a little girl—that too I need, that and being treated like a grown-up. He knew how to do both."

But finally her longing for him overcame her pain and anger, and after a few weeks they were back together, from time to time, up in the room above Hermann's bar. "And then, you know, Hermann sent me up one day and Mario was there, and so was Robert, Heine, and two or three others, and Mario said, 'Get your clothes off, voluntarily. I don't like rape.' And I felt dizzy, I thought I'd faint. I said, 'Rape, what do you mean, rape?' And he said, 'I'm going, I have to go.'

"And then Mario left, but the others stayed and barred the door, and Robert said, 'I'm first,' and I said I wouldn't, and then he hit me, and then Heine pulled me to the bed by my hair and hit me too and I started to cry, and I finally thought, now whatever happens I'm for it, and before I let them beat me black and blue which is what they are going to do before they fuck me anyway, I might just as well do it without any more of that—I thought I might get away with just masturbating them, you know, and it worked all right with Robert, but then there were so many: Heine, Klaus and two others and then I think another one—I didn't even know any more—or care.

"And then Mario came back, and because I was lying in bed, half asleep because I was so tired you know, and when he came in I smiled or something, he thought I'd done it all voluntarily, at least he said so, and he said *he* certainly didn't want to have anything to do with a chick who gave it to everybody. 'All you are good for,' he said, 'is a good beating and that's what you'll get from me too from now on.' When he said that, that was the end, I made up my mind."

What Annette made up her mind to do—and this happened just before we met—was a very curious kind of vengeance. She was deliberately going to get herself infected with VD and then she was going to give it to all of them. "Every one of them was going to get it in the arse, right where it hits them hardest," she said, viciously.

And it worked. "I found out which girl had a dose and made it with one of her guys. And then the very first one I gave it to was Mario. He'd never had one before! Then Heine, Klaus and Arndt and Henne for good measure. And of course they passed it on to other girls . . . it was a ruddy epidemic." She laughed. "In the end the joke was on me. I got my injections and got rid of it and everybody else had, too, except one girl, Maria—and she passed it to Heine, and he passed it back to me . . . "

She had told this whole story in a curious tone of weary triumph and hysteria. We were sitting in my hotel room. At the end of it, she looked white and exhausted and went to my bed and lay down. I had been keeping us going for days with tea, coffee and sandwiches from room-service. Now I ordered soup, cold chicken, salad and wine. She opened her eyes. "You are going straight to the devil," she said. "corrupting a child with alcohol, tut, tut."

"If you could do what you wanted to do, what would you do?" I asked.

"Sleep," she said. "I want to sleep forever."

"And when you wake up?"

"Well," she said, "I've asked my gran whether I can come and live with them. I can't—I just can't go on at the home. I must have a home of my own. I . . . I've just *got* to," and she put her head down on the table, in the middle of plates and crockery and leftover food, and sobbed. . . .

"Well, how about it?" I asked her grandmother the next day.

"I'm not well, you know," she said. "I am not a well woman. I did say to my husband, 'Papa,' I said, 'How about Annette . . . you know . . .' And he said, 'Mother,' he said, 'You've done such a good job bringing up our children, and if Annette comes here now—let's say she does—and starts bringing men into the house . . .'" She stopped. "I couldn't take that," she said. "I have heart trouble, I've had two cancer operations, I have a scar from here to here—" she pointed vaguely from her waist across or down. "Two years ago I had yet another stomach operation and I should really have another one, on the intestines, but I don't want any more operations. I spoke to one of the counsellors at the home and she said Annette hasn't passed any exams and I myself am sceptical that she ever will. If one talks to her about a profession—we do talk, you know, I say, 'What do you feel like doing? Would you like to do domestic work, look after children perhaps?' Well, when I asked her that, she said yes. . . ."

Did the grandmother really think that was a realistic suggestion, from the life Annette had been leading, straight to a household job with children?

"Well, as I told you, what she *wants* to do is to move in with us, and go every day to her school near the home, from here. But that's impossible. As my husband said to me, 'That's just too tiring for the child.' And he said we'd have to get her into a local school."

"So he was willing?"

"I guess so."

"But you don't really want to, do you?"

"I'd be willing to try. Certainly I'd try, but she couldn't run wild as she does, here."

Annette could hardly be expected to lead a nun's life, suddenly, could she? "No, no. But I am old-fashioned; yes, I am that, I admit it."

But she did realize, didn't she, that Annette needed friends, relationships with boys? "Yes, but for goodness' sake, not pimps and Rockers and individuals who've been in prison. One day she showed me a letter she had from a man in prison and I said, 'Annette, what's the sense in corresponding with people like that?' And she said, 'Granny, they are lonely, too.' 'Yes,' I said, 'they are lonely my dear child, but it's their own fault; they only have themselves to blame. They are worthless. . . .' "

But didn't the grandmother realize that by disparaging Annette's friends, she disparaged Annette herself and added fuel to her already disastrous self-image?

"Shall I tell you something?" she said. "That girl is so talented . . . you know what I told her would be the right profession for her? Florist. It's marvellous how she can arrange flowers, and she can paint, too."

"Are you glad when she comes to see you?"

"Well, when she goes to the toilet . . . well, I try not to let her see me, but I go quickly and . . . you know . . . I use disinfectant on the seat, otherwise I wouldn't, I couldn't sit on it."

"Well yes," I said. "I can understand that."

"Oh, I find it so disgusting, you can't imagine it. Or if she picks up my glass or cup and says, 'Granny, can I just have a sip?' I just have to go and get her another glass and wash mine. Do you think she's an actress?" she asked suddenly.

I said that, no, I really didn't: I thought she was rotten as an actress.

"You don't think so? But you can't imagine how nice and sweet she is when she comes here and how happy she looks. She and Renate, they came on Christmas Day last year, and Annette asked whether she could lay the table—you should have seen how beautifully she did it, with my best table-cloth, and the candles and folding the napkins as if she'd done it all her life."

I told the grandmother that the night before I had asked Annette to tell me about her day-dreams. "She said she dreams of four things: a man, a child, a nice flat, and an ordinary life. She dreams of this by the hour."

"You know what I thought might be the best thing for her?" said her grandmother. "To get out of Hamburg altogether, perhaps to the south somewhere—Bavaria. There are lots of good boarding schools there and the people are friendly."

Who would pay for that, I asked. "Well, she could work in one of those . . . you know, sort of *au pair* . . . "

"But what she *wants* is to come to *you*." She shook her head. "It's too late . . . too late to make something of her . . . "

The last time I saw Annette while she was still in care, was at the children's home. She had flu, a cold and a temperature, and was in bed.

"When all this started," she said, her voice very low, very monotonous, as if she was speaking in her sleep, "I had such a mad need for freedom, I thought I had to experience everything, all at once. Silly things, you know: I wanted to drive around in a taxi, I wanted to feel that I had money, that no one could do anything to me or tell me anything, and I got that. I only went in taxis. I went to Chinese restaurants whenever I felt like it. I could go into the best shops, boutiques where ordinarily as a child-in-care you wouldn't even get a look-in. And I went to discos and bars . . . nobody cares how old you are. As long as you have money and good clothes, you can do anything . . . somehow you could really live . . . "

She lay there, with her eyes closed, her hand, now a little warmer, in mine and I found myself almost whispering: "Is that really living?"

"No," she said, opening her eyes and looking up at the ceiling, tears running down her cheeks. "It isn't really living. It's living an illusion."

A few months later, I heard that Annette was pregnant and had firmly refused to have an abortion, or to name the father. She had accepted the offer from the city youth authority of a small flat and with it the obligation to move into a mother-and-baby home for the last weeks of her pregnancy. In addition ("I can't really belive it yet," said Hans, who was holding her hand through it all, "But I'm keeping my fingers and toes crossed"), she had given up prostitution, had abandoned anything or anyone to do with the scene, was learning to house-keep and "making a wonderful job of it," was reading baby-books, trying out recipes, and knitting. ("I think I'm dreaming," said Hans on the phone, two months before the baby was born.)

He wasn't dreaming. Annette lived up to the letter of every obligation she had undertaken. The baby was born and beautiful; she cared for it with talent and devotion. Even while still pregnant, she had met a boy and they had fallen in love. She had hidden nothing from him of her past, he had taken her to see his parents and they had taken her to their hearts.

He is twenty-one, with a good job; she is now seventeen, with two beautiful babies. They have a flat, a family—for her at long last, a family. She is a wonderful mother. There are wonders in the world yet.

11

Gaby

The moment when a child who is engaged in prostitution realizes—as did Annette in West Germany, and Cassie in America—that the life may serve as an escape from intolerable reality but is in the final analysis nothing but an illusion, is likely to be the point of greatest despair. But also paradoxically the return of hope.

Some become weary, fed-up and —the healthiest reaction—angry, but never reach this totality of despair. Not because they are necessarily stronger, or healthier in themselves than others, but because the environment from which they spring is fundamentally sound and their exaggerated actions are caused by, and cause, transitory traumas with which in time they learn to come to terms.

Some are children—one hates to admit it—whom environment and personality may have predestined for this life. Perhaps Gaby is such a child.

Gaby was one of the liveliest, most charming and paradoxically enough, most innocent of the children I met. A honey-blonde with a rather wide, pretty little face, looking not a day older than her fourteen years, she had no pretences whatsoever and a lot of charm. She walked tall, she looked one straight in the eye, she laughed with joy and she seemed to me a young creature full of life and love.

The exceptionally liberal and inventive Berlin Youth Authority had, shortly before we met, given her a flat. The conditions of this experiment, which they were trying with a number of fourteen- and fifteen-year-olds in a desperate effort to stem the veritable flood of child prostitution, were that she should cease prostitution; that her sixteen-year-old boyfriend Rainer, who lived with her, should cease pimping and get work; that both of them should submit to weekly health checks and interviews; and that she herself should return to school.

Gaby—and Rainer followed her lead—had said yes to everything. They set up home with a vengeance and Gaby quite obviously adored playing at house-keeping. She had invited me to a sumptuous tea: a dish of beautifully decorated open sandwiches, chocolate biscuits, cake and whipped cream, coffee and, as a sop to my possible preference, tea made in a specially purchased pot. The flat—living-room, bedroom, kitchen, bath, and a spare room they were using "temporarily" (they said) as a storeroom—was spick and span, with preserving jars and glasses full of flowers on every table.

"You've made a beautiful job of it," I said, and she laughed. "The Authority gave us all that furniture. Rainer polished it all—look how he's got it to shine, and I've got to have flowers. I love cleaning," she added, "but it isn't always *this* clean, and the tea-party is for you. You are our first real guest."

Gaby was a child of the slums. Her father worked for a coal merchant "when he wasn't drunk. When he was out cold, my mum did his job in his stead." He beat the four children black and blue "when under the influence," spent regular periods in gaol, and finally left the family when Gaby was seven. Now he is married to another woman and has turned respectable. "They have a pet shop, would you believe it?" said Gaby.

Her mother, she said dreamily, is of Russian and gipsy extraction. "Isn't it lovely?" she enthused. "She loves us. She's always loved us like mad. You should have seen the row she made when they took us away from her. And she came to see us at the children's home every week." Her feisty mother, with whom I spoke later—a warm-hearted product of slum life in an East German city near the Polish border—is singularly lacking in gipsy characteristics. Her sparse, mousy hair is tightly permed, her eyes are blue and her complexion is fair. She has a broad body, a broad voice, a broad Berlin accent and a laugh that can be and is heard from streets away. It was difficult to sort out her many children. There seemed to be three with Gaby's father, two more which he brought into the marriage, one with another man and —I never could get it quite right—another couple with the step-father.

Gaby was nine when she stayed away overnight the first time. Her mum and the boyfriend she was to marry soon afterwards were out drinking, and the kids—in the nominal care of an aunt on a lower floor—decided to go to the carnival with some neighbouring children who'd also been left on their own. "At the carnival, one of the boys—we were about six— lost twenty marks his mum had given him, so he didn't dare go home, so we all decided not to," said Gaby. They bunked down in the house of one of them.

"And when we went home in the morning, my aunt, she opens the door and says, 'Ah, you weren't home all night, were you? I'm going to tell your mum, she'll skin your ass.' " Their mum was evidently still in bed, not having been in any state to notice their absence when she got home during the night. "We got scared and didn't even go up but just shot out again and didn't come back for four days."

(A few days later I asked her mother what she had done, that day, when she noticed the children were not there. "Good dear God in Heaven," she roared, chuckling heartily, "that Gaby, she'll be the death of me. She's run away a hundred times . . . a *hundred* times, I tell you. How can you expect me to remember the first time?")

Gaby remembered perfectly well. "Well, Mum was cross," she said, "and my older brother, he wanted to give me a beating—he always wanted to beat me, later too when I kept running away. But my mum, she knew it wouldn't help to beat us and she always said, 'You don't beat a girl; she'll get ahold of herself sooner or later.' "

After her mother married her step-father, "He did use to let me have it, you know, when I got caught nabbing things or when I stayed out. Oh not badly, just smacking me, you know, but it scared me, and because I knew I was supposed to be home by seven, if I was late, I just didn't go home because I was scared. And then my step-father was in prison for a while—just a few weeks—and Mum was lonely, so she went out dancing so we went too and all that, and then he came home and I was still staying out and he said, 'Now you stop it. Stay home, be good,' and I didn't, I wasn't, so he got ahold of me and cut me bald. He shaved my head," she explained to this slow listener.

"What did you feel?"

"Well, I looked in the mirror and cried. I looked at myself and then I ran off again, and went to my father—my real father, you know—and he said he was going to the police about it. But I said he mustn't because otherwise my mother would get beat up, so I stayed there, but in the night the dog was crying, so I put a coat over my nightdress to take him out and my step-mother went after me and smacked me and dragged me back, and before I could explain about the dog, my father gave my a real beating because he thought I'd been running away. The next day he apologized but I was fed up, you know, so I ran off again. And then I went off stealing and the police caught me, and my mother said now I've had it, and that's how I first got put in the children's home; I was eleven. Anyway, I ran away from there too, to shoplift—it was our sport, you know, everybody did it—and the police got me and they got me to tell them how and with whom and all that, and then the other girls, and some women we were doing it with, they beat me up and I shot off—I was going to the police about it, but they—the women—got me again."

"What did they want with you?"

"Teach me, you know, how to do it properly, the shoplifting."

Apparently that group of female Fagins took her to a house, beat her again just to remind her, and then "rammed some teaching into me." After that, "they gave me something to drink, I don't know what, and there was a boy there—a Turk, he was sixteen or seventeen I later found out—and that's when it happened: they told him to take me, he told me the next day. Well, I had a good night's sleep and woke up the next morning and the boy—well, he was sort of nice, you know, and he said, 'I'm going to get you out of here'—they were all sleeping anyway. He said he'd take the dog out and he took me along, took me home to my mum. My mum cried when I came home."

Did she tell her mother that she'd lost her virginity?

"No, oh no, otherwise she would have reported the boy to the police for seducing a minor. But he was sort of nice, you know—I hadn't felt nothing anyway—I was asleep, and he gave me money too."

That very afternoon she took off again.

Soon afterwards she met Rainer and lived rough with him, hiding from the Youth Authorities who wanted her back in the children's home. "And a couple of days later, we had no money and Rainer and I were in a Turkish bar and there was this Turk, and he gave me a drink and I liked it, and he gave me another one and some hash too, and then he said he'd give me some money and I was so drunk and we needed it, so I did it with him and he gave me forty Deutschmarks and I said to Rainer—drunk, you know, as I was—'It wasn't so bad, not as bad as I'd imagined it. I can do that from now on, when we need money or something.' "

And the next day they were again without money and she said to Rainer, "What *shall* we do?" "And he said, 'Do you remember what you said yesterday?' And I said, 'No, what?' And he said, 'Well, that you wanted to do that.' So I said, 'Well, okay.' And we took a bus to the Kurfürstendamm, and I got into a car that stopped and I didn't like it at all because the man parked there and said, 'Come on, take me into your mouth,' and all that stuff. Well, so I said, 'Not today—give me your phone number, I'll ring you tomorrow.' Anyway, perhaps he got scared because I was so green. So he let me go.''

But that was the beginning of the year during which she "worked" for Rainer and herself, on the streets and through ads from clubs, as a call-girl. "They put a daily ad in the newspaper," she said. '' 'Young girl, boyish figure'. I had to give the club half the money. I made about a hundred a day.''

And what happened to the money?

"He gambles," she said, looking sadly at Rainer, who had been sitting there silently throughout this whole tale. "I'd make the money and he'd gamble it all away in one day."

After she said that, he got up and said he'd go out for a while. "What will happen when he comes back?" I asked. She shrugged. "Nothing. He wouldn't *dare*."

The year was briefly interrupted when she got VD, was taken to hospital and then back to a children's home, and then to France on holiday with the Girl Guides. "But while I was there, it turned out I wasn't really cured; I got horrible pains and I phoned Rainer every day and he said, 'Come back,' he was lonely. Anyway, I went back a week before the others and ran off again, back to him. And after that I went on working, first back on the *Autostrich*, but I got fed up doing it without rubbers—you can't make any money if you insist on rubbers, they don't want it. Not even the fire brigade want it with rubbers,'' she added.

The fire brigade? I thought I had misunderstood the German word. "What is the *Feuerwache*?" I asked. "What is it you did there?"

"What I always did," she said patiently. "They've got a room there," sounding reasonable, "a sort of dormitory."

"Did they know your age?" A feeble question. Even now, a year later, she looked a *young* fourteen.

"Well, they may have thought I was sixteen," she said, quite obviously to make *me* feel better.

And so how did that work—from one fireman to another?

"Well, no, they'd come in a group, you know, five or six of them, we were all in that dormitory, and I did three and my friend did three. But if they wanted to kiss me, I always said no; I said it from the start, no kissing or other positions, you know, I always said that at once. I couldn't . . . other things . . . I just lay there and that's all, because it somehow made me feel sick. . ."

And her friend? "Oh, she did everything, even . . . " she hesitated, and then said stiffly, "even *Analverkehr* [buggery]."

"But, Gaby," I said, "you were only a baby. How could Rainer let you do this? Did his parents know about it?"

"His step-father found out, just a few months ago though, and he beat him till he couldn't move. He nearly threw him out of the window. 'The girl is younger than your sister,' he screamed, 'and you send her out on the streets and sit on your bum and won't work!' " She shrugged. "But by that time . . . "

"And what about your parents. What do they say?"

"Well, they think . . . they always said for me to be with *Germans*—my step-father always said that. He doesn't like foreigners, and that anyway I was so young and he didn't see why I should go on the street for a man. If I'm going to do that, he said, I should do it for myself and save money or something. I mean if that's what I absolutely wanted to do."

So in fact her parents didn't object in principle to her being in prostitution? What about her mother, what did she say?

"Well, she doesn't think it's a good thing, except . . . she always told me, 'You have to know what you are doing. I told you often enough, come back home'."

So she *could* have gone home? "Not really," Gaby said. "My step-father—he loves me, you know, when I was smaller, he always loved me better than my sister—I had a big mouth, you know, he liked my being so cheeky. He used to take me out with him, to bars and all that," she sounded pleased and proud, "and he'd give me money secretly, you know, so that my mother wouldn't see it." She laughed. "My mother knew it anyway. 'How much did he give you this time?' she'd say. He wanted me to study; he wanted to send me to a high school. The other day he had his birthday—I phoned him and he cried. 'Mousie,' he said, 'I love you so, don't do all this shit, give it up. If things are difficult, I'd always have you back here . . . for a week or two. It won't do for longer, well, you know yourself,' he said. And he's right. But he loves me."

"No," she said, after a little silence. "No, I couldn't have gone home. It wouldn't have done."

So how long did it go on for? How much money did she make?

"Well, about a year; a bit more. I made between two hundred and four hundred Deutschmarks, but not every day, you know. In the end, I had about three regulars . . . I could ring them when I needed money, or they rang me whenever they felt like it."

So what about now, I asked. "What about the future?"

"Well," she said—she sounded thoughtful and wary. "I used to be good at school, you know. When I was small, I always had ones and twos, a few threes, but never a four, never. Now they want me to go back. I said yes . . . and perhaps I can do it . . . but it's going to be very difficult: you know, to pay attention, to concentrate, to be with . . . to be with . . . girls, ordinary girls."

She was scheduled to go back to school for the first time the very next day. I knew some of the teachers there—I knew how anxious they were to help her. "You *will* go, won't you?" I said.

"I have to," she said, listlessly. "There is no other way, I can't live at home. Having my own place is the only solution. And now they've done that for me: they've let me have this beautiful flat. What else can I do, then, except to try it this way? I'm going to try it . . . just try it. . . ."

She tried. The last news I had, a few months ago, was that she had stood the school for a few months, with increasing absences; had lost the flat when she'd gone back to prostitution; had given up or lost Rainer when his step-father (wisely, one must think) had sent him to West Germany; had not been heard from by her family for two years; and had lost touch with her devoted counsellor at the Youth Authority. "It makes me so sad to have to tell you," wrote a social worker friend I'd asked to enquire. "We have enquired everywhere. She has just disappeared."

12

Marianne

Marianne is one of the children whose inner resources proved strong enough to rescue her from the scene. She is nineteen now: a tall slim girl with curly fair hair who lives in a city in south-west Germany. Over the past three years she has passed the German equivalent of final high school exams, completed a secretarial course, held a secretarial job for twelve months, and attended night school for two years in preparation for the intermediary exams as an interpreter which she is about to sit.

For the past year she has lived alone with her dog Blondie in an apartment obtained for her by the city's Youth Authority, which will continue to pay the rent, a clothes allowance, and a generous contribution to her living expenses until she has finished her studies.

Her former boyfriend, Wolfgang, lives two floors below. "I long for him, but I'm better off without him," she wrote me recently. Five years ago, when fourteen-year-old Marianne was working as a call-girl, Wolfgang was employed as a driver by a club-owner who sent her out. "He was supposed to look after me," she said. "He was supposed to stay within earshot, in case I yelled for help."

Had she ever yelled? "No, they were more likely to do the yelling. Still, it was reassuring to know he was there."

Wolfgang is almost twenty years older than she is. She moved in with him when she quit prostitution because she needed this sense of reassurance to continue. "It took me two years to realize that he is too entrenched in the scene," she said. Wolfgang swore that he used to receive a salary, not commission from her earnings, but she no longer believed him; nor did she believe that the antiques business he is now in is strictly honest.

"He doesn't *know* any normal people. All of them belong to the scene, which meant that I had to see them all the time. I asked him to drop them, to make a new life with me in some new place, but he said he couldn't and I can see that. He's too old to change."

Marianne is extraordinarily realistic. Her social worker told me: "There is hardly a girl on my files who has been through worse experiences, and there *isn't* a girl on my files about whose eventual success I feel as certain. She is very intelligent, very strong, and very very nice."

"Oh my God," said Marianne, when I quoted this to her. "Do you know how many men this very very nice girl had in less than a year and a half of prostitution, beginning at fourteen? I figured it out with a calculator. I earned eighty thousand Deutschmarks—I didn't *get* that, of course, but I earned it. Divide that by thirty Deutschmarks per client, and you get 2,666 men." Her laughter when she said this was convulsive.

Did she tell her social worker?

"No. I honestly didn't think she could take it."

"What about your mother? She will read it in my book."

This time she didn't laugh. She shrugged. "Well, if I could take it when it happened, I suppose she can take reading about it."

Marianne's mother, who teaches in an elementary school, is an intelligent woman who dresses quietly and well, and lives in a flat full of plants and pretty things. ("Don't you think her flat is beautiful?" said Marianne. "I hope I've inherited her taste.") She spoke about her daughter frankly, and I could see where Marianne got her strength. Her husband was an architect. He died when Marianne was twelve and her brother Andreas was four.

Marianne knew that her early childhood had been tender, happy and secure, but both she and her mother recognized that she had been fussed over too much. "They spoilt me terribly," she said. "They suffocated me with care."

The child's world went to pieces when her brother was born, although her parents had followed modern teaching most meticulously in their attempts to prepare her.

"They explained that, true enough, they now had only half the time to devote to me, but all it meant was that they had twice as much love available. 'That's how it works,' they said. But it made no sense to me.

I used to think to myself, I can't understand what they mean. I remember when my mother was eight months pregnant, she let me feel him move in her tummy. That was wonderful. But I just couldn't accept the addition, that's all. Either they both loved me best, or they loved the baby best."

The crisis came when she was twelve, by which time it was apparent that her father had heart trouble. "That day," said Marianne, "my mother and I had one of our usual arguments. I had very long hair which I wore falling over to one side, like people did then. My mother wanted me to cut it because she said it got in my way for schoolwork, about which she was fanatic, and into the soup when I ate, which was unappetizing. My father tried to make me compromise and hold it back with a clip—a real pony-tail. 'Just do it for meals, and when you hear Mummy coming to your room,' he said, 'you can always take the clip out again.' That was sensible, I knew—but I just didn't see why I shouldn't wear my hair the way I wanted.

"Anyway, she wouldn't stop yelling about it for days, and finally my father said: 'Now, that's it. Either you go to the hairdresser this minute, or I'll cut it off myself.' I suppose he felt he finally had to support my mother, and in the end he got hold of a huge pair of scissors and chased me down the long hall of our flat, whooping like an Indian. I honestly think he was trying to turn the whole stupid thing into a joke to make it easier for me to give in, you know—he was that kind of person. But you see, he died that evening, and then later my mother said it had been my fault. I was to blame for his death."

("Oh my God," said her mother. "Did she tell you that? Oh my God, I remember it now, I did say it. I was so distraught. How could I have said that to her? How awful, awful, awful of me.")

"The funny thing was," Marianne continued, "when he fell, when he was lying there not moving, she called out for me. 'Come quickly,' she called. I was in bed, she thought I was asleep. When something happened she couldn't manage, the bad girl with no sense suddenly became the good daughter who could be counted on to keep her wits about her. And that used to happen quite often, you know. It was sickening. And . . . you know . . . because I wanted her to treat me like that all the time, I sometimes in my day-dreams wished for certain things . . . well, not *really* wished . . . the moment I imagined it, I was sorry, because of course I knew it would mean someone else getting hurt, so in my imagination I'd quickly make it okay again—you know what I mean?" She had realized what she had told me: that in her need for her mother's love and confidence, she used to day-dream catastrophe.

"Of course," she went on quickly, "I didn't wish for this to happen. I *loved* him . . . he was so warm, he understood . . . and there I was and couldn't do anything to bring him back, and a few days later she started hinting, then saying right out that it had been my fault."

"She didn't mean it," I said. "It wasn't her real self that said it. It was her despair."

"I know. With my reason I know, and I try never to think of it now. But for years I did, and it made me feel sick—literally sick to my stomach. And nothing . . . nothing mattered any more. Nothing."

Within weeks of her father's death, Marianne started to run away.

"She did become impossible to manage," said her mother. "I realized, of course, that the relationship between her and me, even more than her insane jealousy of Andreas, was the source of the trouble. And when it became obvious that she was failing in school, was associating more and more with beatniks and drop-outs and was stealing from me—probably to support them," she spoke briskly, "I understood that I had to get help."

(Marianne said that her mother was the only person she had ever stolen from. It was her school-mates who benefitted, she said: "I bought them chocolates, popcorn . . . I had no friends, you see, only 'chocolate friends'. I think now that I wanted to buy the love I couldn't get from her from other people.")

Marianne was sent to stay first with a great-aunt of whom she was fond, then to a state-run 'home', then to an uncle. Each time it was a failure, and she was dispatched back to her mother, where things went from bad to worse.

"Believe me," said Marianne, "it was pure hell. All I heard was that I was man-crazy and would end up being a whore the way I looked at men . . . she had me believing it in the end. It was true that I was smoking like a chimney, drinking, taking every kind of pill I could get hold of. And my make-up! I took to painting my face all white—but really WHITE. It looked awful. And it became so bad that she started hitting me, pulling my hair, and I finally pulled hers, too—can you imagine the scene? And one day when she did that and I did it back, I burst out and said for the first time that I really hated her. It's the only time I actually said that and I think it really got to her."

At about this time Marianne was more or less raped by a pick-up—she was too drunk to be aware of exactly what happened—and thought for several months that she was pregnant.

"I couldn't think who to go to for an abortion. Finally, on a lovely Sunday afternoon in my uncle's garden, I asked a friend of his, a man I'd known since I was small, whom I liked. You know what he did? He undid his belt and zip and said, 'We'll have a bit of fun and then I'll get you a doctor. You're pregnant anyway, so it won't make any difference.' Me aged fourteen and him a grown man with a big house and a big car—Jesus! I told him to get the hell out, and he was actually *offended*. But that was the first time I really understood that you only get something if you pay for it, and that this thing, the only thing I had to give, could be—no, *was* currency."

By then she knew all about the scene, and she had no wish to be part of it. But anything appeared to her better than "listening to my mother's unending recitals of all she'd done for me, all that money, all that care, all that love, etc etc etc."

Marianne's language was invariably middle class, that of a rather precocious young woman. In some extraordinary way (and it is part of the phenomenon for many of the other children, too) she maintained the standards of her middle-class upbringing throughout.

One could, in fact, always predict when she was going to come up with something outrageous. At those moments not only her tone but even her movements changed. Her head became fidgety, her hands nervous. But above all her voice became artificial, sugary, and she suddenly used horrible diminutives.

"Right, if that was how she wanted it, I was going to show mummykins where she could shove her stupid money," she said, and then—almost another person speaking—she continued, her voice back to its usual low tone, her vocabulary to its mixture of childishness and precocity. "I was going to show her that I could make it without her. I wanted to be, and I very quickly became, financially and psychologically free."

Although Marianne understood very quickly that she was capable of bringing in money, she had at that time no sense of her worth in other terms. "I was convinced that my value, if you like, was purely financial. As a human being, I was worth nothing. And because I was so worthless, if I was going to live—and I never conceived of not living—then my nonexistent human value had to be replaced by a money-value, with a vengeance!" She laughed—the mirthless laugh I heard over and over again when talking with these youngsters.

"Before long I added another eight hours a day on the ten hours' work everyone does. My average working day came to be eighteen or twenty hours. The more of them I did," she said roughly, "the less I saw of them."

Her first pimp, Serge, was a twenty-eight-year-old Yugoslav who started her out on Turkish foreign workers. Totally inexperienced sexually, Marianne found him wonderful at first.

"The only time I'd made love before that, I'd been drunk, so doing it with him was the first time I felt it, and it seemed meaningful and made me feel protected, close. I thought he was feeling the same thing—God, I was ignorant! After he'd got me going with the Turks, he just used to come in for two minutes, sort of to empty his garbage."

He installed her in a one-room flat and brought her Turks in groups of five: "They just lined up in front of the door—mass production. I lay there reading newspapers while it went on. Serge waited outside with the others, and from time to time he brought me things to eat. At one point I got awfully tired, and I even said I wanted to go home. He took my clothes away and put them in the corridor. From then I was just there, with nothing on, and he had his three hundred Deutschmarks a day. "But—I can't remember after how many days it was—then a very big one came in. He . . . he . . . moved so violently I couldn't stand it, it hurt. I cried. And that was when it got to me for the first time, because Serge came in, sat down on the bed, held my hand and told me I had to 'persevere.' " Her voice had become very low. "It was that word—*persevere*. I think that's what got me. This man on top of me, Serge beside me holding my hand, and saying I must *persevere*." She shook her head. "I'd like to find someone I could pay to kill Serge."

Even so (taking the line of least resistance is very common in child prostitution) she stayed with him on and off for most of her time in prostitution, with intervals of working the *Strich* or the *Autostrich* on her own, and trying other pimps, mostly Turks. "They were no better—usually worse—than he was."

Once she got so ill with VD ("I'd had it before, many times, but not so badly. I'd just gone on, passing it on to others. Who cared? They were just pigs") that she turned for help to an uncle who was a doctor. He sent her to a clinic, and from there she was sent to a convalescent home run by nuns. "Their only therapy was cleaning," she said, "but I was tired, so I decided to be good and stayed three months, until they decided I was ready to go into a children's home in the country. I would have liked that to work," she said thoughtfully. "It was in a little village, nothing except country and cows. All the other girls were orphans and the staff treated everyone like babies. It was restful, but I had simply nothing in common with any of them. I tried, I really did, but we spoke a different language, inside and out."

She bolted, without any belongings, and hitch-hiked to Hamburg, which she called "a booming place for baby tarts. After three days I had six plastic bags of new clothes, a train ticket south and a hundred marks." Whereupon she returned to Serge.

He took her to a Turkish foreign workers' dormitory—her lowest point. "You go from room to room. They pay at most twenty Deutschmarks. They won't use condoms, they drink like mad, they don't shave properly and then—they have this way of almost eating you from top to bottom, and constant arguments because one wouldn't kiss them. I drew the line at that—I just wouldn't kiss anybody."

Serge's idea of progress was to get her into a brothel for Turks. "After about three weeks I discovered they had a special trick, the pigs. They'd go to the lavatory and make themselves come before. That way they got more out of the girls. After I found that out, I was really angry and after ten minutes, I'd say 'Schluss! Time's up—out! If you don't like it, get somebody else.' That's the advantage of being young: they want young girls, so the younger you are, the more you can run them. It took me a good long time to realize that, though."

When she did realize it, she began to run Serge, rather than he her, and it wasn't long before she gave him his marching orders.

Around this time her mother's efforts succeeded, the police found her, and she was sent to a closed institution. "Of course I got out. That kind of restraint is hopeless for anyone in that frame of mind. It does more harm than good."

Marianne's last few months in prostitution were spent as a call-girl, to which she graduated via a massage-parlour.

"But these massage-parlours," I asked. "How do people know they aren't really massage places? I mean, they could be, couldn't they?"

Marianne thought that was about the funniest remark she'd ever heard. "What's even funnier, though," she said, laughing, "it happened to me once. There was this place I worked in, it was on the first floor of a respectable apartment house. They'd put a sign on the street-door, 'Massage and Manicure,' and it was run by the owner's mother—she was about sixty, a real classical madame, the kind you read about in Maupassant. Made up to the gills, full of graces, hard as nails. Anyway, one day, sure enough, an old grandpop arrives and asks for a manicure. Of course, she took it for a joke, ha, ha, brought him in to me. He looked around the room, you know, the huge bed with nothing but a paper sheet, a big waste-paperbasket full of Kleenexes, closed curtains and dimmed lights. I mean, it *was* daytime—he looked a bit dazed. Well, I tried to tell him gently—because he said, 'Shall we start?' and held out his hands for me to see—he was real old, they trembled. I was dressed in high-heeled shoes, hotpants, a little waist-coat and nothing else . . . I mean, you did have to be more than naïve. Finally, I thought it was so funny-sad, I got out my nail-file and thought, What the hell, I'll give him a manicure, and got started.

"But then she came in—the madame—because trying to explain and all that had taken time. His reactions weren't exactly quick, and nobody was supposed to stay more than twenty minutes . . . Anyway he finally went. I tried to make him laugh, but he didn't. He just looked puzzled."

Marianne's last few months in prostitution were spent not with Serge (who had been sent to prison) but as a call-girl working out of a club. Did her boss, the owner of the club, know she was fifteen?

"Yes, that's why he had me. After I'd been there some time I once asked him what he would do if his own fifteen-year-old daughter did what I was doing, and he couldn't even answer. I knew that he himself fancied little girls, so then I asked him what he'd do if someone raped his daughter, and he said 'I'd kill him!' He meant it, too." She shook her head. "Funny, isn't it, these double standards? But I can't complain about him. It was he who sent Wolf with me, he was really quite careful," she guffawed—"almost caring, I suppose one might say."

This man—her Chef, she called him, as Germans call any boss—procured clients for her and his other girls by advertising "all over the place, even as far away as Vienna. He invested money, all right. It was worth it to him."

Although Marianne was disgusted by the hypocrisy of "respect-able" newspapers which allowed sex-ads into their columns on condition that they were discreetly formulated, she admitted their useful-ness to working prostitutes. "It's not the safest means," she said, "but if you're properly prepared or looked after, like me with Wolf, then it's the best and the most lucrative."

Was it better with middle-class clients?

"It makes it more pleasant, it's as simple as that. I reached the point where I went only to first-class hotels or to flats in exclusive neighbour-hoods. And most of *them*, you know—they do know how to behave. I mean, one *visits*. One is offered a drink, sometimes a meal; one talks. Quite often, if it was a nice person, I stayed the night—I slept. It's different."

This kind of club arrangement was, she said, highly advantageous. The club-owner (i.e., the pimp) gets 50 DM an hour, or more. "The snag," she said, "is that one has to pay him fifty Deutschmarks an hour from the time one leaves the club, not just for the time one actually works. So say you want to have your hair done—that happened to me once when I was visiting a client at the Hilton. He had a business meeting but he wanted me to stay over, so I said I'd go and have a perm upstairs. Okay with him—he even gave me the money for the perm, a hundred Deutschmarks at the Hilton. But naturally he wasn't going to pay for my time while I was at the hairdresser. Of course not. But I had to pay for it—two hours—to the club. Even so, it's a good arrange-ment on the whole, simply because customers of this kind are generous. I used to end up with at least four hundred Deutschmarks a day, and sometimes a bit more."

She was fascinated by a telephone conversation I had had on the subject of sex-advertising with the proprietor of one of the most respected newspapers in the American Midwest. He had professed amazement at my suggestion that his paper was printing ads for child prostitutes. "That's impossible," he said at once. "I have children myself." I read out some of the ads of that day to him. "But how do we know that's for children?" he asked, sounding helpless. "They are phoned in and paid for by credit card; how can one control it?"

"How about not printing sex-ads at all?" I suggested, but he explained that refusing one kind of ad led to refusing others or being denied others; it was a chain reaction. And anyway freedom of the press demanded the freedom to advertise, "within the limits of good taste, of course," he added, before saying a friendly good-bye and hanging up.

Did she ever make friends with any of the clients? The answer was surprising. "Yes," she said. "Actually quite often. Oddly enough it was a client—an older man—who was the first man to make real love to me, who brought me to orgasm. He was an incredibly nice man. And he changed my feelings, my whole attitude. From then on I was able to look at them as people. And that worked in reverse, too, you see. Suddenly there were quite a few who showed consideration for me, who *gave*. Yes . . . it's extraordinary, but they did. I've always had such a need to receive as well as give—and if a client sensed this and responded to it, then it actually worked both ways."

So what is Marianne's feeling, now, about her past? "I'm ashamed of it," she said. "I don't want anyone I meet in the future to know. I don't want the girls I go to school with to know."

Has it damaged her? "I think I won't know until much later. I don't want—I don't have a boyfriend now. I have my dog to cuddle. But I learnt a lot: it taught me discipline. It takes a lot of discipline, a lot of strength. I am scared to death of the street. No young girl, no one at all, should go on the street."

And the clubs? "None of it should exist," she said. "There *have* to be alternatives for kids like I was, who can't live at home. It has to be possible to create them." She said that if she had been offered anything even half acceptable—anything to do with people, which gave her the possibility of making a living away from her mother—she would have taken it. Just as she would have accepted a really good boarding school.

"But as long as it does exist, and if one wants to look at it realistically," she went on, "speaking from my own experience only, I think one has to go through the worst in order (a) to appreciate and insist on having the better—the less damaging—side of it, and (b) in order to begin to get away from it."

What about social workers? How much help are they? "If they realize one needs help, they should give more personal attention. I was lucky with the one who finally helped me, but too often all I am to a social worker is a file—she has thousands of others. I'm only a job for her so it's meaningless for me. It's understandable, of course—it *is* their job. If they give too much—and some of them do—then it ruins them. If they don't they're useless. It's all wrong, really, because it's a profession only for those who are prepared to risk themselves. Social workers are basically lonely people, that's why they choose to do it. So, you see, they aren't whole either . . . it's the lame leading the blind."

What percentage of young prostitutes, in her opinion, are drug addicts or alcoholics? "I think most young girls in prostitution drink up to a point. I know that specially while I was doing the streets and the porno-bars, I always had one or two drinks before starting . . . otherwise I couldn't even begin."

And drugs? "In my experience, very few take drugs. It's too damaging; pimps know it: At best, it's a wearying business, you very quickly get to look older than you are. With drugs, it's disastrous. I think a book like *Christine F* is misleading. I think only the tiniest percentage of young prostitutes are addicts. Most of them are doing it for the same reasons that I did: conflict at home, a desperate need for friendships, relationships, a need for freedom combined with the obvious lack of judgment one has at that age; and a total absence of choice—no alternative."

So what now? What does she think of herself now? She smiled. "Well, I'm prettier now—I looked really awful, quite awful at fourteen. I felt so ugly. Now I don't feel ugly. I think I'll make it," she said. "Partly, I suppose, because I'm lucky and strong. Partly it is because in the final analysis, my mother stuck to me; even though I didn't see her, she was always there. One does have to have . . . one simply *must* have someone whom you belong with." ("I spent Christmas with my family," she wrote to me early in 1983. "The first time in years. It was wonderful.")

13

Ruprecht

Ruprecht, a boy with a decidedly superior IQ, had no illusions whatsoever about his future. "I will never, never get away from the scene," he said. "Nobody does; the moment I committed myself to this way of life, there was no way back."

We were sitting in—let us call it the Tent—a boy-prostitute "joint" in a side street in Berlin's centre. There were two rooms, eight or ten tables, the customers mostly boys between twelve and sixteen. A few girls—all of them under age—waft in and out, pretty girls who go from table to table, embrace, and are embraced by the boys, kisses on both cheeks and casual hugs. They are pals. The boys refer to them as "brides", slang for available girls. It is very obvious from the way they act and talk to them that few if any of the boys are homosexuals. But the men who come in—who walk slowly through the rooms, who look from face to face and sit down when some signal passes, perceptible to them, not to me—they are all gay, and are here for one purpose only. "*Kalbfleisch*," says Ruprecht tersely, deliberately crude, to impress or shock me.

I was brought to the Tent by a man we will call Fried, a high school teacher who had been introduced to me by friends, and who had offered to help me meet a boy to whom I could talk.

It was to take days, or rather several nights, of "doing" the Berlin scene with Fried before I realized that he himself was gay. It was because of Fried that I was actually able to witness both the nature and the consequences of homosexual relationships between young boys and their teachers.

Ruprecht—he was usually called Rupp or Ruppie, depending on the person or occasion—was wafer-thin. His jeans were so tight they would have cut into him, if there had been anything to cut into. He wore a tight-fitting white sweater which further underlined his skinniness.

He had thick wavy brown hair—dull, not very clean—and a carefully cultivated small moustache. He looked older than his fifteen years and very pale. There was moisture on his forehead and between his little moustache and nose. He seemed febrile, ill, and indeed kept feeling his pulse, looking in a mirror, and leaning his head on his hands. The explanation was not long in coming; it never was with Ruppie, who is a very verbal young man. "*Ich bin jetzt up*," he said—"I'm high"—using, as they all do, the English word "up." He'd taken three doses of LSD over the past twenty-four hours, he said, certainly an exaggeration.

He asked me if I had ever tried LSD, "Because," he said agressively, "if you haven't tried it, you really have no right to write about it. Nobody can understand what it does who hasn't tried it."

Did he think, I said—a tired argument I had employed dozens of times—that in order to write about people who commit suicide, one has to have wanted to kill oneself?

Yes, he did think so, he said at once. "That, too, you cannot really understand if you haven't felt the urge yourself."

"You are talking shit, you know," said Fried. "Dopeshit. I hope you come down soon so that you make sense." He had told me in advance that the boy he wanted me to meet was a one-time pupil of his.

"I *am* coming down," Rupp said. "Can you feel how cold my hands are? They seem humid, don't they?" Yes, I said, they did. "But they aren't," he said, continuing his lesson. "They are completely dry." He went on observing himself closely over the next half-hour, encouraging us in the meantime, somewhat condescendingly, to talk to each other, or to passing friends. "Now I'm down," he suddenly said, and true, his face was no longer so pale or sweating and his voice was darker, quicker.

"How often are you taking the muck now?" Fried asked—we had ordered sausages, bread, and apple juice. "Not often," Rupp replied. "A bride let me down yesterday and I talked to my mother on the phone."

God Almighty, I said to myself, here we go again. There was no need to ask any questions: parents came up in any conversation, within minutes.

"My father runs a factory. As an accountant," he specified, still

unasked. "He keeps changing jobs to 'better himself,' as he puts it."
Rupp's mother works, and always has worked since before he was
born, as a book-keeper at the local authority. "My father," he said
suddenly, with great intensity—"I look him in the face and say to him,
'You are *nothing*. You are nothing to me.' "

It is not possible to judge whether a child who at once brings up the
invariable source of trouble and focus of bitterness is trying one out, or
responding to need and intuition. All one can and must do is accept,
and follow the lead.

But why did he feel this, and since when? I asked dutifully.

"Since I was twelve and saw him beat my mother."

Was that the first time his father had beaten his mother, the first
time Rupp had witnessed it? "No, I'd seen it before. But this was the
worst time and this time I was big and he didn't realize I was. There was
a big knife on the table: I took it and stuck it into his stomach."

What happened? "Nothing happened," he said. His mother told
the police it was an accident; his father spent some time in hospital.
And from that moment on, his father had never laid hands on his
mother, or on Ruppie himself.

Ah, because before that he had beaten Rupp? "Yes, always, since I
was small."

Badly? "Pretty badly. With a strap."

For what sort of offence was he beaten like that? "Oh, everything,
anything. If I got something dirty; if I came late to table; or if I got
home later than ordered."

And his mother, did she beat him, too? "No, never." He loves his
mother more than anyone in the world. He does not feel very loving
towards his sister, who is four years older than he is. "She always got
everything she wanted, she was never beaten, and she went to *Kindergarten*, I didn't." And the sister, he added at once, always had friends.
"I didn't. I was always alone. A loner."

"From what age were you a loner?"

"Three, four."

How could he have been a loner at three or four, I asked. He must
have gone to *Kindergarten*, too?

"I didn't. My father tried to make me, but as soon as he left,
schwupp, I was gone again."

Gone where? "Home. I had my key, always since I was three, on a
string around my neck."

"At three?" I said incredulously. "Don't be silly. It's unthinkable, to leave a tiny boy like that alone at home, day after day. Didn't your mother do something about it?"

He shrugged. "What could she do? She wanted to work; what was she to do with me? They tried to force me, but it didn't work."

(Ruprecht was to prove to me, too, that his will prevailed. I was never allowed to see his parents. "I just can't do it to them," he said, surprising me as he would do quite often. "I've already done enough to them.")

Why, I asked, did he think now that he had been so stubborn about the *Kindergarten*?

"I was determined to bend people to my will."

That was absurd, I said again. For a child of three or four, there had to be other reasons. That was just how he saw it now. Fried had been very good, very silent. He understood that I wanted to conduct this conversation in my own way, but now he came into it. "Tell her," he said. "You were suspicious."

"Suspicious, nonsense," said Rupp. "I was scared."

Scared of what? "I had heard a lot of bad things about the *Kindergarten* . . . " He paused. Then "I don't know why I said I was scared," he retracted. "I've never been scared in my life."

"Except as a three-year-old," I said.

"Well, not really scared. Let's say I was very reserved. The other children—I didn't want them."

What he had wanted was his mother. All her attention, her attention without the presence of his father, the hated interloper. And she had never understood this, had never taken the essential step of staying at home for this needy child, at least until he was ready to venture out on his own. And his father (who though obviously fairly brutal had given his family a "good" and stable home) had never understood that the most important thing for his son was not his intelligence which, oddly enough, the father had recognized very early, but his emotional needs. By openly mistreating the mother the little boy worshipped, he had violated these needs time and again, thereby losing the child for good before he had even grown to boyhood.

Rupp's social worker summed up the basic facts for me. The files confirmed that the very young parents (their daughter was born when the mother was seventeen, the father nineteen, and they were only twenty-one and twenty-three at Rupp's birth), both working full time, put the seven-month-old baby boy into an all-day crêche, leaving him in full-day child care through *Kindergarten* and school until he was nine years old.

"I think I ruined my parents' life," Ruprecht said. "Now they have calmed down a bit, but my mother is almost at the end of her nerves."

For the remainder of this first evening—another seven hours, through much of the night—Rupp told me all about his schooling. He had attended elementary and *Hauptschule* up to and including "eighth" class with "satisfactory" reports. Having begun his life on the scene—and homosexual prostitution—at twelve and a half, he had truanted increasingly over the last two years, and although considered capable of moving up into the ninth class, had left school and home at thirteen. Long before that, however, he had begun his sexual life, having his first experience with a girl at eleven. (Later on, I was able to check through my social worker friends that all this was true.)

"That's very young," I said. "Could you feel anything about her, as a person?"

"Yes, I liked her. She was twelve. But it didn't go on for long. After that I had a pretty Chinese girl, who was in my school—that lasted two and a half weeks. Then she stopped it."

Oh? Why? "Well, she was fifteen . . . "

"And?" No answer. Where did these encounters take place? "At my house. No reason why not," he remarked cynically. "There certainly wasn't anybody to stop me."

Was he happy with this girl? "No. She was a bit wild for me."

Wild? "A bit too passionate." Pause. "Let's say she expected something from me I couldn't—yet—really give her." Pause. "Today I could, but then . . . it was different."

He ran away the first time when he was twelve and a half? "That's right. I closed the door from outside. For two days. Then my daddy got me because I was too stupid and went where he knew I'd go; he beat me black and blue and I went back to school. In fact," he jumped ahead, "even when I left home entirely, I went at first pretty regularly to school."

"Your usual school? And still your parents didn't find you?"

"Oh, they found me all right, but I told my father not to try anything. If he did, I'd just leave again the next day."

"And during that time, where did you live?"

"Oh, with a homosexual man. He was twenty-five, a gentleman, you know; very nice, it was all right, I could go on with school. He took me there every morning on his way to the office."

Was this "homosexual gentleman" his first client then, at twelve and a half to thirteen?

"No, he wasn't my first. I had a few others before, but he was the first I lived with. It was a good year, a good memory for me. I stayed with him for almost a year, did the *Strich* from time to time to increase my takings, went to school and got a very good report that year."

The reason for the break-up of this oddly stable relationship was anything but what one might have expected. Ruprecht became keen on a girl, at thirteen. Again, she was older, but he thought she was as involved as he. When he told this story, very briefly, his voice trembled: before our eyes, this pseudo-sophisticated pseudo-amoral young man turned into an unhappy little boy. We waited quietly till he caught hold of himself. Fried had brought him a glass of beer, at which he sipped without enthusiasm.

"When was the last time you cried?" I asked. It was a long time before he answered—long meaning perhaps ten minutes, during which all of us sat in silence.

"I cried then," he finally said, his voice still not quite firm.

"Why? What happened—you were thirteen, weren't you?"

He answered in slang: "*Sie hat mir ein linkes Ding abgezogen.*" What it meant, I found out later, was a mixture of her having told him he was no good in bed and having gone off with another boy. He expanded this, no doubt in order to save face, by explaining that she was "no longer a girl," but a prostitute. "She wouldn't be a 'bride' any longer, and that really got to me where it counted, to put it plainly, and that's when I cried for the last time. Since then," long pause, "it isn't easy to make me cry."

Having left the twenty-five-year-old man—or been given his walking papers—Rupp's life changed with a vengeance. "All I did was hang around at the Zoo and then, well, that was the start of total *Stricher* life for me, sleeping with different clients every night—that is, if they let me sleep there."

When they did, what happened in the morning? "In the morning one is back on the street and looks for the next one."

This was only the second time that Fried intervened. "I can't stand this," he said suddenly and emotionally. "I can't listen to this."

"Why?" I asked, and finally understood: "Because a boy with whom I was for six years described it almost exactly the same way, and the boy I'm with now and whom I love, he said it too, and"—short hesitation—"it's just how I started, myself. It's awful to hear it."

"Well, the punters come—there's no shortage of them," Rupp continued, apparently indifferent to the interruption. "They come on foot, in cars, on motorbikes, you name it. Then one negotiates, what is wanted, you know, and the price . . . and then one goes along."

Do they all bargain? "Of course."

"I hate them," said Fried softly, almost a whisper, but Rupp took him up on it. "Well, who's going to volunteer more than he may have to?"

"I hate them," Fried repeated.

"Even though you are one of them yourself?" Rupp said, cruelly.

"Surely not?" I asked Fried. "Not like that?"

"Perhaps he isn't like that now," said Rupp. "But he was. You *were*," he accused Fried.

"I never behaved meanly to you," the teacher replied.

"Okay, okay, but somehow you are the same thing . . . "

"Yes, true, I'm gay."

"And somehow we too agreed on a price, didn't we?"

The underlying tension I had not understood had exploded. "Yes, but I know, I know that in principle all I wanted from you was that you should be with me. . ."

"I learnt my lesson all right," the boy said bitterly. "Now I'm a pro."

"I don't believe it. You can't, you wouldn't be; you wouldn't sink that low," said Fried.

"Do you want to come to the station with me?" Rupp said. "You'll find out in a minute."

"But Rupp, you're a *person*, you've got a *mind*; you can't."

"Are you kidding? What's the difference between you and me? Haven't you got a mind?"

"Yes, but I'm older."

"Yes, and that's the only difference between us."

"No," Fried said in a tone of despair, "that isn't the only difference. You'll never reach my age. What you are doing is totally self-destructive."

For a moment Rupp was silent. "You have no idea," he said then, "the hatred I feel for people . . . anybody . . . people who didn't really do that much to me. It's the sort of feeling that makes me want to kill every one of them. . . ."

"Yes," Fried said sadly. "The only thing is, you don't mean *those* people. You mean something quite different."

"I know one thing, one thing I know and that's all: I've proved to my parents . . ." he paused, "I have proved I can make it without them."

"Ruppie," Fried said, his face drawn. "You are not trying to say, are you, you're not saying it's my fault, are you? It isn't through me, not through me you got to this point? Look, how long ago is it when we were together?"—"Half, quarter of a year ago?" They were talking simultaneously now, one sentence running into another, as if both of them knew what the other would say. "But look," said Fried, "we had . . . how shall I put it?"—"Don't put it," Rupp interrupted—"We had a pretty good thing," Fried went on without listening, "warm, human; you remember, don't you?"—"Ah, the hell with it," said Rupp. "But dammit, as 'a pro,' as you call it," Fried went on angrily, "that isn't offering or giving: you can't. You mustn't. You must *use* them, use them and throw them away . . . "—"Really?" Rupp sneered, with heavy irony. "Thanks."

And suddenly he was bitterly angry. "Would you like me to enumerate for you what one does, what one must do if that is what one does?" Fried shook his head and covered his ears. Rupp reached over and roughly, almost violently, pulled his hands down. "You listen. You listen. You know, but you listen. One *works*, to put it in plain German. And in plain German, at the station or the bars, one does it for twenty and fifty Deutschmarks and in ninety-nine percent of the cases one sucks them, and the other percent, one is buggered by them—those are the ones who pay least. They want most and pay least, the pigs . . . " He stopped. All three of us were silent.

"I myself," he went on later, quietly now and conciliatorily, "I didn't do this for long. I found myself a rich one [he named the man, a well-known Berlin millionaire] who became a regular, and I had my two-hundred Deutschmarks several times a week. For that, of course, I didn't mind what I did and did it [anal sex, he meant]. But even rich people like that haggle over every penny—you say fifty, they say forty-five, just to prove something. Still, one has to think that that's for an hour's work, and who gets fifty Deutschmarks for an hour's work? Of course, there are places here in Berlin where they can't even get a hello under a hundred."

"Oh?" I said. "What are those?"

"Places," he said vaguely.

"Come on, Rupp," I said. "There isn't anything I can do with 'places.' "

"For Christ's sake," he said. "*Puffs* in good German."

"Okay then—a brothel for men, nothing under a hundred, right? And can any *Strich* boy go there?"

"No, not a bit of it, only with connections and you have to be of age, because the police, they know these places—the Vice Squad goes regularly—they love it."

So that was not the sort of place *he* could use?

"No, I couldn't and I wouldn't, because there you *have* to do anal and I won't any more, I simply wouldn't."

What Rupp ended up doing was the minimum in order to live. "I did two or three a day and had my regular hundred or a hundred and fifty, that was enough for my room [he gave me the names of the Pensions he used]. Food I didn't have to worry about because lots of punters like you to eat with them, and I had enough left for the occasional grass or trip." For the rest, he said, he led a normal life: kept himself clean (in public baths at the *Bahnhof Zoo*), washed his hair whenever he could, i.e., whenever he stayed over with a man who had a bathroom and dryer. Fried came in here: "I noticed at school," he said, "boys might have dirty fingernails, but on the whole they are cleaner than girls." "True," said Rupp. "Though Miri, who I went to school with and who is about to work for me, she is very clean—I've got to give her that."

"Are you seriously telling me that you've become a pimp?" exclaimed Fried.

"I'm not telling *you* anything. I'm just saying what's what."

"But why on earth don't you come back to school?" cried Fried. "You know you could catch up in weeks. Everybody would help you."

"I'm sure. Specially you."

"Rupp," Fried said quietly, and the boy briefly, very briefly, touched his hand.

"Sorry," he said. "I know you mean it. But I can't. No more."

"Why?"

"Yes, why?" I asked. "Tell us."

"That's what a lot of people ask, but they don't really want to know."

"*We* want to know," I said, and he pretended not to hear but went on anyway: "I tell them, in order to make money."

"Okay," said Fried, "so you need money. You know perfectly well that at fifteen, if you don't want to live at home, the Berlin Youth Authority gives you money for rent and living as long as you undertake not to prostitute or pimp, and to go to school. What have you say to that?"

"I've got this to say: that I can't live on approximately 9,000 Deutschmarks [about £2,800 or $5,000] a year, which is what they give. I suggest nobody can. Over the past year, 'working', I earned about 45,000 Deutschmarks. And anyway, as I told you, it's over for me. I have two girls now, both beautiful, blond and fourteen. At the very minimum, they are going to earn two-hundred and fifty Deutschmarks a day—which I will split with them," he ended provocatively.

"Ha!" said Fried.

"*Which I will split with them*," he repeated. "Also counting only on their three hundred days out of the year, this means that each of them will have 37,500 and I will have 75,000 Deutschmarks. . . . "

"All this is *shit*," said Fried. "It is shit, you know it's shit, I know it's shit and Gitta knows it's shit. So let's stop the shit and go home." He got up. I pulled him back down and suggested we part in a different sort of mood and meet again the next day in my hotel—or rather, later that afternoon, for by this time it was 4.30 am—in order to give us a change of atmosphere.

Ruprecht refused a lift; he was going to stay a while. "I've got to get over you two." He smiled crookedly—not a real smile.

"You'd really rather I didn't come this afternoon, wouldn't you?" said Fried, who had offered to drive me back to my hotel. "I'll have to ask you to forgive me if I insist on coming."

"Are you afraid of what he might say?"

He shook his head, his face pale and his hands on the steering wheel tense as we sat in the car. "There is nothing more he could say that is worse than what he has already said. You know that, don't you?" I nodded.

"He couldn't hurt me more, he couldn't make me feel any worse than I do this minute. Nobody could . . . except . . . " and he named the boy he was living with, also a pupil, but already nineteen years old. "I want to be there," he went on very succinctly, "because that's the arrangement we made, you and I. When you are through with your work, you said, there had to be somebody who would go on with him, and I said I would, because I really and truly feel that if anyone can help—more than you, forgive me for saying it—it is I. There is still something between me and that boy."

I nodded. There certainly was, from both sides. "I give you here and now my solemn promise, I swear it: I would never, never in my life touch him again . . . " he interrrupted his words and thoughts. ". . . except perhaps . . . I must say that, to remain honest with you, one day perhaps to hold him, just hold him if he breaks and needs to be held"—he laid his hand on mine, just for a second—"held by a father," he said. "A father."

We sat there, longer. I would accept his request, for I believed him. But there was something else to say. "You cannot stay a teacher in a school where there are boys," I said. "It's impossible. It's wrong."

"I know," he said, and drove me home.

(Later I would find out that, unknown to him, steps had already been taken by others who had the children's well-being *and* his own at heart to change his appointment to a different establishment, where he could work but neither cause nor come to harm. He was a first-class teacher.)

Fried arrived first, at two-thirty that afternoon, and the desk clerks at the Kempinski in Berlin, where I was staying, could hardly have found anything to object to, either about him or about Rupp, who arrived fifteen minutes later.

Fried had on his baggy trousers and suede jacket, but he had obviously had a haircut and wore a brilliantly white ironed shirt and the most conservative plain-coloured wool tie. Rupp had gone one further—we now saw where at least some of his money had gone. His hair and his shoes were spanking clean, he wore expensive, beautifully cut jeans, a white and beige-striped shirt that could have come from Hermès, a silk cravat I would have loved to duplicate for my husband, and a tweed sports jacket that could have been made to measure by an English tailor.

He put on a convincing act of nonchalance but watched my reaction carefully when he entered.

"Christ!" I exclaimed, "you look *fantastic!*" He beamed and said, in a tone that would have been Etonian had he been speaking English, that yes, thank you very much, he'd love tea with lemon and some sandwiches as he "hadn't lunched."

The atmosphere *was* different: I had Vivaldi playing softly on my radio; we lounged in deep chairs (though Ruppie, taking off his English jacket, soon sat cross-legged on the floor). Two waiters—it's rarely one at the Kempinski—appeared, wheeling a trolley on which, along with a pink rose in a stemmed vase, was a repast called tea that would have fed eight with ease (it would last us until 10 pm). Both young men, left-radical or not, quite obviously and openly enjoyed every aspect of this beguiling luxury.

What followed the appearance of the outrageously prodigious feast was, not unnaturally, a political discussion that lasted (it seemed to me) hours and threatened repeatedly to put me to sleep.

"I am very bored," I finally said, "with all this stuff about the bigwigs in government who are growing fat on the taxes which you, Rupp, after all, have never paid. In your case, Fried, teachers, I happen to know, are very well paid in Germany; you have a car; you no doubt *want* decent roads, council housing, unemployment and health insurances and —as long as they don't interfere with you personally— even police."

Fried took it well, Ruppie didn't, but it served the purpose of getting us back to our subject. "It's easy for you to talk," said Rupp (Etonian tones forgotten). "Look at how you live."

"Yes indeed," I said. "And look how I work to afford it."

"What do you think *I* do?" he said, quick as a whip. "Do you honestly think that your work is harder than mine?"

"It's different?" I suggested.

"Are you saying that I haven't achieved anything?" roared Rupp. "How not, how not? If I have stopped prostitution, then I have achieved"—he stammered in his fury—"have achieved what I wanted. That I *do not go any more* on the *Strich*, that I personally have given it up."

"Ah," said Fried, "you think it's an achievement to have given it up yourself, but to get two fourteen-year-old girls to do it for you? That's your ambition, right, and that's what you call achievement?"

"I am not bloody forcing any. girl," Rupp said. "They came to me and offered."

"You're just justifying yourself," said Fried. "They don't know any better, poor little fools. But you do."

"You still don't understand, do you?" Rupp's voice was suddenly heavy and sad. He got up, walked over to the window and looked out at the wet dark street, and the lights across the parking lot. "You *can't* stop anybody," he said then, turning around, looking and sounding like a twenty-year-old. "I had to learn. They'll have to learn, too, the only way one learns, by getting sick of it, sick to the bottom of one's soul." He walked over to the straight chair at the small desk, turned it around and sat down, very straight, very thin in his beautiful striped shirt. "I know: I know because I know how it happened to me—what happened inside me when I detested the clients, how sick it made me, how I had to force myself, with all my strength hiding what I felt, because otherwise I would have lost them.

"Of course it's bad, more than that, it's hell on earth, that's what it is. Summer or winter, there you are, standing there, waiting. There is nothing else. There is nothing else to hope for or depend on; you can't do anything else, because in order to be able to stand the pace, you must catch a few moments' sleep when you can, morning, afternoon, whatever. Because evening, as sure as God made little apples, you've got to be back there, on the *Strich*, always on the *Strich*, always the same horror . . . " he paused, pulled out a clean folded handkerchief and wiped his forehead. "If I were four, five, six, seven years younger," he said, looking at the grey traces of sweat on his white hankie, "if I had another chance, I would do things differently . . . "

I got up, leaned over and put my arm around his shoulders. He no sooner felt the contact than his head fell against me. "You can," I said. "You can do it differently. The chance exists; one can make it exist."

"What you don't know," he said into my side, "nor you," towards Fried, "I did try, for four months . . . "

"What? What did you try, Rupp?" I asked.

"To study."

"What did you study?"

"I went to night school, I studied, I learned hard but . . . after four months"—he pulled his head away and sat up—"I was back on the scene. You think it's so easy. It isn't. I told you, once one is in it, one can't really get out."

"But how did it happen?"

Again he wiped his face with the now crumpled handkerchief. "I had a bride [he had fallen back into the usual slang]. It was okay and then she dropped me. And so I said to myself, now they can all lick my arse."

"But wait a minute," I said. "Why did she leave you?"

"How could I manage to go to night school, hiding my age, therefore not able to get help from the Youth people?" he asked tiredly. "How do you think I could manage? The only way I could manage was the occasional *Strich*. Well, if she couldn't understand that, if she couldn't take that, then, as I say, the hell with her."

"Oh my God," said Fried, his voice gentle, but he didn't move away from his chair and I too had sat down again.

"My father," started Rupp—"my parents, they knew of course, about the *Strich*, already that kills my mother. They don't know about . . . the pimping and they must never know that. My father hates such people. You say I haven't achieved anything," he said, turning to Fried, his voice suddenly not even fifteen . . . almost back to what it may have been before it broke. "I *did* stop my father beating my mother. I told him I'd kill him if he ever did it again. He knows I would. And I would. But it's true," he went on, although we hadn't said a word, "simply proving to my parents that I could make it without them hasn't really got me very far, has it?"

"No," said Fried, softly. "But, Ruppie, it wasn't all your fault. They do have to shoulder their share."

"No," he said, thoughtfully. "I don't want to blame my parents for everything any more. I have to take responsibility for what I do. Sure, they are to blame for a lot, but still, my decisions are my own and if they have harmed me . . . well. . . . "

I brought a bottle of champagne and some orange juice from the fridge and we drank and ate peanuts. "What I'm thinking," said Rupp, sounding quiet and adult, "what in the final analysis has harmed me most, has hurt most, is that I was exploited. I exploit others, of course, but I think they exploited me more than I them. I've been thinking . . . and let's now leave my parents and my sister out of it, out of everything . . . but I was thinking of the girls, the two girls. They want to work for me; there's no stopping them. If I say no, they'll do it on their own and fall in with someone else." He shrugged. "I know the macks, I know who they'll fall in with. If I take them on"—he hesitated—"if I take them on and help them . . . "

"Yes?" prompted Fried.

"I'm just wondering . . . I'm just talking, you know, wondering. If I were to *help* them, I mean will myself to help them, never exploit them, not allow others to exploit them either, it would be a funny way, but is that perhaps then also my helping myself?"

And that was Rupp's decision. It seems an odd one to feel some hope for, but when we said good-bye, I did.

Part Three

GREAT BRITAIN
The Game

14

Nellie's Story

The trial had lasted two and a half days. The jury returned after one
hour's deliberation. Nellie, aged twenty, was convicted of murder and
one minute later was given the mandatory life sentence.

It was two minutes past mid-day when the small girl with long limp
hair and a nervous smile, flanked by two police officers, left the
courtroom. GIGGLING GIRL KILLER GETS LIFE was the headline in London's evening paper that afternoon.

I telephoned her parents that night, at their home in a small
Scottish town. The phone was answered before the first ring had
finished. "I've been sitting here waiting," said Nellie's mother, who is
a little delicate woman with a light, warm voice. "I did so hope you'd
call."

I told her as gently as I could. "Life?" she said, unbelieving. "Oh
my God!" Then there was silence, except that in the background I
could hear the happy, child-like voice of Nellie's sister, beautiful Janie,
now nineteen, with the mind of a five-year-old.

"I'm holding onto myself," Nellie's mother finally said, "but her
father, he's been crying all day . . . "

"All the tears in the world won't get me out of here," Nellie wrote me
from Holloway Prison, outside London, ten days later. " . . . I've
really done it this time, haven't I. What did my parents ever do to
deserve this?" And she was right to wonder.

When I first met Nellie, she was seventeen and looked even
younger. She was small, compact, with tiny breasts, black, shiny,
short-cut hair, a lovely complexion, brilliantly blue eyes and long, soft,

black lashes. She wore no make-up whatever, but was dressed dramatically in black jeans, a black turtle-neck sweater, a black jacket and
boots. Her knife—which I was to find out later was always carried in
her boot—that too had a black handle, though it was probably coinci-
dence.

By the time I met Nellie, she had been "on the game", in Scotland
and in London, for six years, she said, since she was eleven. According
to the story she told in minute detail over our initial few days together,
she had first run away from home at the age of eight. Nellie, as it turned
out during the months we worked together, is both the most honest girl
and the most accomplished fantasy-weaver I met in the years I spent
preparing this book. Of all the youngsters I talked with, she was the
most desperate and the most able to mask and hide her despair. But
her knowledge and understanding of London's teenage street life was
phenomenal, and her compassion and generosity towards youngsters
with the same dire problems she herself had faced a few years earlier
was unique.

For the year before our meeting, Nellie's most frequent "stand"
was right smack in the centre of Kensington, one of London's most
desirable residential districts. Here, in front of the Gloucester Road
Underground station, the girls sat on or leaned against a stone border
that frames a carefully maintained flower-bed (just as the boy-
prostitutes in Hamburg line up like birds on a telegraph wire along a
wall in front of the main railway station). At the time when I was
researching, they were there during almost all of the day and the early
part of the night— none of them older than fifteen and most of them
younger. Now, two and a half years later, they have moved north to
King's Cross. In Gloucester Road there used to be a good deal of irony
in the contrast between the care lavished by the rich Kensington
Borough Council on the bright red geraniums, the petunias, the
pansies and the red, white and pink Busy Lizzies, and the public
indifference of which the children were—and still are—the victims.

"There are loads of little girls here," said Nellie. "I had a chat with
one last night, Katie, she's thirteen and she's been on the game for two
years. I asked her whether she'd come and talk to you. I said, 'She only
wants to talk with you, she's not going to fucking *eat* you.' But no way.
She's fucking terrified."

What this thirteen-year-old—I did meet her later—was terrified of
was being arrested as an underage vagrant and sent back to where she
came from. Her mother had died years before and she had been put

into a children's home rather than with foster-parents because her father, who couldn't both look after her and work, wanted to see her regularly. And he did, every weekend, until she finally ran away. No doubt the social workers, in their statutory enthusiasm for maintaining family relationships, did everything to facilitate the meetings. "They used to drive me to me dad's home," the child said bitterly. What they didn't know—one wonders how they could miss the tell-tale signs—was that when she was nine, the father had raped her, and from then on had intercourse with her every weekend and all holidays.

"When I met Katie first, it was in the Piccadilly Underground station," said Nellie. "She was filthy, man—she'd been sleeping there for three nights. I said, 'How old are you?' and she told me, and I said, 'Fuck it, but you're only a baby,' and I took her back to my flat [her flat was a room 6 feet by 8 in a condemned building in Kensington, a bathroom with a rusty tub on the lower landing]. She had a bath and something to eat and I gave her some clothes and —it was only lunchtime, man, I had to go back out to work—I told her to get some sleep and we'd talk later.

" 'I'm going to do what you do,' she said, half asleep but still in that fucking cheeky way. And I said, 'I'll fucking bust you first,' and she started to cry and said, 'I told you, I can't go home.'

"I put her to bed and tucked her in after she'd had a bit more of a cry, and she went right off to sleep and I went off to work. And when I came back, she wasn't there. Well, she came back in at three in the morning with about a hundred and fifty quid and tried to give me half of it. Of course, she was clean, you know, and had clean clothes on. She looked real good. She had guts: she'd gone straight back to Piccadilly and found herself four punters that first night. If I'd told her to go away, she would only have had a rougher time—she certainly couldn't go back with that father around. So she stayed with me for a little while.

"There were already two of us in there—me and my boyfriend, Rick. She slept on the floor, but at least it was clean and she had somewhere to stay. And I opened a bank account for her and she put half of her earnings into it every day. Of course, she doesn't look so wonderful any more now, after two years—thirteen and she looks about (what do *you* think?) nineteen, twenty? But she's got her own room and money in the bank and, as you could see, she's very determined. She is so scared, she hasn't any choice. When you met her, did you see how she goes into a cold sweat and starts to stammer when you ask her about her dad? I don't mention him any more, but I did at first, because I was curious. But it scared me, the way she'd . . . you know . . . almost go into a fit. So I stopped."

But Nellie is obviously selective about whom she encourages. "A few weeks ago, there were two girls in the pub and one of them was crying and all, and I said, 'What the fuck's wrong with you?' And she said, 'The hotel man—he's trying to put us on the game.' There are these two hotels in Earl's Court, and a Scottish guy works in one of them. Well, he got the manager's watch and some money out of the safe, you know, and he put it in the girls' luggage and then he conveniently found it. And then he went to them and said he wouldn't say where he found it if they got him money. So they said, 'How can we get you money—we are only kids, man,' so he said he'd show them. One of them was a fucking *virgin*, man! I told them to stay put, not to *move*, and I went out with a punter and I gave them the money and took them to Euston and told them to get the fuck home. They really were too young—they weren't the kind of chicks who could handle it, you know. And they went.

"There are thousands of wee runaway lassies in London, man," she said. "You usually very soon meet some 'kind' chap who'll point you in the right direction. But most of them don't even need pointing, 'cos if a chick's already having intercourse before she comes to London . . ." She paused. "Girls don't keep their virginity any more, you know," she explained earnestly, "so that really applies to most of them, and then, you know, it isn't *so* difficult. Because, for most of them, at twelve, thirteen or fourteen, what they had at home with their boyfriends wasn't so fantastic either, you know. I mean, they do it to be grown-up, or to show off to their pals. If they have any sense, they're usually sorry afterwards.

"Anyway, they run away, right? And the first thing they need is money. They head straight for Piccadilly, everybody does: the bright lights, you see. And then they spend what they've got. On hamburgers, most likely. They're always hungry and it's . . . it's a sort of freedom, you know, to go into a place and order food. And they spend the rest on amusement arcades, Cokes—perhaps a movie. They don't think, you know. They just live for the moment. And a few hours later, they suddenly realize they haven't got any money. A chick—no matter how small she is—if she's got a decent enough body, some guy will pick her up. Oh yes, they know how old the lassies are. Guys aren't stupid, you know, they can tell the difference between a twelve- or thirteen-year-old kid and a seventeen-year-old woman. There's a big difference in the way you act, your attitude, whether you fall about giggling, whether you can have a conversation. It shows. Sure, good guys will try to persuade small kids to go home, but there are enough bastards, and it's bastards, always bastards, the small ones end up with. . . "

I met Debbie by pre-arrangement, through a detached social worker, in a snack-bar in the Earl's Court Road—a lively street in the Middle of Kensington which with its many snack-bars, pubs and small hotels had been a centre of child prostitution for a long time. She is the middle one of three children. Her home is in the north of England where her father runs a small electronics factory. She was fifteen when we met, and had run away from home for the eighth time. It was the morning after her thirteenth birthday, but because she had stolen a pen at Woolworth's two weeks before, her parents had cancelled her birthday plans. (Her mother has been repeatedly hospitalized for nervous troubles, her father is a strict Methodist.) Debbie arrived at Euston Station one late evening, with £5 she had stolen from her mother and a few pence in change in her pocket. It was the first time she had run to London. Her seven other escapes (again classic) had been to cities nearer home.

She consulted the Euston hotel information office about cheap lodgings, and was directed to a small hotel in Earl's Court. When I checked this part of her story, it proved quite accurate: five hotels in the Earl's Court area were among those the information personnel regularly recommended at that time. "What are we supposed to do?" they asked when challenged by one of the social workers who helped me in the research. "We have listings of inexpensive accommodation and give people the information they ask for. We're not equipped to act as police officers or social workers."

"I just fell into bed," said Debbie, "I was bushed." She is about 5 feet 4, thin, with curly black hair which looks very much at odds with her face. Her natural colour is blond—"almost white," she said. "It's horrible; my dad always said I looked like an albino." She still spoke with that special melodious northern lilt where every sentence ends in a half question.

Debbie had spent the next day—the sun was shining—walking and "stuffing" herself with hamburgers and American ice-cream. "Piccadilly, Leicester Square, Regent Street, Bond Street, Oxford Street," she said. "And Buckingham Palace. All the places I'd always heard about. It was so exciting. The shops were fantastic." By the time she got back to Earl's Court that night, she had £1 12 shillings left. The next day, Sunday, she walked, too. "I went to Hyde Park; I listened to the speakers. I lay down in the grass in the sun. Yes, some guys tried to pick me up, but I told them to go away."

In the late afternoon she went back to the hotel and went to bed. "I only had 40p [pence] left and I didn't know anybody." The very next morning she found out what London meant to a thirteen-year-old on the run. "The hotel man came in my room at eight o'clock. He didn't even knock, he just used his pass key. He said I owed over fifteen pounds." [The £5 a night charge is often a ploy. Once these hotels know a girl is on the game, the price of the room may go as high as £100 a week.] I said, "My God, I have only 40p left,' I was so stupid, I thought I had to tell him—I thought it would be dishonest not to. I said, could I work it off? I asked him whether I could clean rooms in his hotel till I found a job. He said," she laughed bitterly, "you know what the bastard said? He said, 'I'm not allowed by law to employ you—you are underage.' Of course, he could see I was. I looked a kid—my God, did I just. Anyway, he said I shouldn't be so silly, that it was easy to make money. This was *London*, man, he said, and I wasn't a bad looker; he reckoned I ought to be able to make a hundred pounds a day without trying. Yes, I knew what he meant. My mum had told me often enough I'd end up a whore."

Although she had had "a few boyfriends," as Debbie said, these had been hapless sexual experiences. "I told the man I wouldn't even know how to start. So he said he'd send somebody up, but that I was not to be stupid; by lunchtime he wanted his fifteen pounds or he'd get the police." Again she laughed her unmerry laugh. "The *police*—and my God, I believed him. Anyway, ten minutes later a man came to my room. He was a foreigner, I don't know what—Turkish, Arab—I don't even know now."

What was he like to her? How did he behave? She shrugged. "I think he'd been told he was my first; He was allright, you know . . . he didn't . . . hurt me or anything. I was so scared I was sweating all over, but he didn't say nothing, he didn't talk any that I remember. We just did it and he gave me ten pounds."

Debbie had been on the game for almost two years by the time I met her. "Once you've done it a couple of times, it doesn't seem so bad," she said. At fifteen, her minimum per client—"on bad nights, in the winter" as she put it—was £15. And she learned all the tricks: carrying condoms for the punters; chatting them up; sounding merry and vulgar—"They like that," she said and added, with horrible wisdom, "specially the posher ones. They must think it'll make it different, different from their wives, I mean." She guffawed again. "It doesn't. There *is* no difference; they are just getting their rocks off, whether with me or with their wives, what the hell. And anyway . . ." she added (a remark made by almost every girl I talked with), "wives are just as much prostitutes. They just do it for jewellery and furs or whatever. In the end I'm more honest. I do it for cash."

But how did she feel about it all? Couldn't she possibly go home? "Never," she said. Her parents knew she was in London and okay that's all they needed to know. "And they know now that I can make it without them." (That horrible sentence I was to hear time and again.) "I should probably have left much sooner." She suddenly sounded very grown-up and oddly reasonable. "It would have been better." But couldn't she get out of this life? Get a job now she had reached the legal age; learn something?

"I suppose I could," she said, listlessly. "Anyway, I'll get a job sometime. I won't always be doing this." And she added with false bravado: "*I'm* not going to turn into an old slag."

"She will," said Nellie, who knew Debbie as she knew everybody in Kensington. "They all turn into slags."

"What sort of child *can* handle it, at eleven or twelve?" I asked.

"Nobody, really. They can *do* it if—like for Katie, too—the pressure is strong enough and they have some brains. But unless they stop in time—Nellie was always realistic and wise about everyone except herself—"it ruins them. You'll never stop it," she went on, "because there's always one man in every—I don't know—hundred, say, that likes to go to bed with a real wee lassie. And there'll always be runaways."

Because of Nellie's exceptional know-how and the relationship we developed, she (along with Elana McCreaner, the social worker through whom I had met her) became my guide in London's teenage underworld. As far as others were concerned whether children or young people her own age—everything Nellie described, undertook for me, or promised, turned out to be true and reliable. About herself, it was a different matter. Here her capacity for interweaving the strict truth and quite extravagant lies with perfect aplomb was astonishing. Four violent years later—after she had killed—her mental capacities by then dimmed by alcohol and fear, she would fatally misjudge the effect of her fantasies, which had by that time become second nature. By then accounts she gave of her life and feelings to two psychiatrists appointed by the defence and to the prosecution proved so diametrically different that her lawyers would decide they would only confuse the jury and be worse than useless in her defence.

In my work with her, it took me weeks to realize that some of her tales had to be fantasy; and it was literally years before (with her help) I finally unravelled her story.

Her parents, she told me, hadn't been strict in the way a lot of Scottish parents are strict. Her father was a Roman Catholic of Italian extraction, "a very handsome man, and a bit soppy like Italians are." Her mother was pure Scots and Church of Scotland, and had only beaten her once—"I mean, really *beaten*. That was when I was eight, because I was running around with a crowd of boys. I was a tomboy, you know? Well, I was running with these boys, and they decided to break into a factory, a lemonade factory . . ."

"But you were *eight*?" I said, incredulously. "Is that what all of them were?"

"There was nobody younger than eight," she said. "Some were older—fifteen, sixteen. Anyway, we got caught. But because I'd never been in trouble, and because of my family—we were quite well off and money counts, you know—nothing happened to me. A couple of them got sent away, and some got put on probation, but not me. The police came to the house and said, 'We might have to charge her,' and my father said, 'Could I have a quiet word with you, in the next room?' And because my uncle had been a chief constable of Glasgow and all that, they just went away."

One of Nellie's brothers had been part of this youthful factory break-in gang. "My mother took a strap to my brother and a strap to me. It took about three weeks for the bruises to heal. Anyway, I ran away and came down here. . . . "

"How does an eight-year-old girl run away?" I asked.

"I hitched it," she said.

"But you must have been tiny?"

"Yes, I was about *that* size," she said, holding her hand less than four feet from the floor. "The lorry drivers said, 'Where're you going?' and I said, 'I am going to my auntie's in London'—because I was always an imaginative child, you know. And they said, 'Didn't yer mem 'n dad give you train fare?'—'Oh yeah,' I answered, 'but I want to keep that, I don't want to spend it.' I reckon they thought a kid that young, you can't just leave her, so I got really good lifts, you know. They were arranging lifts for me at the caffs where they stopped, and they brought me food and were real nice. I only had sixty pence in my pocket. Anyway, the last one dropped me in London, at Swiss Cottage—that's where a friend of my sister's lived, I told him she was my aunty.

"I told her I'd run away and she said, 'Look, do you want to go back?' and I said, 'Oh no, no way,' and she said, 'Well, phone them anyway,' so I called and just said I'd got to London all right, and put the phone down. And a bit later, my mother phoned up this girl—it was the only place she could think of—and I was in bed, but the girl, not being able to lie, told her I was there. And the next day they came down and collected me and I went back. I was fucking unhappy."

Although I would discover, as the days went by, that as a result of good Scots schooling Nellie could speak and write the purest of pure English, her everyday language was peppered with colloquialisms and four-letter words. Did she use words like that, at that age too, I asked. She sounded horrified. "Oh no, never! I never swore that way . . . I had great respect for my parents."

In her family, she said, they had all been pretty nice to each other. She had only heard her parents argue three times in her whole life, "Oh, they fought all right, they fought like everybody else's parents. But usually, if they were going to have an argument—that's what I think was wrong with my parents"—she interposed oddly—"they always used to send us out. We had money, right? I was the only kid in my class that got three quid pocket money."

"At *eight*?"

"From when I was five years old."

Was that what her parents gave to all the kids? "Yeah, all of us, till we were fourteen. At fourteen, my father expected the boys to have a paper-round."

What was their house like?

"Oh, it was like a fucking palace, you know, just fantastic. It's got three storeys. The bottom storey is kitchen, dining-room, lounge and a little recess bit, you know, a sort of conservatory for plants and all that, and a sitting-room and a porch. Upstairs it has three bedrooms and a bathroom and a playroom—we used it as a communal room where we just messed about, you know. The next floor was all bedrooms, and in the loft was a flat for one of my sisters. It's a beautiful house. We didn't expect to have to do anything ourselves. . . . "

But in fact her parents expected the kids to start doing some kind of work at fourteen, didn't they? "The boys, yes, not the girls—the girls were just expected to study homecraft at school, so they'd be prepared to get married, you know."

How many children were they? "Eight girls and five boys," she said. Her parents said no to the older ones but not the little ones, least of all to her.

Considering how many children there were, one would think the parents wouldn't have been able to spoil Nellie. Why just her?

The question—I only understood the reason weeks later—threw her into confusion. Listening to her voice now, on tape, I can hear how it changed, both in tone and speed. "Of course, what my mother called giving me loving was giving me a quid," she said. "I can't remember her paying any what you'd call real *motherly* attention to me." She paused and then, sounding even younger, much more hesitant and much more broad Scottish, too, she repeated, "I can't remember at all."

"When you were little, did you cuddle on anybody's lap?" I asked.

"Yes," she said, the voice still with that child-like timbre. "My Nana . . . my father's sister, I lived with her when I was six," and then her voice changed back to the darker pitch and her usual quick fluency. Only much later would I understand these accent and voice changes. "That was another of my decisions," she said, the words almost falling over each other. "I told them, I'm not fucking living with you. I'm living with my Nana . . . . " At this point she warded off my next question and suggested a break. "Excuse me, could I have something to eat?"

Later, once more the Nell with the faint Scottish burr and laughter in her voice, she returned to descriptions of her home. "My father loves cooking," she said. "He's a typically Italian man about his food, loves it, eats all the time and drinks wine. My mother used to give me wine in my bottle when I was a baby to make me sleep. Delicious. A lady came to clean the house. My mother spent quite a lot of time in bed. The woman came at nine in the morning; we were all gone by that time. She'd get up and see the house was okay and then she'd go back to bed."

"But how do you know that? Weren't you at school?"

"I'll never forget coming home from school one day," she said. "My mother fucked around . . . "

"What do you mean, 'fucked around'? Other men?"

"Yeah. One time I came up and found her in bed with a guy. My father suffered it for his children because of his religion. Well, yes, maybe I'm a little biased about my mother, but that's the way I looked at it, I favoured my father. I used to hate my mother, as bad as any kid could hate anybody."

"Since what age do you remember feeling that?"

"After I found her in bed with that man—I was about nine . . . " She and the other children had always known about sex—"From the very beginning. Our parents taught us. That was one thing my father was very strong about. If I said, 'Where do babies come from?' I'd get an explanation. A child's explanation, you know, like, 'Out of my tummy.' An if I said, 'How did it get in there?' They'd say, 'Mummy and Daddy love each other and they go to bed together. And the baby comes—' see what I mean? A kid's explanation, but just right at the time. Also, all my schools taught sex-education. Mind," she went on, and laughed, "I really learnt about it in the bike shed, from a little boy."

She started to menstruate at nine, she said, and by ten had a regular period. At ten, too, her parents decided something had to be done about her, so they sent her to a "Young Ladies' School."—in Glasgow. "My first day there I beat up three of the girls because I didn't like their smell or their accents."

"But surely you had the same accent, didn't you?"

"I could, but I wouldn't. I wouldn't talk like them—or like my mother," she added. "She speaks very very nice. My sisters do, too," and she suddenly put on her pure English. "You thought I couldn't, didn't you? Oh yes, I can. I just don't want to"—again she laughed— "except with the Arabs," she said. "You've *got* to speak English to them or they can't understand you." The irony of speaking Oxford English in order to be understood by her Arab clients produced unrestrained mirth.

Her first sexual experience, "*and* my second and third," she quipped, was at eleven, on a weekend or during a holiday. Nellie, a school friend with her "boyfriend" and a nineteen-year-old boy Nellie had known all her life, had experimented with cocktails one night when her parents were away. "I woke up in the morning, quite sore, you know, and I vaguely remembered something. So I went over to that boy's house and said, 'What happened last night, I'm sore and it doesn't feel like fingering. What did you do?' And he said, 'I screwed you. You're not going to tell anybody, are you?' I said, 'Would you mind doing it again, because I missed it last time.''

Later that day, she told her father. "I said, 'Look, I've been with this guy.' My father and I, we were always honest; I never told my father a lie in my life until I came here. I told him I had been with this guy and he immediately said, 'Who is the bastard, I'll kill him!' I said, 'I won't tell you. I'm not going to tell you any lies. I just want to tell you because I love you, Dad, and if you love me, you are not going to try and make me tell you, because I won't.' He said, 'I fucking well will,' and he went on at me, but I wouldn't, so I was told I had to stay in, not go out at all, and that's why I ran away . . . ''

Didn't her father ask her whether she was hurt, or take her to a doctor? "Oh yes," she said. "He took me to the doctor and I was examined and all that crap, and the doctor said, 'She is all right. She's only been broken, but she's okay.' Anyway, I think I lost my virginity earlier, on horseback, because I didn't bleed.''

She couldn't know that, could she? Because she had in fact been drunk. "There wasn't any blood on my clothing. Anyway I asked my dad about it and it was he who said, 'You lost it riding.' I used to ride a lot.''

Did she have any pictures of herself at that age? "At home, but not in England," she said. "I had long hair when I was a kid. I could sit on it, but at one point I caught lice from some of those kids I ran around with and gave them to all my family. My mother went fucking crazy and attacked me with a pair of scissors and cut it all off. I cried for three days; I loved my hair but after that I'd never grow it again." And suddenly she connected that experience with the one her father had allegedly punished her for. "My hair was chopped off and I was kept in. So I said, 'Fuck this, I am off.' So the first time I could, I was away.''

This time, again hitch-hiking to London on lorries, she said, she had £15 savings. "And this time I dressed, put on some make-up and looked quite a bit older, you know. One of the drivers thought I was eighteen. He wanted me to 'pay' for the lift and I said, 'I'll get you arrested—you know how old I am? I'm only going on twelve.' He said, 'You are a liar. You're fucking eighteen if you're a day.' But in the end I rubbed the make-up off and he believed me.''

This time, too, she went to the girl in Swiss Cottage, Fee. "I told her all about me being kept in, about me having a dog's life. I made it sound worse to her than it was, you know. So finally she said, 'There is no point in me phoning your parents because they will only come and get you and you'll only come fucking back up.' "

Nellie stayed for two days with Fee and then, because Fee didn't have the space, she moved in with a former boyfriend of Fee's, a young Pole called Ivo.

"But did this Fee think it was all right for you to move in with a young man?" I asked.

"Yes, because I was only a kid. He was a really good guy. She knew he wouldn't touch me." She grinned, wickedly. "I was the one who started with that. He gave me a couch to sleep on—it was a very little hard couch. But that wasn't the reason. Me, with my 'grown-up' mind, I wondered, you know, whether a Polish guy would be any different from a Scottish boy. So the second night, when he was making up his bed, I said, 'You have a fucking pretty marvellous bed there, man, with lots of space.' And he says, '*What*?' and I said, 'Lots of *space*'—I mean, you would have had to be a moron not to get my meaning, and he wasn't. And he said, 'You're only a little kid, you haven't even got anything to wear in bed.' And then he said again. 'You are only a kid.' And I said, 'Look, I've screwed before, man.' He said, 'You *what*?'

So I went and sat on his bed and told him all about it, and then I was a right little bitch and I really made him, you know—he wouldn't have, otherwise. He wasn't happy about it, ever. He was," she searched for words, "he was very very gentle with me, I think because I was so young. I am glad I had that experience, right fucking glad . . ."

Her parents, it appeared, had not called the police. "And after two months I told Ivo and Fee I was fed up and wanted to go home. I'm not brainy, you know, but I'm not a stupid person either—I know how to play chess, you know," one of her curious non sequiturs. "I don't kid myself. I know what my limits are and I really knew I should go home. And Ivo, he'd been very good—I mean, now I know he was very good. He didn't go on about it, that would have had the opposite effect. But when I said I wanted to go home, he said, 'Okay, I'll take you,' and he came up with me on the train and paid for the train, too. I introduced him as Fee's boyfriend, he stayed the night and then went back to London the next day."

*

Nellie and I had now been seeing each other every two or three days for over two weeks, and I had begun to realize that some of her accounts had to be fantasy. I knew, too, however, that if I wanted to get to the "real" Nellie, I'd have to let her direct the pace, let her act out the fantasies until she was ready to stop, or be stopped. She ate with us often, and after her initial shyness became comparatively relaxed with my husband. Despite Nellie's vast experience of life, she was in no way condescending about my daughter Mandy's own rebellion against middle-class mores, but warm and interested in her. And now, in every letter she writes from prison, she asks about our doings and sends love to my family.

When she was with us *en famille*, her manners were faultless: she never forgot that she had been taught to mind them. In an odd way she was the epitome of the well-reared classless Scottish child. She loved to be amongst pretty things and had a special way of not just touching but almost caressing or fondling perfectly ordinary household items: a bread-basket, a wooden cheeseboard, silver cutlery, earthenware coffee cups. Also, when with us, she was always very conscious of her language. Almost deliberately, I felt, she would draw my attention to her "wrong" way of talking by sometimes hitting her mouth, her face, or her own hand quite hard when she said "fuck."

"Please don't do that, Nellie," I said once when she had smacked her own face so hard it showed bright red. "I've got to," she said. "My language is something awful. I've got to stop . . . " And then she added, in what she obviously thought was a challenging tone of voice: "I'm using you, don't you know it?"

"I *want* you to use me," I answered. What I didn't say, but always worried about, was whether *I* was using *her*—something I was more afraid of with Nellie than with any of the others, because she was the most lost, most isolated and most entrenched in the marginal world of the streets. As the weeks went by, every time she left us to go back to her own life which was so very different, and which—I became certain—she hated, the gaiety of her good-byes became noticeably more artificial. More than in any of the other children I worked with, I sensed in Nellie a deep nostalgia for "ordinary" life. And this in spite of the increasingly clear probability that her ordinary life, in the idealized form she described, had never existed.

After her return to Scotland from her second flit, she said, she was sent to another school, this one a day school near home. Did she like that better than the boarding school?

"The subjects I liked I loved," she said. "The subjects I didn't like I hated and just wouldn't work at at all. I was in love with my arithmetic teacher, so I got to be fantastic at arithmetic. And I was in love with my history teacher, so I got fantastic at history. And I loved cooking anyway, although the teacher was a woman and I wasn't into that. And I liked statistics. And I just loved English, never mind the teacher." And she also liked—though not "loved," she emphasized—chemistry.

"But there were a lot of other subjects we had to do. Music, art, physical education and religious education, and all that bored me to distraction. So, quite often, I just wouldn't go to school and I stayed out late and I didn't come home but stayed at friends or whatever guy I happened to fancy that night. But," she added quickly, "none of that guy business ever got back to my parents."

"Were you sleeping with these guys?"

"Quite a bit, yes. There were about three-hundred guys in our town and I reckon I've been with two hundred and fifty of them."

"You can't really mean that?" I said.

"Maybe. I don't know. I sat down one night and made a list, an honest-to-God-with-myself list. I had a piece of paper"—she held her hands a foot apart—"that long and that wide, and I wrote the names side by side and I covered both sides of the paper. That was an honest-to-God."

"Did these guys pay you?"

"No, no. I was just gaining experience," she quipped.

"You were just twelve; how old were they?"

"I never went with anyone under sixteen, seventeen and some were much older—one was thirty-two. After a few months of this, my parents decided I was out of control and put me in front of a panel, and they said that I either strictly behaved myself for the next nine months or they'd be putting me in an institution. I said, 'It's all fucking lies, you can't touch me, you know. I am Nell, man, I can fucking do whatever I like. I always have.' But then my father had a talk to me and I started attending school and behaving myself and being a good little girl."

But before that—before the panel, before her promise, she said— she had run away to London once more and stayed for about five weeks, the beginning of her prostitution. "I left early in the day when I was supposed to go to school, and got there that night. I think I had a quid on me, that's all."

This time she didn't go to Fee in Swiss Cottage, or Ivo who had been so good to her. She went to Piccadilly. "And there was this guy, looking like a fucking prince, my ideal man. He starts chatting away to me and says, 'What are you doing in London?' and I said, 'What's it got to do with you?' At first I was a bit cautious because I thought he might be an Old Bill . . . a policeman.

" 'I live here, I've lived in London all my life; I was born here,' I said with my fucking Scottish accent. And he said, Yeah, yeah, have you got anywhere to go tonight? I could see he didn't believe me—he knew I was a runaway. So I said, 'No,' and he said, 'You can stay in my house,' and I said, 'I'm not staying with you; you are fucking black.' There's a lot of racial prejudice in Scotland. Now I don't like it any more, but when you're brought up with it—well, *you* know.

"Anyway, his name was Ron; he was twenty and a drummer in a group. I went back to his place, in Bayswater, it was. I said, 'It's the first time I've been with a black man,' and he said, 'There's a first time for everything, sweetheart.' And we just got on with it. He didn't know how old I was, but when we had finished that first night, I told him, and he said, 'Don't you realize you could end up in gaol and so could I?'

"But anyway, I stayed with him for three weeks—and then he took me to a gig, and while he was playing I met another black guy . . . they called him Cat and I know now why they called him that, he's a sleek and slimy bastard, he should have been a snake. That's where it started . . ."

That night she told Ron she was moving out, "if he didn't mind," and she moved in with Cat who, it appears, lived in the same block of flats. "And two days later, we are sitting in his sitting-room—he had a nice place—and he said, 'Would you like to make some money?' That was the big introduction, the big fanfare and a fucking roll of drums. So I said, how could I? I couldn't get a job; I didn't like living off him, I said, but there was fuck all I could do. 'I'm paying you with my body,' I said. So he said, 'Well, I know how you can make money, I'll show you.' I said, 'What does it entail?' and he said, 'Nothing you don't know already.' There wasn't a thought in my mind about prostitution: I went to bed with a guy because I fancied him. Well, we went down to Piccadilly and he said, 'Just walk around. If anyone approaches you, you say, "Do you want business and how much?" And if he offers you anything less than fifteen pounds, say no thank you and walk away.'

"I said, 'Wait a minute, do you mean go to bed with them for money?' I said, 'No, I'm not fucking doing it, man, I'll go home to my fucking parents first.' So he talked and talked at me and finally he persuaded me. He was really a smooth guy, and the stupid thing was I liked him, the slimy bastard. I didn't want to lose him; I was getting feelings for him.

"Anyway, so I did my little bit and a Welsh guy was my first, for twenty quid. He took me to his flat in Half-Moon Street. That place was stinking, with Durex lying all over, and he was fat and smelly. Cat told me to make them use Durex so I wouldn't get pregnant."

Had she ever used precautions before? "No, never."

For the first week, "Cat" went to Piccadilly with her. "But after that he stopped coming; I'd just get back late at night and give him the money—about sixty pounds a night the first week and then more . . . "

Did he give her any of it? "No, but he gave me quite a lot of clothes, and he was always bringing me little things, stuffed animals and that like—I loved it. I was only a fucking little kid."

She also kept house, shopped and cooked. "It all came to an end about three weeks later," she said, "I'd been getting real worried because I had missed a period. And that night I had gone to a pub with a Scots girl I met in the [Piccadilly Underground] station, Mary was her name. I thought I might be able to talk to her—I needed to talk to somebody, you know, because I was that worried. Anyway, we didn't get to talk about it, because she had worse troubles than me and no money and she told me all about it, so I gave her some money, and when I got back to the flat it was late, I only had sixty quid left and I was drunk because I was not really used to drinking at all.

"And when I came in, I put the money on the table like I had done every other night, and he [Cat] said, 'What's that? Is that all you've got? What do you fucking well mean? I have been sitting in this fucking house all night, waiting.' So I said, 'What about all the money I gave you last night?'—'That's fucking gone,' he said, 'And I need some.'

"Need some—that was rich. He had a wardrobe as big as a room full of clothes. I told him, 'I'm going to bed. I've got a sore head,' and he said, 'What you've got is fucking drink,' and he called me an alcoholic. I turned around and said, 'You fucking cunt, don't you come to me for anything, you can leave me alone.' He walked across and spun me around and he slapped my face and I just slammed out of the door and ran down to Ron.

"The whole story came out, and he said, 'I'm going to have a quiet chat with him.' He came back and his knuckles were all red and he had blood on his hands, and I said, 'You've killed him.' He said, 'I don't kill; I just taught him what fucking being a ponce is like. Tomorrow I'm going round to collect your things and you are going back to Scotland if I have to take you there.'

"So later that night I said, 'I've got something else to tell you—I haven't had a period.' He said, 'Whose is it?' And I said I just didn't know, it could be his or that slimy bastard's. And he said—would you believe it?—he said he hoped it was his. And I started to cry and said I was trying to get rid of it and that was why I had gone to the pub with Mary, to ask her to help me find an abortionist, and he said not to do that, 'I want that kid,' he said.

"And the next day he went and got my things and I went back to Scotland. My mother wanted to know where I had got all these new clothes—because I had a lot of them—and I said I'd met this guy, Ron, but I didn't say he was black and that I'd been staying in his house and he was really nice to me.

"So my father said, 'Have you been to bed with him?' and I said, 'Yeah,' and he said, 'Well, aren't you ashamed of yourself?' and I said, 'hm' and 'sort of,' and that's when they said they were going to ask the Authorities what to do about me and I went before that panel. And that's when I went back to school, and was a daughter again."

Three months later, she started to show. "My mother noticed straight away and said, 'You are pregnant,' and, of course I was. I got really enormous and . . . well . . . then she was born: I called her Kim. She was a really big baby and now that she's four, she is a really big girl. She takes after my father's side and Ron's side—a big strong girl. After she was born, my father said he would like a little talk with me. He said, 'You are too young to bring her up, what do you want to do about her?' And I said, 'I don't know. Can I keep her?' And my father, he said they would take care of her, and they eventually adopted her when she was two.

"I wish I had a photograph of her," Nellie said. "Ron, he was a very beautiful guy and she's got his grace."

"Is she black?"

"No, she's brown, brown like a nut. She walks like a queen, man. She knows I'm her mother, and my parents are her grandfather and grandmother. She calls me Nell: I told her, 'I might be your mummy, but you call me Nell, there's only thirteen years difference between us.'"

"How often do you see her?"

"Not very often. I went to see her when I was in Scotland. She's at a private school because everybody is racially prejudiced except the people with cash: they accept anything."

"Isn't she very young to be at boarding school at four?"

"There's nothing I can do about it," Nellie said. "I've got to work, you know. I'm saving money for her. I went to a lawyer and he set up—they call it a trust fund. That means it's not my money once it goes in there. It's got seven and a half thousand pounds in it now. For college or whatever she wants to do. For six months I put in half of what I earned. I kept it till the end of the week and then put it in. Then I slacked off—now I just put twenty pounds in once a while. I haven't done it for about five months now. She'll stay in boarding school till she's sixteen; my parents pay her fees and clothes and books. Really she's their daughter as much as mine."

Did Nellie think she could protect Kim from going the way she did?

"The only thing I can do is help provide for her. I can't see her more than once every few months, which I do try to do."

I found the thought of that four-year-old banned to boarding school hard to take. "Do your parents go and see her in school?" I asked.

"Yes, yes," she said, sounding impatient; and then, as if it was nothing at all, just one more bit of information, she added: "They can't have her. They've got a mentally handicapped child, Janie, my sister. She's sixteen, now. She's a year and eleven days younger than me. She's a beautiful-looking kid as well, normal-featured physically, but she has the brain of a five- or six-year-old. She got pneumonia after she was born."

Continuing immediately with her own story, Nellie said she had lived at home quite happily while pregnant and for a time afterwards. "Except for my going with guys," she said, "and not always attending school. But because of that, a year or so later, I was again put before a panel as being out of control, and they sent me to an approved school. I was fourteen and a half then." ——

While she was there she asked to do voluntary work with mentally handicapped children.

"That was because my oldest brother is in an asylum. He was born like that. He's an old guy now . . . no, I don't know exactly how old, perhaps thirty-eight or so, but he still wears nappies. The last time I saw him I was twelve. I suppose he's quite happy but it does upset me. He *is* my brother, you know."

Did she like this work with the children? "It was tough, and it broke my heart. There was a wee boy and he thought I was his mother. He was sixteen, but he was like a baby, and he used to bash his head on the cot they had him in. I had a fight with the Sister because she slapped him and I thought that was wrong . . . "

Had she ever thought of learning how to work with children like this?

"Yes, I'd love to do that, but it's too late, isn't it?" They wouldn't let her do O Levels at that school. "They said it wasn't part of the system. I said, 'If I study, could I just go and sit them at the local school?' But they said, no, the local school wouldn't accept us criminals, not even for sitting exams. Well, I was put in there for dodging school," she said, "so I didn't consider myself a criminal."

So after she was told she wouldn't be able to study toward O Levels, she decided in that case it wasn't worth her while to study. "I decided I might as well enjoy myself."

But she did pottery and tried painting. "That was part of the school's recreation and we were allowed to go to the teacher's house for it and he was a really good guy."

They had a disco in the school every second weekend, and on alternate weeks five girls could go out to a disco in the town. "But the guy who picked the names for the outside disco always let me go—I went every week. His name was George. He was about forty and he smoked a pipe and his tobacco was imported from another country. He was fucking fantastic. Really, I loved that guy—like a father, you know."

The school was evidently one of the experimental institutions—somewhat like later German ones—set up by the English local authorities before and just after World War II. No pressures were applied to force the thirty-four teen-agers to attend lessons. "It really was more like a commune than an approved school," said Nellie. "The only thing we *had* to do was make our beds, keep our rooms tidy and on a rota, serve and help with the dishes. And then we also had to volunteer for some other household chore, like I did laundry."

Every two weeks or so, she claimed, she absconded, staying out a few days—on several occasions as long as two weeks—but then always returning voluntarily. "I guess they knew I'd come back and they always took me back; I got 'talked to,' but never punished."

And what did she do when she absconded? "Oh, stay with guys. Sometimes, too, I sneaked my guy in; this was a very old house and in the coal cellar there was a trapdoor to my room. So you could come in from outside into the coal cellar and into my room, quite easy."

If she didn't get much academic instruction, she learnt a good deal about other things: about gangs, about burgling houses, about picking pockets, and about selling to fences. And for three months she had a lesbian relationship with a roommate. "I had never heard of such a fucking thing, but it was something new and I thought I'd learn about it. Quite a few of the hard chicks at that school were into it."

Did she like it? Did it give her any reassurance, any satisfaction? "I quite liked it at first. Living with only girls . . . it's very emotional, you know, it makes . . . " she searched for the words, " . . . it's a different atmosphere than anything else is. I can see now that it was probably to prevent this that they allowed us the discos, asking boys in, you know, and allowed us to go out. But still, most of our time was spent with each other. I had a boyfriend . . . well, several boyfriends, but one I really liked, in Edinburgh, and emotionally the lesbian thing really fucked me up. I reckon what I learned was that it isn't for me . . . " again she paused. "I wouldn't go into it, ever, permanent. But those first months at that school—you weren't allowed out for about a month or two—it gave me something. You know, something to feel."

The children were allowed home-leave every few weeks or months, but Nellie never went to her parents. "I didn't have any communication with them all. My sister and grandmother were in Edinburgh, and one of my brothers was in Stirling, and I used to go to them."

It was as a result of one of these home-leaves (with which the school tried to prepare the girls for their return to normal life) that Nellie got herself into bad trouble. Finding on her return that another fifteen-year-old, a recent arrival at the school, had been "making time" with her boyfriend, she beat the girl up. Contrary to the girls' own unwritten rules, this one then "shopped" her to the headmaster, and Nellie was disciplined. "When I found out she'd shopped me, I got her up to my room on a pretext and I hit every bone in her body and smashed up her face for her with my boots. They called the ambulance and the doctor. He said, 'Every one of her ribs is fractured. Who did this?' I said I did. I really didn't mean to hurt her that much," Nellie said. "If she had pressed charges on me, I would have been in Borstal, but she didn't, and she became my girlfriend till I came out and we even stayed together for a few weeks afterwards. . ."

The violence of this incident would have surprised me less had I known then what I learnt later: that Nellie had been sent to the approved school at the age of fourteen and a half, not for "going with guys and not always attending school," as she had told me, but for attacking someone with her knife. This incident from her past was to have a crucial and tragic effect on her fate six years later, and was indicative for the future. Now, once again in prison, she is in deep trouble because of violence against other prisoners.

15

"We always feared the day when she would go to London"

Nellie knew before we began to talk that I would eventually want to meet her family. I mentioned it repeatedly over the months, in order to keep this essential aspect of the undertaking clearly in her mind. It was she herself who called her parents to make the arrangements for the visit, and she gave me exact instructions how to get to their home. In view of what was to happen, this ready cooperation is very significant for an understanding of Nellie's personality and problems.

Virtually everything she said about her life in London eventually proved to be almost entirely true, although the sequence of events was sometimes different. Her stories about her parents, however—so real and detailed in the telling—turned out to be such extravagant fantasies that my trip up to Scotland to meet them became an astonishing voyage of discovery.

The home town where she said she had slept with almost three hundred men proved to be an ultra-respectable village most of whose male inhabitants, one felt sure, wouldn't be caught dead copulating with a pre-teenager, if for no other reason than that in a place of that size nothing remains secret—anybody's doings are everybody's business.

The house she had described as a "fucking palace" turned out to be a pleasant little semi-detached working-class dwelling in a street of identical homes.

"This can't be right," I said to the taxi-driver who brought me from the station. "You must have the wrong address."

"Who is it you are visiting, then?" he asked, and when told the name, he pointed at the couple who, evidently on the lookout for my arrival, now stood in the open door. "That's right," he said. "There they are."

Dougie, now sixty-two years old, the "sexy Italian" father of Nell's dreams, far from being the lighthearted, free-spending business man she described, is a big, paunchy, silent Scotsman. He has been an engine-driver all his working life, and—one feels sure—copes admirably with the huge responsibility of hundreds of lives whenever he takes out his long-distance train.

And Nellie's mother, the flippant semi-courtesan of her story, is a small slim woman with a wonderfully humorous ready laugh, tired eyes and unending patience with young Janie who, I suppose, until Nellie's recent conviction for murder, represented the family's overriding tragedy and preoccupation. A beautiful girl ("That's what worries us to death," said her mother pointedly. "How can we protect her, bonny as she is?"), Janie was brain-damaged by pernicious pneumonia soon after birth and has remained with a mental age of three to five. When she was born and became ill all the children were still at home. "They kept her in hospital for over a year," said her mother. "I went to see her every two days; it was far away and took all day just to get there and back and stay a couple of hours. It was that tiring . . . "

It must have been extraordinarily hard to have this happen, again, with the youngest, I said, after they'd already had the tragedy with their eldest.

They looked puzzled. "Our oldest?" Nellie's mother finally said. "That's Maggie. She's fine, she's lovely. She's married and has her own bairns. She was fourteen when Janie was born."

"No," I said, "I mean the boy."

"What boy? We have three, but we haven't had any troubles with them, have we, Dad?" she said.

It was a difficult moment. Was it possible that they were hiding this severely retarded oldest son to whom Nellie had referred as being in "an asylum" and still wearing "nappies" at thirty-eight? I carefully apologised if I was intruding into something they perhaps didn't wish to talk about.

"You think we have a son who is mental?" Nellie's father said. "Is that what you mean?" I nodded.

"Is it Nell who told you that?" asked his wife.

"Yes, she did."

She shook her head in wonderment. "But why would she say that?" Suddenly she laughed—she has an exceptional gift for laughter—and hugged Janie who had come to sit next to her. "It's only our Janie we have, and we wouldn't have her in any institution, would we, pet?"

Janie smiled and stroked her mother's cheek.

I told them Nellie had also said she had two younger brothers, now thirteen and fifteen. They both shook their heads. "She just has the three brothers—Euan, Colin and Andrew—Janie here, and her three older sisters. And there isn't a handicapped boy. Oh," she laughed, "we sometimes say Euan's weak in the head, but we don't mean it."

By this time, watching these exhausted parents with Janie, who they so obviously adored and gave all their care and love to, I had a pretty good idea of the reasons for Nellie's fabrications, dreams and childhood transgressions.

But I said I didn't know why she would invent an older brother in an institution; she had told me about this in the context of describing her volunteer work with mentally handicapped children while she was in the approved school near Edinburgh. "She *was* in an approved school, wasn't she?" I asked.

"Yes, she was that," her mother said, sounding unhappy. "We just didn't know any more *what* to do about her, she was that difficult, and yes, she did work with handicapped children when she was there."

"How is Nell?" asked her father. "It's so long since she's come to see us."

Nellie had told her parents that I was writing a book about runaway children and their problems, and had made me promise not to tell them what she was doing or had done in the past. "I don't mind anybody knowing, except my parents. I don't want them to know."

In Scotland that day, I suggested that before talking about the present, perhaps they wouldn't mind my asking them some questions about the things Nell had told me of her childhood and her running away.

"Och yes, she ran away all right," said her mother. "When was it the first time she went, Dad? Was it when she was eleven?"

"Yes, eleven, I think that was it."

I said I thought it was earlier—eight, wasn't it? "Eight?" her mother repeated. "Did she run away at eight? Did she, Dad? I can't remember, but I don't think she did, that wee. When she was seven or eight, Maggie—she was twenty-one then—she took Nell on a trip to Venice. And we took her and Janie on a holiday to London. Of course, quite soon after, with us so busy with Janie and the other children leaving by and by to go to work, half the time we didn't know *where* she was or who she was with. That's why in the end we asked the panel, isn't that right, Dad?"

"Yes, that's right."

"The stealing, you know," she said. "I just couldn't understand why she would steal and all . . . "

"Yes," I said, "specially since you gave her so much pocket-money."

"Pocket-money?"

"Yes," I said. "I gather all the children got three pounds a week from the time they were five."

"Three pounds, at five? *Our* children. . .?" she exclaimed, and then laughed. "Guid heavens!" Her husband laughed too, quietly. "If we'd given three pounds to seven children," he said pensively, "that would have been twenty-one pounds a week." The mother said, "Twelve years ago, when Nell was five, that would have been practically all Dougie's basic pay." She laughed again. "Fifty pence each, that's what the children got."

Now of course, she said, Doug earned much more as a senior engine-driver in charge of British Rail's fast trains. And anyway, salaries had multiplied by five since 1970, and his old grade, then £21.55 basic pay, now in 1982 was worth £104.15.

Yes, she said, all the children were still at home when Janie was born. The oldest, Maggie, had been a real good girl that year, when she had to go back and forth to the hospital every two days. "I was that worried, with Nell only a baby—there's only eleven months between them, you know." But Maggie, even while going to school, had looked after her splendidly, and the others too.

"And of course my sister took Nell too," said Dougie.

How much time had Nell actually spent at her aunt's, her Nana, as she called her? She had lived with her for a time, hadn't she?

"Not *lived* with her," Nellie's mother answered quickly. "She took her for the days, but I always insisted she had to be brought back to sleep." Nana had spoiled her dreadfully, she said, dressed her like a fairy, let her do what she liked.

"As a baby?" I asked.

"Later too . . . we were that busy with Janie," she repeated. "And then she started stealing, already in primary school, stealing and fighting. We were that ashamed, that upset . . . "

Did they not realize that Nellie was very disturbed, very unhappy?

"I knew. The moment came when I saw she was rejecting me," her mother said slowly. "She was that bad to me; I never knew why, never understood. We wanted her more than any of the others. She came five years after the next in line, we waited for her with so much . . . " She paused and looked at the quiet man across the room. "Dougie, he was over the moon when she came. Do you remember, Dad?" He nodded, and a few moments later blew his nose and surreptitiously wiped his eyes.

"Well, she wasn't unhappy all the time," I said to him, hoping to lighten the atmosphere. "She tells me you love cooking—your Italian background, she thinks."

"Me, *Italian*?" he exclaimed in his thick Scottish accent, for a moment losing his habitual equanimity.

"Him *cooking*?" said his wife, and went off into peals of laughter, immediately echoed by Janie. "Why, he'd as soon put on wings and fly as go into the kitchen."

I tried once more. "Well, at least as far as learning about the facts of life is concerned, she seemed content with the way it was handled by both of you."

Again total incomprehension, "The facts of life?"

"Sex, where babies come from. She said that was one thing her father was very strong about and that you too always provided a totally acceptable, clear answer the moment she asked."

"I never . . . " Dougie started, then stopped in utter perplexity.

"I used to look at the books," his wife said, "to see how they said one has to tell kids, and then I'd pray they'd never ask. And they didn't. And I thanked God they didn't. We never said anything about it to any of them."

Hadn't Nellie, when she was eleven, told her father that she had had sexual relations with a boy?

"Me?" he said, beginning to sound exhausted. "No, she told me nothing. I wouldn't let her speak to me like that."

"Him?" said his wife. "He'd have fainted right off if she'd mentioned the word 'sex' to him." She sat for a moment, thinking. "But it *was* at eleven she ran away . . . I'm sure it was."

"She stayed away for two months, didn't she?"

"Oh, I don't think so. She was never away for two months that wee, was she, Dad?"—"I don't know," he said, wearily. "I just don't know."

About then, their middle son, Colin—a slim, handsome young man of twenty-four—dropped in, evidently having been told of my impending visit. When I mentioned the little room Nell had described, a sort of conservatory where her mother grew plants, he guffawed. "That would have been the window-sill," he said. And when his mother quoted Nellie's invention of a room where they "all played together," he said, "She never played with us or anybody. She was afeared of the lot of them . . ."

The lot of whom? I asked. "Everybody. Nell has always been afeared, of everybody," he said with perception.

"You never said that before," his father remarked.

Colin shrugged. "What's the use? What was the use?"

"One time she was real unhappy I *do* know," his mother said. "That was when Nana's daughter gave birth to her bairns. After that, Nana dropped Nell."

"Dropped her?" I echoed.

"Yes. From spoiling her for years, the moment she had her own wee grandchildren, she dropped Nell."

There was only one detail of Nellie's account left to explore, albeit the most significant one. "What about Kim?" I asked.

"Kim? Who's Kim?" said Nellie's mother.

"Nellie's baby."

"Nellie's *baby*? My God, has Nell had a baby?"

"When she was thirteen . . . ?"

"Did Nellie have a baby?" her mother asked the room. "She had no baby," she continued. "She *can't* have had a baby; we would have known if she had had a baby."

"She says after she had it, you asked her what she wanted to do about it." I turned to Nellie's father. "And that after she told you she wanted to keep it, you said you would take care of it and that you later adopted it. She says you both were terribly terribly good about it. . ." If there *was* such a baby, and they were too ashamed to admit it, I wanted them to know how much Nellie appreciated what they had done.

"Dear God—it's all in her imagination." Nellie's mother looked over at her husband. "He would simply have died if that had happened—if she had told him. And I . . . I just don't know what I would have done. . ."

"You would have coped," I said, and for a while we sat in silence.

"How is Nell, can you tell us?" asked her father.

I told them she was coping. That friends and I were hoping to get her to go back to school, to study for a profession. Her brother laughed out loud.

"What are you laughing at, then?" his mother asked.

"I'm laughing at you," he said. "It's pathetic, that's what it is. Both of you know what Nell is doing. You've known all along."

"Yes, she's a model . . ." her mother began.

"Model, that's a laugh! She's on the game. You know it. I know it. And of course *you* know it," he said to me, not at all unkindly.

"On the game?" his mother said, surprisingly calm, her tone of voice hardly changing. "I don't think so. Do you, Dad?"

"Yes," he said, with what I thought great dignity. "I reckon I do." He looked at me. "We always feared the day when she would go to London. . ."

16

"I *knew* it wasn't true"

"Colin, the blue-eyed boy," fumed Nellie a few days later. " 'She's on the game.' How *dare* he!"

Why was she so angry? Her brother was right, wasn't he? "He had no right to say it, he doesn't know. He has no right to say anything of the fucking kind about me."

But she had never minded before when people talked about her being on the game. "I mind *him* opening his big mouth he doesn't know what he's talking about . . . "

"But Nellie," I said, "what is it that Colin doesn't know?"

She didn't answer, she hardly heard. "When I go home for Christmas," she said, sounding quite vicious, "I'll get him. I'll tell him about his fucking slut of a wife. If he makes my life his business, I'll make his life my business."

"But all he said to your parents was in essence, 'Be honest, you know what she's doing.' "

"All right, that's what I'll say: 'C'mon, be honest, your wife's a fucking slut. I don't like his child, either. Last time I was home, he never even brought the child."

So that was it. She was hurt because Colin hadn't brought his child to meet her?

"I'll get the bastard for that," she said.

"He's the one who's most like me," Nellie said, now three years older, when we talked in prison a few days before I wrote this. "I think that's why I'm more hurt by what he says, and I reckon he's more hurt by what I've done with my life that anybody else."

I had asked her mother on the telephone if any of the sisters or brothers were writing to Nellie in prison. "They don't know anything about this," she said. "How can I weigh down their lives by telling them their sister is a murderess? And can you imagine what Colin would say?"

I asked Nellie why she had invented the baby, Kim.

"I don't know." She laughed, in an embarrassed way. "That was weird, fucking weird . . . you see, like, I *knew* it wasn't true. I knew once you met my parents, you'd know it wasn't true. I didn't have to let you go and see my parents. I know it was a condition of our talking, but I could have got out of it. But I wanted you to find out." She sounded astonished and puzzled about herself.

It was a healthy, a hopeful sign, I said.

"It's fucking silly," she answered. "That's what it is . . . "

Could it be, I asked, that she very much wanted a baby, and as she had had VD repeatedly, was afraid she might not be able to have children? "I don't know," she said, sounding sad.

The second version of her story, which she told me about ten months later, was mostly true. "When I was thirteen my cousin was staying with us. He was in the Army in Ireland and came to stay with us on leave. I was sitting up in bed reading a book—I shared a room with Janie because she gets fits and always had to have somebody there—and he came in and said, 'Can I get in bed with you?' And I said 'No, we've got the same fucking blood, you're my cousin'—he is my mother's sister's son, and if I got pregnant from him, the baby would be a mongol. I don't know if that's true, but that's what I was always told.

"Anyway, he got on the bed with his clothes on and we started kissing, and he said, 'I love you,' and it just sort of happened, and that night we did it again and we done that for about a week."

Were they still friends now, I asked. "Yes," she said. "I like to keep as many friends as I can."

Now that she is older, does she feel bitter about this grown-up cousin having made love to her when she was little?

"I don't feel bitter about anybody," she answered. "It was my own fucking fault. All I had to do was kick him out. It's I that didn't. Any man will ask, you know; if a chick doesn't have the sense to say no, she can't complain later. I listen to these chicks at the clinic [the VD clinic] raving against guys who made them. *Who* makes them? They make themselves. I know this guy Bébé—he's a ponce in Mayfair, he's black. He's got fourteen girls working for him, none over sixteen."

"Where does this ponce Bébé get the girls?"

"He gets them off the street."

"Runaways?"

"Mostly. But he also gets some when they are just amateurs . . ."

"Amateurs?"

"Yeah—don't you know? There are thousands of wee amateurs around, boys and girls. Stupid cunts they are, going out on Friday night and thinking it won't harm them."

It was not long after that conversation that I met two of these "amateurs": two girls looking like any other West London teen-agers on a Saturday afternoon: boots and ethnic shoulderbags, jeans and tee-shirts and little underneath. Their breasts bobbed up and down aggressively as they walked, and the tiny pants were clearly outlined under their jeans. One, a truly voluptuous figure for what turned out to be her age, had long luxuriant dark brown hair and was made up to the gills—shiny foundation, shiny lipstick, shiny mascara and scintillating blue on her eylids. The other one, a curious contrast, was thin as a rake, blond, very pale, hair pulled back tightly tied into a pony-tail, and no make-up whatever ("I hate the stuff," she was to tell me later, with a shudder of disgust).

Their names—first names only, of course, and those manifestly false—were Patsy and Joey, they told me, giggling, when by means of my press card and a copy of *The Case of Mary Bell* with the photograph of a child on the cover, I eventually convinced them that I was a writer, not a policewoman. "I'm scared of pigs," said Patsy, while Joey nodded ardently.

How old were they, I asked. They started with eighteen and gradually came down until we settled on fourteen. They were, in fact, both just thirteen.

How long had they been "working" the Underground station?

"Oh, we're not regulars," said Patsy quickly. "We just do it on Saturday afternoon"—"Well, sometimes also Fridays, for a couple of hours," corrected Joey, who was a manifestly honest child. "Yes," admitted Patsy. "Friday sometimes, for a bit, just . . . you know, to have enough for Friday night."

"Enough for Friday night," meant of course, enough money for the disco and the "grass" they all smoke. "Doing it . . . regular" meant engaging in prostitution.

After an hour's chit-chat we had become friends, and both girls admitted that their parents were professional people. "Well, mine almost, but not quite," said Patsy (her father, it turned out, worked for the borough council). Joey's father was an accountant.

But then why on earth, I enquired, couldn't they just ask for enough pocket-money?

"Do you *know*," they replied, addressing me, as they well might, as though I were the man on the moon, "how much 'enough' would have to be?" And they jotted it down for me on a paper napkin. An evening at a disco would set them back a fiver each—"and that's without any food," said Joey; a taxi ("We can't *walk* at that time of night") £2 each; "grass"—"well . . . maybe another fiver." And of course, clothes. "I've got to have some nice things," said Patsy, "and look at the *prices*" she added, sounding like a middle-class housewife.

Would they consider taking a Saturday job, in a boutique or on a market stall?

"We're too young," said Joey. (Not true, incidentally. I happened to know from my daughter's forays into Saturday work that many of the West London boutiques and market stalls are only too happy to employ youngsters for small wages.) "*You* tell *us*," Joey continued, "how one can manage to get by."

How much pocket-money did they get? "I get a pound a week," said Patsy. "My dad just doesn't have more to give me; I don't blame him, not a bit. But what can I get with one pound? It won't even pay for a film, a hamburger, a drink or transport—not to speak of anything to wear."

I found myself shrinking away from discussing the actual details of their prostitution with these children who, confusing the concept "I want" with "I need," were well on the way to corrupting their childhood. Any word I made them say about their activities might make it even worse.

Had they any idea, I asked feebly, hearing myself utter cliché words, what could happen to them?

"Oh my God," said Patsy, the surface charm gone in a trice, hard little eyes now glaring at me from under all that make-up. "She's going to say—wait for it," she announced loudly to Joey, and to the fascinated coffee-shop at large—"VD. Right?" she asked triumphantly.

It was pointless to continue. In their case, unfortunately (contrary to the runaway children), the only solution was to signal their activities to the social services who, one would hope, could get the parents to persuade them or to exercise more control. At fifteen, I said, they could legally work—did they think they would? Patsy shrugged. "Maybe."

"They won't," said Nellie. "Can you see them working in a shop, say, for eight pounds all of Saturday, when by doing two guys on Friday night they can make thirty, forty pounds? In a pig's eye they will. Hustling is good money, man," she said. "That's the problem. And wee chicks like these, they are playing games—they don't know what's happening inside them.

"It's an emotional strain. Not what you feel towards the clients— it's what you feel towards yourself. Ay, man, everybody feels it who's in it, you know, properly." She guffawed. "That's a funny word to use, isn't it? Och, the money isn't worth it," she continued. "I'm like a carrier bag from a shop—once used, that's that. I think, though, that you should talk to Alan," she said. "A wee Scottish rent boy I know. He can tell you a lot."

17

"There's a wee Scottish rent boy . . ."

Alan, at thirteen—which was when he ran away and came to London—
knew very little of the world he was about to enter. "Two nice lesbian
girls who found me huddling in the Brompton Cemetery and took me
in, asked me whether I was gay," he said. "I wasn't that sure." A week
later, in Mayfair, he became sure. A man "in a super car" invited him
to get in. "He took me to a garage. He asked me what I liked doing. I
said, almost anything. I didn't know what the hell gay people were
meant to be doing. He said, 'Would you like to be fucked?' I said no.
He said he'd give me ten. When he said ten, I thought, I wonder what
that means: it could be ten pence or ten pounds, you know. But he gave
me this ten-pound note and told me to wank him off. He spoke very
posh. He was about thirty-five, forty. Well, it was sort of good fun,
getting paid for just doing that. Half an hour later, I got someone else
and I asked him for fifteen pounds—that was in Mayfair, right near the
Hilton. By that evening, I had more than forty pounds and got myself a
cheap room in Earl's Court."

Nellie had met Alan in a youth club she used to go to. When she
suggested my talking to him, she said, "He's a real bundle of misery, as
confused as they come. Just up your street."

Alan was fifteen then and had been in prostitution in London for
two and a half years. Now he is not so "wee"—"I've growed," he said.
"I was five feet when I came to London—I'm five feet seven, now."
And he's not really all that Scots either.

Alan had a pale narrow face and coal black hair. "I dyed it last
week," he said. "My natural colour is dead boring, sort of mousy, you
know?" He had thick velvety eyebrows, meeting above the bridge of
his nose, which were unexpectedly attractive, giving his face character
and strength.

He was perpetually hungry, childishly happy when given the run of the kitchen, and intent on examining the contents of the fridge. "Cheese," he enthused. "Oh, you've got Brie. Oh, pâté . . . ohhhh, lovely bread!" When we got ready to have lunch, he sat down gingerly. Earlier, too I had noticed that he walked with a curious sideways gait, as if he hurt. "I've got piles," he said ingenuously, with that homosexual inflection that seems so easily acquired. "I've had them for nine years."

His Irish father has worked as a civil servant in South Africa for years. His mother is Scottish. His sister, one year older than he, was finishing her education in an English boarding school. When Alan was seven, on a holiday in Scotland, an eighteen-year-old cousin raped him. "I think that's what did it to me," he said. "I could have been straight: I like girls. You know, they turn me on. But what happened to me then, I think turned me gay. It was the first time my parents had been back home for seven or eight years—the first time, too, all the relatives got to see us children. We were staying up in Perth with my great-aunt. It was a big house, five bedrooms upstairs, a living-room and another bedroom downstairs. Every bed was full because all the relatives had come for the whole family to be together before we sailed back to South Africa a week later."

They'd put up a bed for the little boy in his cousin's room. "It was okay the first days, but just two days before we were leaving, he started messing around and that."

What had the cousin actually done with him? "About three in the morning, you know, he put his arms around me. He said, 'You'll like what I'm going to do to you.' He always told me never to tell anybody about it. I never did, not even my aunt or my parents."

But had the eighteen year old cousin actually buggered him? "Yes, he did."

That must have hurt: Did he cry? Did he ask him to stop?

"I was trying to get out of the bed, but he was holding me down; he was quite tall, he had some muscle on him. I told him to stop because he was hurting me. He said, 'In a minute.' I said, 'Stop it, stop it, I'm going to be sick.' So he stopped. But in the morning, before we got up, he tried to do it again. Luckily my mum knocked on the door and came in. I asked her if I could go and sleep in her room. She asked why and I just said I missed her. But she said not to be silly so I had to stay."

And did he do it again?

"No, he didn't. He just put his arms around me and crushed me tight."

Alan's parents hadn't "cuddled" him when he was small—they cuddled his sister, but never him. He never had a proper birthday—she did, but he didn't. "I don't know why," he said. "As the time would come near for my birthday, nothing would happen. When I asked my mum for a birthday party, she'd say, 'Wait till nearer the time,' and then nothing happened. They'd say, 'Happy Birthday. Here is your card,' and that was all. My sister always had a cake, presents—really nice things. Me—sometimes I would maybe get a pound or two. They'd say, 'Run down to the shop, buy yourself some sweets.' I asked my mum why; why my sister and not me. And she said, '*She* has friends.' "

What about him? Did he not have friends as a little boy? He hesitated. "Well, I had friends when I went to school in South Africa."

What sort of school was it? "Day school. It was . . . " hesitation again " . . . it was a black school. I'm not prejudiced," Alan added quickly.

But wasn't it very rare then for white children to go to school with black children in South Africa? "Not that rare. We were about eight whites and fifty or sixty blacks. It was a good school. I liked it. I loved it."

The experience with his cousin when he was seven was the only one of its kind until much later. "About two years after that trip to Scotland, back in Africa, there was a very nice boy; I used to go and stay with him, sleep in the same bed with him."

"A little white boy?"

"Oh yes. Little black boys weren't into this sort of thing—at least, I don't think so, certainly never with me."

This little boy was ten—Alan was then nine. "We used to muck around. Everyone thought there was something funny about us because we always hung around together. He had blond hair, really lovely. We saw each other nearly every night for nearly two years."

Was he saying that they had sex together? "Yes, we did."

But how could they, at nine and ten? He shrugged. "Having sex" to him had a different meaning. They masturbated each other—that was it, wasn't it? "Yes. He's somewhere in England now, in London I think. The last I heard was that he had got into the police force as a cadet but was chucked out almost at once . . . "

Because he is gay? "I reckon he would be."

Does Alan think people are born gay or made gay? "I think probably you can be born gay; I think I probably was, I don't know."

Had he thought about it a lot? "Yes, I do . . . I do, specially when I find that girls turn me on: I don't understand why girls turn me on when

I'm gay. It makes me want to know more, understand more . . . But on the whole, I'd rather stay as I am, except . . ." he fooled with the salad on his plate, "I would like to have children," he said. "I love children." And then he added, strangely, "If I had children, we wouldn't sleep in the same bed."

Why? Did he sleep in the same bed with his parents? His mother, his father? He shook his head and only repeated: "I wouldn't have them sleep in the same bed with me."

Would he like to sleep with a girl? "Are you scared, in case you can't?"

"Yes," he said. "Thinking of it worries me."

But sex with a man didn't—had never worried him? "Yes, I was scared. When I started, I was awfully scared, I didn't even know what I was scared of, I didn't know anything: I didn't know what one did, what they wanted, what it was all about."

Except for that experience at seven—that *had* shown him, hadn't it, what it was all about? "Oh, I'd blocked that out. I tried never to think of it again, for years."

When he was twelve, his parents told him he was going to his aunt in Scotland on holiday for two or three months. But when he got there, he found out that he was to be sent to boarding school. "I said I wouldn't, I just ranted and raved and said they could do what they liked, but I wouldn't go. So finally my aunt entered me at a high school—a day school, and I lived with her."

His aunt owned a restaurant. "She worked very hard—I didn't see that much of her but even that was too much."

Did he make friends? "How could I make friends?" he said, sounding tired. "My aunt said school was one thing and her house was another, and the two didn't mix. Just as long as I didn't ever—and she meant *ever*—bring anybody into her house, she didn't care what I did at school." If he wanted pocket-money, said the aunt, he'd have to earn it. "So I got myself a job washing-up in a hotel—and on weekends she let me work in the kitchen in her restaurant and payed me ten or fifteen pounds for that."

After about six months, he had saved £130. "And one Friday in October I took it all out of the bag I kept it in in my drawer, skipped school, and went to Edinburgh. I had a great day: I went to the castle, and to Jenners—a big shop—I had lunch in the restaurant there. I bought all kinds of clothes; I went to a sauna." When the day was over, more than half the money was gone.

Three days later—he was just a few days under thirteen—he ran away to London. From the start, Alan had expensive tastes. "I had a rucksack, and in it my suit and all the things I'd bought: two pairs of nice jeans, about six pairs of socks and underpants, five short-sleeved shirts—nice ones, you know. By the time I'd got all that and brought the ticket, and had supper before leaving and breakfast in the morning, I just had four pounds left." Realistically, he had also taken five tins—baked beans and soup—and a tin-and-bottle opener.

Like all of the runaway children, he found the first day a great adventure. "I felt free; it felt wonderful. I thought the streets were paved with gold, that there would be no hassles, that it would be easy to get somewhere to stay. . . . "

He spent another two days walking the streets, living on the tinned food he had brought supplemented by the odd cup of tea. And the nights he spent in the cemetery. "Cemeteries are nice, really nice," he said. "I love them."

It was here he was found by the two young women. "Then, of course, they seemed quite old to me, but they were only in their early twenties. They said what was I doing there and was I okay and, you know, I suddenly heard myself say, 'No, not all that okay,' and they just said, 'Come on, you can crash at our place.' They lived just a few streets away, in a flat near the Embankment; a nice flat. They gave me some hot soup, they ran me a bath, they put sheets on a divan they had in their living-room. God, it was heaven. I reckon they saved me."

When he woke up late the next morning, he was alone in the flat. "There was a note on the kitchen table saying they'd see me when they got back from work. To help myself to food and take it easy."

Did he tell the girls that evening about himself? "They asked whether I was gay. I said I didn't know. They asked about my parents; I said I couldn't go back to my aunt and my parents wouldn't understand."

Did he tell the girls his age?

"Not in so many words, but I think they knew—they guessed. They said I could stay for a bit and think about things, but that if the police got me, I wasn't to mention them."

Over the next two and a half years Alan had innumerable "encounters" and several "affairs." This—and the high incidence of violence—I found to be the main difference between what happens to boys on the loose and to girls. The majority of girls' clients want nothing beyond a

quick and anonymous release, but many homosexuals seek relationships even when on the prowl. A terrifying number from among
the veritable armies of boys engaged in prostitution all over the United
States and Europe end up injured—or dead. But almost every runaway
boy I spoke with, whether in Britain, West Germany or America, had
at some time or other been offered more than casual sex.

A few weeks after Alan arrived in London, he found out that one of the
best pick-up places was in front of a notorious nightclub in Earl's Court.
"This man invited me to come down to the disco with him," he said. "I
was very scared—there were all these gay people dancing—it was
weird. But then there was the DJ. He told the man I was with to leave
me alone. He made me sit down at a table near the band and sent over
soft drinks. And later in the night he took me back to his flat in the
West End, a beautiful place. He was about twenty. He was very nice.
We had steak, eggs, chips, mushrooms and tomatoes at four-thirty in
the morning. It was cosy. He asked whether I wanted to sleep with him
or in a separate bed. I slept with him. Nothing happened—he had his
back to me. I stayed with him for two nights but he never touched me.
He also worked in records aside from being a DJ. In the morning he'd
squeeze my hand very tightly, say, 'See you tonight,' and go to work.
He gave me a key to the flat and said I could stay as long as I liked and
come back there whenever I liked . . . "

Why did he think this young man never touched him? "I think he
was probably shy. He spoke very little, too. I tried to make conversation, but somehow it wasn't even necessary: it was really nice."

Was it, perhaps, that the young man just thought he was too
young? "I don't know." He laughed in an embarrassed way. "After
two nights—three days—I left because I didn't think I should just be
living on him like that, you know." Alan's moral scruples were really
quite remarkable.

After that he went into prostitution systematically. "It was obvious
that it was the only way I could keep going. Nobody would employ
me—I really did look my age and there was nothing I could do to look
older. I thought I got away with telling people I was fifteen. Later I
found out that nobody had really believed it."

He got a room in one of the small hotels that litter Earl's Court, for
£3.50 a day. "Nobody asked me my age and nobody bothered me." He
went up to Mayfair two or three times a week, sometimes for ten

minutes' sex in a dark corner or a car, sometimes to spend a whole night with someone. "They'd take me out to dinner—a good dinner, you know, in a posh place—and then they'd take me back to their flat. It was always nice places, nice to be in even for a night, rather than my crummy hotel. That was the difference," he said, "between prostituting in the streets or finding people in discos. Street hustling would have been maybe four a night, twelve a week. Discos usually meant just one person—it was nicer."

After three months, Alan had an "affair" which lasted six months. "He was a very rich bastard, he was about thirty-five. First I stayed with him in Notting Hill Gate, then we got a bigger flat. He was living off his parents; he was on dope. His sister works in Parliament. He was nice to me—like a sugar daddy. He gave me money, anything I wanted, a stereo, clothes. The only thing was, he kept going away for weekends and wouldn't tell me where he was going, and I was that worried. And when I complained, he kept threatening he would commit suicide. In the end I got very sick of it and—I suppose just to spite him—I went out on the weekends and made my own money.

"After I got to know my way about, I went to the bar at a swish hotel—I made a hundred pounds a night, between two and three hundred the weekend. But half the time I felt like committing suicide. You can get very fed up with it: I got fed up with going down Mayfair. I'd say to myself, Why am I doing this? I'd earn a hundred pounds a night; the next day, if I went out for a meal with a friend, I'd spend fifty, sixty pounds . . . It's only worth having money so that you can show you've got it."

Was that what made him feel secure, I asked. "Yes. Now I don't care. I don't care about anything any more . . . "

Did Alan think that being a prostitute was wrong? "I used to think it was all right. I was not ashamed of it. You're a prostitute, you're a prostitute. I didn't think there was anything wrong with it."

What did he think his parents would feel? "Oh God, I don't know. My sister knows—I told her a year ago. She just said, 'Be careful, don't get caught. Look after yourself.' "

His sister hadn't indicated that she thought it wrong?

"No."

But aside from what Alan felt about himself, did he think it was right for grown-up men to use little boys sexually?

"No, I don't. But when you're a kid, you don't think, you know. Now I think because I'm older. I think, My God, these men and all this pornography. You think, My God, what horrible men and what stupid children we are. At the time you think it's okay, you know, it's great, it's money, but when you really start thinking, it does make you feel, you know. . . ."

Alan's happiest time was with twenty-five-year-old James, who was the son of a peer. He lived with him for three months, not so long before I met him. "That was different from anything else. He used to take me home with him to stay with his parents; his mum really loved me. You know, she gave me an account at Harrod's, wasn't that amazing? And she took me to Wheeler's in Knightsbridge [a very exclusive fish restaurant] and said any time I wanted to go there for a meal, I could charge it to her."

So James's mother knew her son was gay? "Oh yes, of course. She loves gay people. His father didn't. And he didn't like me. He thought I was common. I *was* common by comparison. But his mum was really lovely."

Did Alan ever make use of the Harrod's account? "Only if I went shopping with James. I'd never use it on my own. We split up when his father said he had to get married, to carry on the title, and he got engaged. He was the only son and he had to have a child. I loved him. We had wonderful times, just being together. He was very shy. We'd just sit and read. We'd go to the philharmonic and the ballet; we'd eat at home—I cooked. I do so love cooking. I so much want to learn really how to cook. We went for long walks in the country. And he took me to museums—he knew such a lot about paintings. He was so nice. When it all came to an end I thought, Christ, why did he have to be a bloody Lord?"

I asked whether he had seen James again. "No. He said he would invite me to the wedding, but he never did. I sometimes go to Harrod's, just to look around or to have breakfast. If I see his mother, she always comes and speaks to me. But we never mention James. I still love him and she knows it. She once said I was like a son—a younger son to her."

How much time on average did he spend with one man on "encounters"? "When it's in a car, about ten minutes. If it's back in their hotel or flat, say fifteen or twenty minutes."

Did he take any precautions, before or after? "Well, you go for a check-up to the clinic, and you try . . . you know . . . you try to be clean. When it's in cars, you go to a pub afterwards and clean up in the toilet and make sure everything's okay."

Did he care about any of these men? "I care about a lot of people," Alan said, and laughed bitterly. "I think that's what's wrong with me—I care about too many people. If I spend a night with somebody, I care quite a lot. If I spend a few hours, I care too. I don't care about myself," he said, and laughed again. "I think that's the problem. I am all wrong," he added. "All the nice people like girls . . . "

Why does Alan think boys go into prostitution? Why do they run away? "Because parents don't give them enough attention and they have a bad time at school," he said, quick as a whip.

But he wasn't with his parents when he ran away. "Yes, precisely," he said. "And my aunt nagged and nagged me, told me all the time what to do, not to do, she never said anything happy or good to me."

"Couldn't you have written to your parents and asked to go home?"

"How could I complain about her?" he said. "She is my mother's sister. And anyway, you know"—he was very often on the point of tears—"they didn't care. I wish I were older," he said a few minutes later, then paused. "No," he added, very quietly, with not the least attempt at drama, "I wish I were dead."

18

Nellie's Truth

In all the months—years now—that I have talked with Nellie, she has only once spoken of death, and then with the comparative detachment instilled in a Roman Catholic child from the moment they can think.

"If I die," she said, "I'll die whichever way I'm supposed to."

Did she feel like this because she believed in God? "I'm not positive whether I believe in God or not. Like everybody else, when I'm in trouble I say, 'God, please help me'; everybody calls on God when they want something. I don't think that's faith, do you? But there has to be something above—no—something beyond us. People who go on about being atheists make me sick. What do they contribute to anything? To me, somebody who babbles on about being an atheist is usually somebody selfish. But I'm not a true Roman Catholic. I go to confession—oh, at Christmas, at Easter, sometimes in between."

Why bother to go to confession at all? "I do it as a duty, I think. I think it's my last link with my parents, with my father. I don't want to break it; I don't want to lose it. But all the time when I confess, you know, I know with my brain it can't be right. I said that to the priest, both up in Scotland and here, too. I said 'How can I be doing what I'm doing and then just get absolved by you when I confess?' The one up in my home town, he is a very good man, a fantastic priest. He said, 'As long as you come to confession and say you need to confess, that's quite enough. God knows anyway what you are doing, so you don't have to go into all the details'—the 'gory details,' he said. 'Just keep coming to church.' "

As I wrote in beginning this account of Nellie's life, she was seventeen when I met her, and therefore at liberty to do what she wished with her life. The events and feelings she described thus had to be carefully related to the subject of this book. Interestingly enough, when I compared Nellie's experiences in prostitution with those of boys and girls still under age as I talked to them, I found time and again that all the details she had told me matched those told by the younger children. The advantage of talking to Nellie was that being just that much older and considerably more intelligent, she could both articulate and in retrospect evaluate what she had lived through so recently as a child.

It was from her that I learnt that the money a girl earns in the street in Britain varies even more widely than in America or West Germany, depending not only on the time of year, the weather and the locality, but above all on the nationality of the punter.

"I charge twenty quid, right?" Nellie said. "In summer I charge more. It depends on the punter, what he looks like, what he sounds like. But in Gloucester Road—whether it's me at seventeen or the wee lassies at thirteen, it's thirty quid cold whack in summer, right? Unless you get one that's feeling fucking splashy with his money, you know." She laughed. "You always know the ones that's going to pay more. It's a routine, right? 'Hello, how are you? You want business? How much?' The ones that aren't splashy will ask in return, 'How much?' The ones that are, they'll say, 'Ah, fifty pounds,' and you'll say, 'No, not enough, darling.' " She laughed. "You laugh with them, you know; you make it like a game . . . that's why it's called the game, you know. It *is* a game, in a way. Anyway, if they are splashy, I usually get seventy from those. And if they say no or something, then you say, 'Well good-bye, try somebody else, darling,' and then usually (the game, you see) they'll say, 'That's a lot of money,' and I say, 'Well, I'm a lot of woman.' It's crap, you know. It's a routine . . . what the Yanks call a spiel. You say it to every man."

But how would a child—such as she herself was when she started—how would a child know how to do all this? "One listens, one watches, one hears. But picking up punters off the street carries a lot of risk. I would never advise any chick unless she was really strong, in mind and body, ever to be a street hustler. Bars and hotels—they aren't any more agreeable, but it's safer . . . "

I said that I knew now how it worked when a child was edged into it by hotel managers or desk clerks; but how did it work when it was done on an organised basis?

"Well, they all get their wee cut. If the hotel agrees, you've got to put out ten pounds at least before you can even sit in the fucking bar. Earl's Court hotels are handy—they'll let anybody in. In one of them, you had to have a twenty-pound subscription—that one's been closed down. But no matter, they'll open up again in minutes. They call it 'under different ownership'—all they do is pass it on to their brother-in-law or something. Just another creep who'll do exactly the same as the last one and the police haven't even got enough men to watch them all."

But why did Nellie call them creeps, when it is they who provide her livelihood?

"I don't have to respect them, do I, because I use them? Can you imagine grown men, whether they are English, Scots or Indians, taking money off kids who they force—or if you like enable—to hustle? Oh, it's all right when one's grown. But kids! And all of them allow kids in there—they just take more money off them, because it's a risk for them. And you don't want me to call them creeps? What do *you* think of them?" she asked me, in a challenging tone.

"I think they are creeps," I said, and she laughed and laughed.

"Anyway," she went on, "the subscription covers sitting in the bar, and a room for the night. But the room finished at six the next morning; if you wanted it later, you had to pay another twenty pounds. Then you had it until six o'clock that night. You were also entitled to one free drink. The punters don't do any of the dealing, you do it yourself. It's just sitting in the bar. The barman arranges it for you, usually. You tip him five quid and say, 'I'm looking for some business.' I often did eight punters in there in one night, but more often than not I'd go over the six o'clock limit so I'd end up with a laughable amount, like sixty pounds. A lot of the Earl's Court hotels are last resorts. If the weather's miserable, it's better than nothing. Punters *crowd* in there . . . you could do fifty men a night if you had the strength, but none of them will pay more than ten pounds each. ("That's blasphemy, don't leave that on your tape," she stressed.)

"Of course, if I stay with one man all night, I earn a hundred, wherever it is, but I rarely do it. I don't like to. If they ask for that it oftens means they're kinky and I won't do anything kinky—I'm just straight sex. And I wouldn't advise any wee lassie to even think of doing anything kinky. She wouldn't know what she's letting herself in for. Sometimes funny things happen, though: I met one young Iranian student who was upset because his father had forced him to take this course and he didna want to. Iranian parents are really strict—they are

Persian, you know, not Arabs. He was very lonely and he said, 'I just want someone to talk to, I don't want to fuck.' I said I still wanted paying for it. But then I gave him the address of a club I knew where I knew a couple of Iranians were members, but he didna come.

"On the whole," Nellie went on, "I prefer to go with foreigners—coloured men, you know, because with white men there are two possibilities: they are either fucking kinky, or they are Old Bills. One day I was running very short—bad weather—and I met this white man and he said, 'How much do you want?' I said eighty pounds. He said, 'Actually I don't want a fuck.' So I said, 'What do you want, because I am not one for going about with chains.' 'No, no,' he said, 'it's nothing that'll hurt you, I promise.'

"Well, I went to his hotel with him . . . I had my knife in my boot, you know (you remember I told you about that carving knife I always carry? And if he tried any funny business with me, I'd cut him up before he could say one two three, I wouldn't give it a second thought and I told him so). Anyway, when we got up there, he pulls out a wee black suitcase with four canes, a cat-o' nine-tails, I think you call it. It had four strong prongs. He said, 'If you just beat me for fifteen minutes, I'll give you anything you want.'

"I said I wanted a hundred and fifty pounds for ten minutes, because if I did it any longer I'd end up losing my temper and kill him. He had a pair of leather handcuffs, too. I left the poor bastard bleeding. I didna believe a man could want such a thing, but he did. I took the money first, and as he was handcuffed I could have taken his wallet—it had a lot more in it. But I felt sorry for him so I just untied him and went. Poor bastard."

How did she feel about herself when she did this? "I hadn't got the slightest notion that I could even do it. I think it upset me so much, I hit out hard because I was sick about him and me. But that was the only time I did anything like that.

"Though I did once . . . well, there was this guy I knew, not as a punter, but in my travels, and he said, 'What would you do for money, Nellie?' So I told him what I *wouldn't* do. And he said, 'Would you treat a guy like a baby?' Well, like I said, I had heard of that one before, it's an English speciality. *God*—the English! Anyway, he said he'd pay me for doing him a harmless favour. He took me to his flat and he had a specially built high chair and baby clothes, in his size. I fell about laughing and said, 'What do you want me to do?' He said, 'You'll see.' He took off his clothes and he had a nappy on. I was still treating it as a joke. But he said, 'Just treat me like a baby.' I said, 'I don't know what to do.' 'Just tell me to get into the high chair, and help me,' he said. So I did, you know, and he starts saying Mama and googoo and I just keep bursting out laughing. I mean, he is a public school boy—about twenty-two he was then, I think. He went to Eton and did terribly well at university. He has real brains. He's as posh as they come. He had a nanny until, oh, very old—his parents were always abroad.

"Anyway, he says, 'Take it seriously, otherwise it's no good.' So I put on my professional face and treated him like a baby, bathed him, fed him, changed his nappy and played with him on the floor as if he was a baby. I rolled a wee ball to him and all that. Oh fuck," she said, suddenly falling out of her baby-playing role. "Anyway, it got to me after a while so I said, 'Time for bed now'. 'Whehwheh,' he went. I said, 'Don't fucking play me up,' and he went again, 'Whehwheh.' 'Right,' I said, 'You asked for it,' and I gave him a few smart spanks on top of his nappy and he looked at me, all gentle-as-a-lamb-like and said, 'I'm ready to go to bed now.' I said, 'You're fucking right you are, my hand's getting sore.' He said, 'You've got to tuck me in.'

"He had a bed like a cot, a double bed with the sides folded in. That was so his girlfriend—he had the most beautiful fiancée, I guess he's married now—so that she wouldn't see the sides. He wanted me to put the sides up around him. I gave him a wee kiss on the foot and said, 'Night, night, darling, see Mummy in the morning.'

"I wouldn't take any money from him. I wasn't sorry for him, but he was my friend. I haven't seen him for about six months now, but I did see him about three weeks after this happened."

Was he embarrassed? "No, he came into the coffee-shop we use in Park Lane. He came up behind me and went 'gagagaga' and both of us fell about laughing. That's the kind of guy he is. He'll be very unhappy with the snippy-faced bitch he's marrying, beautiful but hard—it's a shame. She'll never understand anything; he'll never be able to tell her anything; he'll be going to prostitutes for as long as he lives."

And she thinks child prostitutes are asked to perform this kind of "service"? "Yes. Oh, it didn't happen to me professionally, so happens, but I've heard of it many times from wee lassies. They don't mind none; they enjoy that. There's no harm in it, you know. It's just sad that a man should need that. It's funny," she said again, "it's always the English who want this sort of thing. Arabs don't."

*

In Britain, foreigners, and particularly Arabs, provide a large percentage of a child prostitute's clientele. "It's incredible how much you get from an Arab," said Alan. "They've got this incredible amount of money, they peel off notes as if it was so much paper—I've seen them do it. It makes your eyes pop. I've seen girls who go for the whole night and come out with fourteen or fifteen hundred pounds."

"That's true," said Debbie who was then fifteen. "You'd certainly never go with an Arab under a hundred. But once, just once," she added dreamily, "there was one that gave me one thousand two hundred pounds. I was only fourteen, you know, and I see him take this heap of notes from an even bigger heap on the dresser without counting, and just hand it to me and would you believe it, I say, 'But that's too much.' Well, he was nice. He just waved and said in his funny English, 'Enjoy . . . you enjoy.' So I did."

What did she do with that enormous sum of money?

"Two girls and I went on a spree for a whole day. We went to the King's Road and we just went into one boutique after another and we each got goodies coming out our ears and we had a slap-up lunch and a fantastic dinner in a posh place, all dressed up we were to the teeth, with all those Italian waiters making eyes at us, but this time we were *ladies*—ladies like the others and nobody thought different."

I tried without success to find an Arab visitor or resident in Britain who used child prostitutes and who was able or willing to talk to me. My attempts failed principally because of the language barrier. Those men I was able to find spoke only the most basic English and no other foreign language. I did not think that, given what I wished to discuss, I could involve an interpreter, either Arab or English. The only one to whom I managed to get across the nature of my project on child prostitution waved me away with a laugh and a stream of Arabic. "You must understand," said a British academic specializing in the Near East, "that the vast majority of Arab males view such a matter entirely differently from us. Not only is their general attitude to women one of master to servant, but in addition the female child has an entirely different meaning for the father than a male. Leaving aside princes or sheiks, the average Arab visitor abroad, particularly in England, where the class and caste system is still so much in force, lives a totally isolated life, limited for all his social needs to his own community. Of course, there are some Westernized Arabs. They're highly intelligent and can be very sophisticated men—most of them will have attended a British university or the Sorbonne. Incidentally, in France, Arabs—or for that matter people of any colour other than white—have a much easier, a much better time. The French are and always have been far more open, far more civilized not only in their attitudes, but *feelings* towards foreigners, than we are.

"In Britain," he went on, "it's virtually unheard of for a non-Westernized Arab to have sexual or even social contact with 'respectable' English women. Let's face it, this is irksome to some men. In addition," and he laughed, "it is intriguing for them, a challenge. Forbidden fruit and all that. But for white women, they *are* virtually restricted to prostitutes, many of whom, incidentally, reject them, in spite of the money they are willing to give. Given all these circumstances, you can see, can't you, that it's almost grotesque to expect them to know or to care what age a white girl is who solicits their favours?

"Now that I think of it," he concluded, "I've never heard of an Arab visitor to Paris seeking out girl children. Boys, yes—anywhere, if that happens to be their taste—but not little girls. And one more thing, I bet you've never come across any story of an Arab being cruel to a white girl. They are curious about them, but, I would gladly wager a bet, never cruel."

19

Meena: "All of it was a bit rude"

Twelve-year-old Meena, a Pakistani child with shiny black hair, soft brown eyes and a plump little body, all puppy-fat, had horrible experiences with foreigners, mostly Arabs. But it is true that none of them hurt her deliberately. Indeed, on several occasions she had not been sexually used herself, but had been made to play the role of spectator. When she ran away from a children's home—a carefully structured, caring place in one of the most beautiful parts of England— it was at the instigation of an older girl.

"It wasn't me, really, who decided to run away," she said. "It was Rita. She's sixteen." Although Meena has been speaking English from infancy, she often uses literal translations of Urdu words. "She goes to me that she can't blink," she said.

"Blink," Meena repeated, and winked suggestively. It could have been funny, as she meant it to be, but in the context it looked obscene. "She can't blink for men, you know," she said. "Get men, for money . . ."

We were having lunch in the almost empty dining-room of a "chic" country pub, a place I thought might give her pleasure. "Ohhhh," she said, glancing in mock alarm at two men busy with their lunch at a far-off table. "I'm glad those men didn't see when I did that. Anyway, she tells me on the morning when the counsellor wakes us up that she's gonna go straight outside and wait for me, and I say, 'No, why?' and she goes, 'Well, I want some money from men and I go.' And I say, 'Why do you want money? You can't just get money off men.' And she goes, 'You do it with them' . . . I didn't rightly know, but I think [guess], you know, what she means and I don't like doing it. . . ."

Meena had not in fact known about the facts of life—Rita told her after they got to London. "Well," she said, "I did know what I saw on TV, you know, but . . . you see, I don't like seeing that. Our religion don't really like a lot of sex; they don't think about sex. Well, she was talking about it [all] when we got to Piccadilly, you know, and what happened: she said, 'You have to take your clothes off,' and I said, 'I don't like doing that, it's not my religion to do it,' and she goes, 'You really have to. Otherwise, how are you going to have money?' and I go, 'I don't want money, it's *you* who want money.' Then she goes, 'If you are not gonna do it, I'm gonna slap you right in the face.' "

The two girls spent a week in London after that, in deliberate pursuit of Arab clients. "Rita, she goes blink at them, always at *them*—they pay most," said Meena.

My talk with Meena could only take place because the highly qualified medical man running the children's home she had been placed in a year before felt that he and his staff (specialists in disturbed children) had got about as far with her as they could over this recent unhappy escapade to London. He considered it just possible that she might open up further to me and thus enable them to help her more effectively.

Meena's problems, which led to her becoming an habitual shoplifter—the reason for her being taken into care—lay in her parent's alienation from British life. The parents, with their deep attachments and needs for their native culture, and the children, with *their* needs and allegiances to Britain where they were born, were locked in constant and unremitting collision. This is a conflict to be found in many immigrant families in Britain. It is made worse by the traditional closeness of family life, which is impressed or imposed on the Indian and Pakistani child from the moment it is born. As the growing child becomes increasingly exposed to external influences, the differences in language, interests, and customs intensify, and the emotional demands on the child can become overpowering.

Meena was a remarkable case in point: the youngest child of four, she loved her parents deeply, and desperately wanted their affection. She also needed, equally desperately, the approval of her older siblings, who were much further along in accepting the inevitable generation gap, and who, in order to protect or confirm their own self-images, deliberately adopted their peer groups' largely anti-social conduct. Thus, two years before we met, Meena, in a desperate attempt to "belong," had accompanied her sixteen-year-old sister in shoplifting expeditions. But, for a very special and extraordinary reason, her attachment to her parents remained uppermost and came to dominate all her thoughts. For Meena believed that her parents had killed one of their children in babyhood . . .

The story only emerged slowly.

"How many of you are there at home?" I asked.

"Well, this is a secret and I don't want to tell nobody at all. I had three sisters, but the one—my first sister that was born—died as a baby."

"How did she die?" I asked.

Meena squirmed in her chair. "I don't know the whole about that . . . my big sister told me that she died, and my mum and dad found out I knew and said that I wasn't to tell my brother or my other sister, ever at all."

"But why not?"

"Because we don't want nobody else to know about this."

"But why, Meena? Babies sometimes die. There's no shame in it; it's only sad."

"Well, we tell—they told—people it was a disease or something, that she was sick, but people might say it is a lie or something. My dad doesn't even like people to know about it, you know, if they just hear us talk about it, they start crying . . . "

"Do they get angry?"

"They cry."

"Do you want to tell me what it is that worries you so about this? You are worried, aren't you?"

"Well . . . " she started to cry.

"Would you rather not talk about it? Perhaps it would be best if you talked to the doctor about it [the psychiatrist in charge at the children's home]. Would you like to do that and forget about it for now?"

"No. Because I'm so worried, things are worrying me so. I want to go back home because my parents—they need me, because, see—I *know*."

"You *know*?"

"Yes, and they . . . my mum and dad . . . they are scared, see . . . my mum, she twice had a heart attack."

"Have you told anyone before today about the baby who died?"

"No, oh no; my mum and dad," she said again, even more urgently, "after my sister told me, they said, every day, every night, 'Never tell anybody,' so I never did . . . "

"And now? Why are you telling me now?"

She cried again. "I don't know; I cry so much because I'm really worried."

Meena never actually pronounced the words "killed" or "murdered," but there was no doubt at all that that was what she thought; nor was there much doubt that this knowledge—quite possibly a mistaken suspicion, which she had gained two years before—had put an intolerable burden on her. It was four weeks after she learnt about it that she was first arrested for stealing, and less than a year later, after numerous other misdeeds, that she was taken into care. At the end of our talks, I told her that I would tell the doctor all she had said. I had to do that, I said, because he was responsible for her, and he was her friend. He would help her after I had gone. She agreed.

Why did she think she had run away to London with Rita, I asked.

"Because I was scared of her?" She put it in the form of a question.

Was that the real—the only reason? "Nobody likes me," she said. "Only my parents: they did, they do," she repeated, vehemently. "They love me a lot . . . Pakistani children never do run away, they always stay near to their parents. I never run away before . . . this was the first time . . . because that school doesn't really love me a lot. I think the doctor loves me but in the meeting [some weeks before] Rita, she said to the doctor that the other children, they don't like me . . . I was a bit scared, shocked to be told that in a meeting . . . nobody likes me down in England because I'm fat, see? In Pakistan, in Karachi, when we go there two years ago . . . a boy, he was thirteen . . . he goes [said], 'I like how you look like,' and when we leave, he asks my mum if he can gave me a kiss, and she said, yes, a *little* one, and he gave me a big one." She laughed. "But then, at my school at home [in England], the children called me 'flea-bag.'. . ."

"Why, darling? Did you perhaps have fleas? That can happen to anyone."

"Oh no . . . Pakistani children are very clean—never fleas or things in the hair, never, never dirt in the house like in English houses. Never bring dirt in from outside, never wear shoes in living-room or kitchen or bedroom . . . I don't know why they called me 'flea-bag,' " she said in a depressed sort of way. "The only one who likes me here," she said, equally sadly, "was Rita. And she's gone now; they sent her away."

Sixteen-year-old Rita was sent home after the escapade to London, because the staff of the children's home found her influence on the younger children impossible to deal with. "In Meena's case," said Dr

L, "she actually played the role of the pimp. As you saw, it is quite tragic, because this is a deeply dependent child who was sexually totally innocent. We cannot even begin to estimate the harm that has been done to her."

I could never pin Meena down as to just how many men they had intercourse with during the six days they prostituted in London, mostly in hotels around Victoria Station and Piccadilly, with Rita accepting grotesquely small sums of money for services rendered and getting half of anything Meena "earned" as well.

The first man who took them up to his hotel room near Victoria kept them with him all night and gave them each £3 in the morning.

"What happened there?" I asked.

"She, Rita, she got right drunk and then she got sick and then she undressed. I just got up and went."

Where? "Outside . . . "

"All night? Where did you sleep?"

"Outside there," she tried.

"In the corridor?"

"Mmhm," she said.

"Mmhm?" I repeated. "Is that perhaps a bit of a fib?"

She laughed. "What really—I was scared to tell you—both of us slept . . . I slept on the floor . . . I didn't really like seeing it when they, you know, so I just slept on the floor . . . and then, she was so rotten drunk, she fell asleep and he fell asleep as well."

And in the morning, what happened then? "Well, those two did it again and . . . I saw them . . . I don't like to—I never have," evidently she was being paid for assisting as a voyeur.

"But at home," I said, "you and your brother slept in a room with your parents—your brother in a small bed, and you on a mattress on the floor. So you knew about people making love, didn't you?"

"No, no, they never do it, they never—they don't like sex—I mean, they don't go just and do it, you see what I mean?"

"Do you mean that Muslims like your parents only make love to have babies?"

"That's all they want it for—they don't, they don't," she repeated, urgently. "And I didn't like it, it's not my religion . . . "

"I see. Well, anyway, what did you do after Rita had been with that first man?"

"We went to Piccadilly to find another man, that's what we did. I've forgotten some of these men's names, which is silly . . . "

"We don't need their names," I said. "How many men do you think there were, all together, for each of you?"

"Oh, I don't know," she said, after a long silence.

"In the end you had to do it yourself too, didn't you?"

"Yes, I didn't like it . . . it was a coloured man, they were all coloured men. The first one, he looked a bit old, about thirty-five. Rita, she said, 'All Arabic men are rich, we take Arabic men.' "

That first man she was actually with, was that in a big hotel or a small hotel? Silence.

"A big building or a small building?"

"A little bit big."

And was she alone with this man or was Rita with her? "She was still with me."

Did Rita have another man, or did they just stay together, all of them?

"The three of us stayed together . . . " As was to happen time and again, both girls had sex with the man, one after the other.

"Did this first man hurt you?"

"It pained a lot." Had she told him she had never done this before?

"No, I think he knew." Rita told all the men that Meena was eighteen. "And she goes, 'I'll bash your face in if you say different.' " The man gave each of the girls £10 and he also gave them supper, curry and rice.

The second man she had sex with, did it hurt her as much? "Yes, it hurt me a lot. I was, you know . . . I was so small for them . . . "

Did she like anything about it? Silence. Did it sometimes feel nice? Silence. She had watched Rita several times, hadn't she? So when she had to do it, because Rita said she'd beat her if she didn't, did she try to move the same way Rita moved? "I hope so," she whispered.

Had Rita told her, described to her what to do? "Yes."

Had she seen Rita do all kinds of things? "Yes."

And had Rita told her she too must do whatever they wanted?

"She was telling me to, but I said I don't want, I was just keeping saying no." Her parents, Meena said, would get angry with her if they knew what she had done. "Right down angry." There had been, she thought, fifteen men, but she wasn't sure. "Could be more, could be fewer. Two of them didn't give us money. Rita was really in a temper because of that." Four of the men she said, had been "really young," one was old, the others "in the middle."

One—just one of the men—"didn't want to do it," she didn't know why. "But he said, 'We will not' . . . he had his pants off and he kissed me a lot."

Just kissed her? "Yeah, a lot . . . "

And had she quite liked that, perhaps? She smiled, shyly. "Yes. And . . . he gave me, gave us forty pounds: twenty to her and twenty to me." She *had* liked that man, the kissing. "But I don't like doing it undressed." And she didn't like it when they used bad words, as some of them did and as Rita did all the time.

Was Meena cross with herself for having done this? "I have to be, don't I?"

No, she didn't have to be. It was her own decision. Did she think she had done something wrong? Or didn't it perhaps really matter all that much?

"I think I did do something wrong. I talked to the doctor about it and he said it is not good for me and I think that's true."

But it was an exciting week, wasn't it? "It was scary."

"Of course, parts of it were scary, but weren't there things about it that were fun too, or funny?" I asked.

"Funny?" she repeated, sounding indignant at my choice of words. "It was a bit *rude*."

"Rude?"

"All of it was a bit rude. . . ."

In principle I consider it wrong to subject young children to this kind of questioning, so when I talked to Meena I was, in a way, doing violence to my own feelings. I would not have talked to her at all without the ready agreement of the expert in charge of her, who had worked with her over several weeks following her experiences in London and thought that such a conversation with an informed outsider might help to break down the barriers Meena had erected. And apparently it did, in fact, help. It did make it possible for the staff to take over where I had left off, enabling her to enlarge upon the story she told me, and thereby continue to free herself of the guilt she felt so deeply.

But my main reason for quoting this inarticulate child so fully is that in the course of research I have so often been told that the children to whom such things happen *provoke* the experiences; that in our progressive era, children are quite sophisticated enough to deal with such experiences, and "being what they are," do not suffer any ill consequences. This, basically, is the same argument as the one which claims that no woman can be raped. By demonstrating verbatim how this totally innocent child reacted to direct but carefully formulated questions, I have tried to show her inner revulsion and, at the same time, the consequences of her inevitable submission on this child's spirit. There is no way of demonstrating this except by letting her speak.

And this applies equally to all the children. It is only by letting them speak, by listening to their fantasies, their dreams, their nightmares, and their poor small hopes that one can get a glimmer of understanding.

20

Nellie Pays

By the time we got towards the end of our original conversations, which had stretched over several months, Nellie told no more lies. I had seen her parents and had been told by her afterwards of her own amazement at wanting me to find her out. I had also watched her repeated attempts to form normal, or semi-normal, relationships, and the failure of these attempts. With Elana McCreaner, her friend and mine, who was as concerned about Nellie as I was, I had tried to motivate her away from prostitution towards training or study for a career, or some job she might learn to enjoy.

We had seen her slowly change from the lovely, clear-complexioned girl who looked much younger than her seventeen and eighteen years to a drab, tired-looking woman, an obvious drinker, who could have been anything from twenty-six to thirty-five.

"If we said to you, 'we'll try to make it possible for you to do anything you really want to do,' " I'd asked her one day, perhaps nine months after we met, "what would you want to do?"

She thought about it for a long time. "Babies," she said finally. "I'd love to work with babies."

I explained at once that with her record, which could not be hidden from anyone we would have to talk to, this might turn out to be impossible. What would be her second-best choice?

"Animals," she said. "If I could work with animals."

It took some doing, but we obtained interviews for her towards fulfilling both these ambitions. One of the most enlightened directors of social work in England, from a town in the north, achieved a conditional agreement (depending on an interview) from an equally generous woman who was in charge of a baby-home in his area. And through friends, benefactors of the Battersea Dogs Home, she was given a chance (this, again, depended on an interview) to work in these famous kennels for lost dogs.

She didn't show up for either of the interviews, nor did she come when we managed to set them up a second time.

"Why didn't you come?" I asked her later knowing the answer only too well.

"I thought and thought about it, but I think I'm not capable of handling such jobs . . . I don't think I'm responsible enough." Instead, she had found herself a job as a barmaid. "It's probably the work I'm best suited to. It's not much money—just forty-five pounds a week—but everybody takes some, from the bar, it's the perks of the job."

Takes money? "Yes, I take about five pounds a night. I know it's wrong from your point of view, but not from mine—if I wasn't taking it, somebody else would. You see," she went on, when I reminded her how she had loved the idea of working with children or studying, "I can sit and listen to you and I can agree with everything you say and inside I can say to myself, I wish she'd fucking shut up. I used to do it all the time, listen to people and agree with them and then fuck it up. Now I don't; now I won't, because it just gets too bad. I'm just bullshitting myself. And what's the point? If you're going to start bullshitting yourself rather than just others—that's *really* the end. I think I know what I can do and what I can't do. That doesn't mean I'm lying, that I was lying when I told you what I'd *like* to do. That was the truth. But I can't, that's all there is to it. I'm not good enough. Just think, if something happened to a baby I'm supposed to be taking care of? Or even a little dog? How can it be right," she said, echoing Marianne's morality, in West Germany, "for somebody who's had VD *twelve* times to go and look after *babies*?

"You know what really shit me up? A little while ago, a punter I knew two years back, came back. I was really fond of this punter, he was a nice, nice guy. We were lying in bed and talking, and he said, 'Before, you used to look sixteen, now you look sixty,' and I just cracked him across the jaw, man, because he was saying what I was thinking. He didn't mind none, he just turned around, turned the light on me full and said again, 'Before, you looked so young.'

"I haven't hustled for two weeks now," Nellie went on, "and I'm hoping to get off it. I'm fucking *praying* to get off it. I don't want to become an old slag. Every hustler says, one more season. That's me, I say, two more weeks, a month. Hustlers don't save money. Any hustler tells you she saves money, she's a liar. When I met you first—when was it, less than a year ago?—I was making seven hundred pounds a week, easy, on good weeks. It's all gone, every penny."

"But what on earth can you do with that kind of money, given the way you live?"

"I drink it," she said, simply and starkly. "That's what I'm most frightened of. Like something that happened the other day, with that guy Mick I've been going around with. I was in the kind of mood I get into sometimes now, and I was having arguments with everybody, and Mick, he pulled me into the bedroom, told me to lay off, and slapped me. I told him, 'Never lay a hand on me again, or I'll stab you to death.' I don't want to hurt anybody: my head just gets filled up and then things just happen, you know. Mick, he went out and came back with his buckle belt, and I swear I tried to stab him. I can't stand anybody slapping me. I just can't stand it. I was never so relieved in my life when he forced me down on the floor and I realized I hadn't done it—I hadn't cut him. Of course, I was drunk. . . ."

The man Nellie killed three years later was twenty-three years old. She had been living for two months with Greg—a boyfriend, not a ponce—in a "half-way house" flat just behind King's Cross, now one of London's most disreputable areas, and had just decided to leave him. The morning before the final day, she had rung her mother in Scotland and asked whether she could come home. Her mother said, yes, that it didn't matter she didn't have any money. "Just come home," she said.

Nellie went to try and get a ticket for the long-distance bus, but they had no seat until two nights later.

The following morning she, Greg and several others started drinking at about ten o'clock. By noon, the mood was belligerent. When Steven joined them—the boy who was to die, who was no more than a casual acquaintance of theirs—he started a fight with Greg and was thrown out. The drinking continued on and off all day. (When Nellie's blood was tested by the police that night it showed an alcohol content of 192 mg/100 ml—80 mg is the legal limit for drivers—and Steven's blood, tested after he was dead, showed 227 mg.)

By ten o'clock that night, Greg had passed out in the bedroom; one of their friends, Bob, was there, asleep. Nellie was in the kitchen, cooking, when Steven appeared at the door of the flat saying he wanted to see Greg. "I don't want him woken up," she said. "Get out."

Steven called her a slag, not worth fighting over, and slapped her. "You touch me once more," she screamed. "I'll stab you!" He took her by the shoulder to turn her around.

Nellie stabbed him five times. The boy bled to death.

If a person by an act of his or her hand causes the death of another, said the judge in his summing-up to the jury, he or she is guilty of that death. If there is intention actually to kill or to cause grievous bodily harm, it is murder. If one cannot be sure of such intention, or if the act was a consequence of intolerable provocation, then it is not murder but manslaughter. And if this young woman committed such an act in the course of self-defence, then she must be acquitted.

This was his general explanation to the jury. But his final words were more specific and, one must assume, of decisive importance to the twelve men and women who were to decide Nellie's fate. Later her lawyers were briefly to consider an appeal on the grounds of the summing-up, but they finally decided it would be pointless.

Is it reasonably possible, in this case, asked the judge, that there was sufficient provocation to make "a reasonable woman" act in such a way? If the jury thought so, then they must bring in a verdict of manslaughter. Is it reasonably possible that the accused was provoked into losing her self-control? If not—if in the opinion of the jury the story she had told in court was "transparent nonsense" and they were sure she was not provoked into losing her self-control—then they must bring in a verdict of murder.

It took them less than an hour to reach that verdict, and it was unanimous.

They had heard nothing of Nellie's background, or of her childhood experiences. Two psychiatrists had seen her, but their findings were not made public. The defence lawyers felt that if they brought up her childhood, the prosecution, using the same documentation, would have brought up her record of violence. As for the psychiatric evidence, the stories she had told the two psychiatrists had been—as one lawyer put it—"as far apart as the moon," and would only have shown her up as a liar. These stories included, once again, the story of her child, Kim.

Why, I asked Nellie when it was all over, had she trotted out that old fantasy?

"It was my only mitigation," she answered, an irrationality which surely any twelve human beings might have found proof of a disturbed state of mind rather than criminal inclination.

During the period of her trial and the first week of her life sentence, Nellie read Dostoievski's *Crime and Punishment*. Three weeks later, when I first visited her, she gave me a vivid and clear analysis of this difficult book. "It really meant something to me," she said. "It was as if he was talking to *me*."

Nellie's situation is, of course, different from that of any of the other children with whom I worked. For she was the only one amongst them who ended up committing a crime, a fatal one at that. Even so, a truly enlightened society would never send to prison, for *life*, a girl of that age and that background.

Nellie's original intention, indeed, her determination was to change her life. To use this awful but perhaps fated opportunity to make something of herself; to study English, history and psychology—the subjects she has always been interested in—toward O and then possibly A Levels and the university education of which, in principle, she is eminently capable.

She stuck to this plan, at some sacrifice (the permission to attend classes depends on the degree of willingness to do menial jobs) for the first six months, the same period during which she also asked us to visit her, agreed to talk with psychiatrists and social workers in the prison, and kept up a fairly constant correspondence with me (seven letters in the first five months).

There have been no letters since, and it is now a year and half since she was committed. Indeed, about four months ago, she sent a specific message that she wanted no more visits from anyone except her "pals".

It was the step backward we had feared, which could probably only have been avoided if she had been transferred away from a huge women's prison to a different, more open facility catering to young prisoners. During her first months of prison, the drinking stopped, her physical condition improved dramatically, and she was open to influence from well-meaning adults. The turn-about came when the expected and hoped-for transfer did not materialize and she realized that this sort of prison, with these prisoners, would be her life for many years to come. Already—the promises of the transfer broken—she felt betrayed, and reacted exactly as we feared. She abandoned the short and long-range plans she had made with us, the outsiders; and probably quite deliberately, decided to get the best out of the only life she would have in the foreseeable future.

A doctor reports that she is physically well, but "getting heavy" ("I'm going to be very careful in here," she told me the last time I saw her. "The women who are fat are the ones who've given up").

A social worker says she is working in the sewing shop but "not attending classes" ("I've GOT to go on with classes," she said on that last visit. "I know it's my only chance").

A friend who is a prison visitor and sees some of Nell's friends says: "Oh, Nell, she's running the joint."

Nellie is and always has been the kind of person who ends up "running the joint." ("I've got to stop running other people's lives," she once told me. "It takes all my energy and always, invariably, makes me angry because they are all so stupid.") In just one year of prison she has come full circle. Her ambitions and her dreams have vanished away, and she has become part of the system.

CONCLUSION

What you have read here was not intended as a scholarly study. There are no sociological or statistical tables because information of this sort does not exist. The children I write about are—except to those who seek them out—invisible.

At the end of three years working with them, with their parents and relatives, their social workers and teachers, their pimps and their friends, I am left with a sense of outrage, despair and frustration. It is not the children who shock me. They are almost invariably warm and sensitive, with open and enquiring minds and—given their atrocious experiences—a strangely unsullied innocence. If I feel despair it is over their parents and relatives, many of them basically good people but unaware of their own deficiences and how to deal with them. And if I feel frustrated it is with our own inability to face squarely a problem which is at least partly of our own making.

Where have we gone wrong in our sense of priorities and responsibility, when children of a prosperous society—children like Patsy, Joey and Alex—see nothing wrong in selling their bodies to supplement their pocket-money, and find a ready market for their wares? How can it be that in the midst of the unprecedented social care available in Western countries, thousands of young boys and girls who cannot endure living with their families find themselves at the mercy of their own lack of resources and of those who prey upon them, with no recourse whatsoever to helpful adults or public means? And finally, how is it possible in these enlightened times that judges—the guardians of our rights and custodians of our laws—should in countless cases deliver minimal sentences—if any—to men who sexually abuse young children?

The economic ills of the Third World, and the obsession of the West with material possessions are, of course, relevant to the subject of this book, but these immensely complicated questions, and the changes in society which they demand, require other forums. But the children and adults speaking in these pages should enable us to take issue with the other questions, and with their causes.

Most of the causes are to be found in individual character traits and individual deficiencies, some of which may exist independently of societal pressures. But nobody lives in a void, and the young—especially those of them who are particularly vulnerable—are the people most subject to influences from without.

No other age has encouraged violent crime, as ours does, by constantly exploiting it as entertainment. No other age has subjected so many people to such a bombardment of artificial stimulation, so that our children are urged or forced as never before into adult behaviour and pleasures, and are brainwashed into readymade decisions on almost every puzzling subject under the sun, particularly that of sex. Every day of their lives, from newspapers, magazines, advertisements, pop music, and above all from television, they are presented with images and interpretations of sex which have little to do with its reality. They are supposed to be able to absorb and come to terms with all this without being damaged. Is it possible? Demonstrably, for quite a large number of them, it is not; and that should give us pause.

Although we are accustomed to think that the rejection of traditional values—those of family, religion and disciplined education—by the young is a nearly inevitable part of adolescent rebellion, the children we have met here appear to demonstrate a desperate *need* for family life, for structure in their environment, and for the kind of support found in a faith or in some degree of intellectual discipline.

Every runaway child who goes into full-time prostitution has a history of continual and profound family conflict: conflicts invariably the result of actions, words and above all feelings of adults, to which the children have reacted with anger, fear and confusion. Of course, one child—or one set of parents—may have the inate resources to withstand dissension; but others do not. One child can control jealousy; another is overwhelmed by it. While many children can manage their awakening sexuality, and many parents can help them, there are some children who find it difficult, and some parents who (quite possibly damaged themselves when they were young by equally inhibited fathers and mothers) are unable to help. Insecure in their own sexuality, they in their turn inflict damage on their own young; who, rendered even more vulnerable by the pressures of our times, break apart under the strain.

Some children are driven from their homes by sheer brutality, much of it in subtle pathological ways sexually prompted. Even graver—and surely a cause for far more concerted action by the public sector—is the extent of overtly sexual interference with children by fathers and male relatives. It seems extraordinary that in an age when anything is open to discussion, incest—arguably the most widely prevalent childhood sexual experience and certainly the most stunting—is still taboo.

Even less bearable for children than physical cruelty is persistent psychological pressure from parents, of the kind which occurs when quite commonplace deficiencies in adults—possessiveness, ambition, immaturity, coldness or inhibition—go beyond the norm and end by ruling family life. Children have an instinctive faith in their parents' strength and goodness and, as they grow up, try—often against considerable odds—to maintain it. In the cases of the children we are talking about here, this faith, after a long period of erosion, has crumbled, and with it their central life support. Parents can neither understand nor accept the child's growing awareness of their frailties. And the child's attempts to fight back, resist, or—saddest of all—even help, are misinterpreted and resented. The conflict escalates until the child's pain and confusion are beyond bearing, and he or she runs away.

The reasons for parental failure are various, but the consequences for children are always the same. Defeated by the loneliness of their decision to run—and stay—away, they feel valueless as children in a world of adults who cannot help them, and valueless as sons or daughters of parents whose lives, they are convinced, they hinder rather than enrich. Their value as children—their right to be protected—having been taken away from them, they feel worthless as human beings. Prostitution, this act of extreme self-abasement (and let no one believe that children do not very soon perceive it as such) serves both to feed their self-contempt and vengefully to express the anger and fear stored up against those who caused it—their parents.

So we have come almost full circle. We are forced to admit that prevention of the family–child breakdown may be impossible. There will always be individual parents who fail, and children who can no longer tolerate that failure. There will always be runaway children who cannot return home. What need *not* always be the case is that they must turn to prostitution in order to survive.

To prevent this fatal step, we must accept that some children cannot live with their parents; and indeed that some parents cannot live with—cannot endure—their children. Recognizing this uncomfortable truth is the essential first step towards any attempt to create the kind of public awareness, and the services and facilities, which would be able to take over before catastrophe strikes rather than afterwards.

Even were such measures established, there would still be the need for "first aid" (it can never be more than that) for children who have experienced prostitution. This can take the form of "safe houses," such as are being tried out in various American cities and very successfully in Holland, where the children can have a period of physical and emotional respite, safe from both family and pimp, while they and those helping them consider their future. Or it can be institutional care of some kind (such as was successfully offered to Rachel, Anna and Julie), where they can if necessary receive medical care during their period of respite. Or it can be "youth flats" such as the enlightened Berlin Youth Authority provided for Marianne, where a child can live on her own, or with a legitimate boyfriend, on condition that she completes her schooling. An additional possibility would be foster-care on the lines of the excellent American "foster-grandparents for handicapped children" scheme: carefully chosen and trained older couples, supported by counselling, could offer these children the parenting they so desperately want and need.

No such measures could be easy or fool-proof. But in some form they are essential. And what is equally essential is to face the fact that no children would go into prostitution if there were not adults who wanted to use them, men often so emotionally starved or damaged in their own childhood that their perception of other human beings and their sense of morality have become distorted beyond repair.

There are three types of sexual crime being committed against children daily, all over the world. The first is incest, which although not the subject of this book, has to be included here because the essence of the crime is the same as that of other masculine abuse of children. (The active agent is almost always male, although women are frequently passive partners by their silent consent.) The man tends to go from one girl-child to another, and the whole family is bonded into a conspiracy of guilty silence. The incestuous relationship between father and child is particularly complex because there is more often than not a degree of tenderness, and the child is therefore driven into a perverted kind of love.

The degree to which those who should be capable of understanding and doing something about these disastrous cases sometimes misjudge and mishandle them is exemplified by a priest and—more recently—by a judge. Some years ago, an international conference on child abuse in London was told by the priest (who was later relieved of his functions by his bishop) that in his opinion, the nature of incest was misunderstood. In his parish, he said, where there was a good deal of incest, these families were among the "most closely knit and most loving." And only days ago, as I write this, a judge in California ordered a nine-year-old girl to be held in solitary confinement for several days in order to force her to give evidence that her step-father had sexually assaulted her. When, predictably, she refused to speak, he ordered her to be returned to her step-father's custody.

Homosexual acts between adult males and young boys—again the incidence is enormous and increasing—appear, in Great Britain, to be primarily a middle- and upper-class phenomenon. (Interestingly, no cases have been reported between lesbians and under-age girls.) As such, they seem to be considered bad form rather then criminal, and are often subject to a particularly objectionable kind of class solidarity. On two occasions in recent years police in London presented the Director of Public Prosecutions (who must approve any case the police wish to bring) with evidence against several men of good professional and social standing, only to learn that the Director, in spite of evidence described to me by a senior police officer as "overwhelming," did not consider that there was a case to answer. "What's the use?" asked the police officer bitterly. Two of his best men had resigned as a result, and he said that it would be a long time before any British police force bothered to try again.

In America, too, prosecutions of males for sexual acts with minors are so rare as to be almost non-existent; and in West Germany the possibility can hardly arise: it is the only country I know where older people still look painfully embarrassed if homosexuality is even mentioned.

But before we limit the blame to any one social class or any one country more than another, we should remember that a congressman in America who was *convicted*—and widely mentioned in press reports—for having sexual relations with boys, was re-elected two years later by a large majority. I visited a number of his constituents. How *could* they re-elect a man like that to represent them and their families, I asked. In every case I was told that what he did in the privacy of his home had nothing to do with his effectiveness; he was, they all said, a particularly good congressman.

Finally, there are the men of all nationalities, classes, ages, colours, religions, who again daily, all over the world, make sexual use of young girls, often no more than eleven years old. If and when such men are apprehended—and it hardly ever happens—the punishment they receive is invariably minimal. "It's the kind of thing that could happen to anyone," said one British judge recently about a man who when drunk had sexually used a girl of ten.

To allow men to use children with impunity, and to ignore the children as though they were invisible, seems to me indefensible. "Do you think anyone cares?" Cassie asked me: a justifiably bitter question I was to hear time and again from these young victims. For victims they are: no child in prostitution *wants* to be a prostitute. They long to be wanted—as children. They long to be loved. They long to *be* children.

Martin O'Brien
All the Girls £1.95

In Buenos Aires she had a closed circuit TV covering the bed. In Rio she worked with another girl, taking turns. In Paris she trussed, blindfolded and lashed him. In Caracas she turned out to be a man. In Tokyo she sprayed him with Coke. In Budapest she cost 3,000 forints. In Munich she stole 1,600 marks while he slept. In Melbourne she accepted credit cards. In Moscow she preferred dollars . . . One man's odyssey across sixteen countries, to seek and buy the professional services of the girls of the night.

Jeanne Cordelier
The Life £1.95

There is no such thing as a happy prostitute, and Jeanne Cordelier gives us the truth. Brought up in a Paris slum by an alcoholic mother and a father who violated her, as a teenager she was offered temptation in the shape of a wealthy pimp who promised her money, bright lights and an endless supply of eligible young men . . .

'Fascinating on the physical drudgery and financial exploitation of prostitutes, no less so on the brutal theory and practice of pimps' NEW STATESMAN

Rosie Boycott
A Nice Girl Like Me £1.95

Rosie Boycott was a nice girl. She was also an alcoholic. This is her story, a frank and moving account of a girl who made it from the top to the bottom — and all the way up again.

'It is the story of growing up the hard way in an easy age, with a round-the-world ticket in one hand, a glass in the other, and fear and loathing down below' SUZANNE LOWRY, SUNDAY TIMES

Alan Burgess
The Small Woman £1.95

The amazing true story of Gladys Aylward, the parlourmaid who became
a missionary in China where, with great faith and indomitable courage,
she worked for twenty years.

When the Japanese came to bomb, ravage and kill, she led a hundred
homeless children on a terrible twelve-day march over the mountains
to the Yellow River and safety. Translated into many languages and
filmed under the title of *The Inn of the Sixth Happiness*, the book is the
inspiring record of the struggles and achievements of a most remarkable
woman.

The Diary of Anne Frank £1.95

The intimate record of a young girl's thoughts written during two years
in hiding from the Gestapo, to whom she was at last betrayed.

The *Diary* has appeared in twenty-eight languages, and over a million
copies have been sold in Pan alone.

'Few more moving and impressive books have come out of the war'
NAOMI LEWIS, OBSERVER

Piers Paul Read
Alive £1.95

There were 16 survivors. Despaired of by their families, they had
survived against all odds a plane crash and ten long weeks of endurance
in the icy wastes of the Andes mountains. Piers Paul Read was chosen
by these young men to tell, quite unsparingly, their story: a story of
constant faith, unbounded determination and immense courage – and
of how they broke the greatest taboo of mankind . . .

'One of the classic survival stories of all time'
DAILY MAIL

J. H. H. Gaute and Robin Odell
The Murderer's Who's Who £2.95

An illustrated anthology of 150 years of notorious murder cases: Manson, the Boston Strangler, the Acid Bath Murders, the Brighton Trunk Crimes, the Brides in the Bath, the Hammersmith Nudes and the horrific cannibalism of Albert Fish – plus countless lesser-known but equally horrendous and bizarre murders. According to Colin Wilson's foreword, 'Perhaps the most valuable single volume ever published on murder', fully indexed for reference use.

'One of the best-organized encyclopedias of crime' DAILY EXPRESS

'Compulsive reading' DAILY MIRROR

Gerold Frank
The Boston Strangler £2.50

The most bizarre series of murders since Jack the Ripper; the greatest man-hunt in the annals of modern crime; Albert DeSalvo, brutal sexual psychopath, who murdered thirteen women and held a city in the icy grip of terror for eighteen hideous months.

'Tells us everything about the case . . . chronologically, as it happened . . . the result is completely satisfying' NEW YORKER

Gordon Burn
'Somebody's Husband, Somebody's Son' £2.50

It seemed the case of the notorious Yorkshire Ripper was finally closed when Peter Sutcliffe was sentenced to life imprisonment in May 1981. *Sunday Times* journalist Gordon Burn spent two years researching Sutcliffe's life, living in his home town of Bingley, talking at length to everyone who knew him. His definitive account of the man and his crimes is a penetrating examination of the mind of a murderer.

'A book that will undoubtedly become a classic in the field of investigative criminology' COLIN WILSON

Emlyn Williams
Beyond Belief £2.95

The story of the Moors Murderers, Ian Brady and Myra Hindley.

'I keep remindin' myself,' Superintendent Talbot said to me, 'that this isn't a tale – that it's been happening . . .'

'Perhaps the greatest value of this book is that it shows us that the human monsters Brady and Hindley were not one and the same, but two different kinds of monster' TIMES LITERARY SUPPLEMENT

'An appalling subject, and overpowering book' SUNDAY EXPRESS

Frank Smyth
Cause of Death £1.95
the story of forensic science

A smear of blood, a flake of paint – the raw materials of the police work conducted on the lab bench and under the microscope lens, the evidence that brings the killer to justice. This compelling history traces forensic science from Bertillon and the early pioneers to the expert pathologists, chemists, toxicologists and ballistics specialists of today.

'Gruesomely fascinating . . . gory, bizarre reading' SUNDAY EXPRESS

Martin Gosch and Richard Hammer
The Luciano Testament £2.50

America's most notorious gangster tells all . . . Bribe by bribe, killing by killing, Charlie 'Lucky' Luciano came to be *capo di tutti capi*, boss of all the bosses, from Capone to Dutch Schultz and Bugsy Siegel. Companion to society women, confidant of politicians, he bought judges, union leaders, policemen to change the face of the Mafia. Told against the violent backcloth of America's underworld from the twenties to the fifties, this is the controversial story of his rise and fall.

Francis Hitching
The World Atlas of Mysteries £6.95

From the origins of the universe and terrestrial life, throught the unique development of man, to the secrets of ancient civilizations and bizarre phenomena in the sky and beyond – the enormous scope of this encyclopedia, its exhaustive research and copious illustrations (maps, photographs, diagrams) make it a unique and fascinating book. Francis Hitching, author of *Earth Magic*, is one of the world's leading authorities on the inexplicable and the unexplained.

'A book of absorbing interest to anyone who believes that there are more things in heaven and earth than science will recognize'
DR KIT PEDLER (creator of DOOMWATCH), EVENING NEWS

Jay Anson
The Amityville Horror £1.75

On 18 December 1975, George and Kathy Lutz, with their three children, moved into their new home at 112 Ocean Avenue, Amityville. Twenty-eight days later they fled from the house in terror . . .

'One of the most terrifying true cases ever of haunting and possession by demons . . . heart stopping . . . chilling' SUNDAY EXPRESS

'The scariest true story I have read in years' LOS ANGELES TIMES

Colin Wilson
The Psychic Detectives £2.50

The phenomenon of psychometry and psychic detection has its roots in the extraordinary powers, recorded through history, of those who can 'see' things otherwise totally unknown to them as a response to handling clothing or other inanimate objects. No established psychological or criminological science can explain this ability, through which psychics have been able to solve a crime, identify a murderer, locate a corpse, even predict where a killer will strike again. Colin Wilson, a bestselling authority on the paranormal, has investigated in this book subjects ranging from psychic archaeology to the Yorkshire Ripper case, from Madame Blavatsky to the mysteries of Atlantis.

Stephanie Norris and Emma Read
Out in the Open £1.95

At last, a book which shares the first-hand experiences of gays and bisexuals with others. Drawing on hundreds of letters and interviews, the authors provide fascinating insights into the lives of men and women from all walks of life. Simple honest and down-to-earth, this book bravely attempts to bridge the gap between gays and heterosexuals and provides revealing and enlightening reading.

Shirley Eskapa
Woman versus Woman £1.75

Wives and mistresses – a frank and fascinating account of the conflict between two women battling for one man. Read about the wives who saw the other woman as a challenge rather than a humiliation and fought back. Learn to recognize the early warning signals of an affair and how to tackle them. Discover the true feelings of the man in the middle. Compulsive, controversial and essential reading for every woman, and the man in her life.

Louise Roche
Glutton for Punishment £1.95

Imagine a girl at university, obsessed with food, buying bagfuls of biscuits and malted fruit loaf and chocolates and bingeing on them. Then the starving reaction – no more food for days and massive doses of laxatives. This was Louise Roche's life. She was a victim of *bulimia nervosa*. She was diagnosed as anorexic. When she began to eat again, she left hospital and the problems really started. Now, she is cured. With the help of friends and family and professional therapy, she's beyond the craving . . .

Larry Gurwin
The Calvi Affair £2.95
death of a banker

The discovery of the hanging body of banker Roberto Calvi under Blackfriars Bridge in June 1982 made headline news The mystery was heightened by the collapse of his Banco Ambrosiano, revealing a twisted net of intrigue. Journalist Gurwin has produced a thrilling account of Calvi's financial and political wheelings and dealings, his involvement with the notorious masonic lodge P2 and links with the Vatican Bank.

'Takes a hard look at those who played Mephistopheles and Lucifer to Calvi's overweening ambition . . . leaves the reader in little doubt that Calvi was murdered' FINANCIAL TIMES

Jimmy Boyle
A Sense of Freedom £2.50

Jimmy Boyle grew up in Glasgow's Gorbals. To survive he had to fight and steal. Approved schools led to Borstal, a career in crime . . . then they nailed him for murder. The sentence was life . . .

A Sense of Freedom is a searing indictment of a society that uses prison to destroy a man's humanity and an outstanding testament to one man's ability to survive.

Derek Wilson
Extraordinary People £5.95

An illustrated encyclopedia of the world's greatest eccentrics, visionaries, geniuses, enthusiasts, adventurers and criminals through the ages. William Blake and Captain Blood, Walt Disney and Mozart, Ronald Biggs and Nostradamus, a random sample of people who had one thing in common — by any definition of the term they were extraordinary people.

Brian Moynahan
Airport International £1.95

The sensational book that takes the lid off the world of international air travel. How smugglers operate, and how they're caught . . . when and how luggage is pilfered . . . how air traffic control really works . . . how airports cope with a crash landing . . . which are the dangerous airports that pilots try to avoid . . . your chances of survival in an air crash.

Based on extensive research by Brian Moynahan of the *Sunday Times Insight* team.

Hugh Miller
Casualty £1.75

The vivid story of one weekend in the front line of a big city hospital. The drunken skinhead from the pub punch-up who didn't tell the doctor he was diabetic. The twenty-seven-year-old mother raped by the babysitter's boyfriend. The middle-aged lady who turns up regularly after her suicide attempts. The man who had a massive coronary in the public bar. The two-year-old girl with both legs scalded by boiling water. And the endless trickle of drunks wandering in to cause chaos . . . It's all in a weekend's work for Casualty.

'Startling in its realism and riveting in its revelations'
BIRMINGHAM EVENING MAIL

Elizabeth Longford
Victoria RI £4.95

'A wonderfully vivid portrait built up with skill from massive research and presented with a beguiling artistry' C. V. WEDGWOOD

'It is hard to imagine how Elizabeth Longford's detailed and vivid volume could have been bettered. Her book is scholarly yet racily readable, witty yet wise' JAMES POPE-HENNESSY, SUNDAY TIMES

'Easily the best life of Victoria that has yet appeared'
PROFESSOR J. H. PLUMB, NEW YORK TIMES

Reference, language and information

☐	**Pan Dictionary of Synonyms and Antonyms**		£2.50p
☐	**Travellers' Multilingual Phrasebook**		£2.50p
☐	**Universal Encyclopaedia of Mathematics**		£2.95p

Literature guides

☐	**An Introduction to Shakespeare and his Contemporaries**	Marguerite Alexander	£2.95p
☐	**An Introduction to Fifty Modern British Plays**	Benedict Nightingale	£2.95p
☐	**An Introduction to Fifty Modern European Poets**	John Pilling	£2.95p
☐	**An Introduction to Fifty Modern British Poets**	Michael Schmidt	£1.95p
☐	**An Introduction to Fifty European Novels**	Martin Seymour-Smith	£1.95p

All these books are available at your local bookshop or newsagent, or can be ordered direct from the publisher. Indicate the number of copies required and fill in the form below   12

Name_____
(Block letters please)

Address_____

_____

Send to CS Department, Pan Books Ltd, PO Box 40, Basingstoke, Hants
Please enclose remittance to the value of the cover price plus:
35p for the first book plus 15p per copy for each additional book ordered
to a maximum charge of £1.25 to cover postage and packing
Applicable only in the UK

While every effort is made to keep prices low, it is sometimes
necessary to increase prices at short notice. Pan Books reserve
the right to show on covers and charge new retail prices which
may differ from those advertised in the text or elsewhere